CLARENDON ARIS

M000308341

General E
LINDSAY JUDSON

Also published in this series

Categories and *De Interpretatione*   J. L. ACKRILL

De Anima books II and III   D. W. HAMLYN
New impression with supplementary material by Christopher Shields

De Generatione et Corruptione   C. J. F. WILLIAMS

De Partibus Animalium I and *De Generatione Animalium* I   D. M. BALME
New impression with supplementary material by Allan Gotthelf

Eudemian Ethics Books I, II, and VIII   MICHAEL WOODS
Second edition

Metaphysics Books B and K 1–2   ARTHUR MADIGAN, SJ

Metaphysics Books Γ, Δ, and E   CHRISTOPHER KIRWAN
Second edition

Metaphysics Books Z and H   DAVID BOSTOCK

Metaphysics Books M and N   JULIA ANNAS

Metaphysics Book θ   STEPHEN MAKIN

Nicomachean Ethics Books VIII and IX   MICHAEL PAKALUK

On the Parts of Animals I–IV   JAMES G. LENNOX

Physics Books I and II   WILLIAM CHARLTON
New impression with supplementary material

Physics Books III and IV   EDWARD HUSSEY
New impression with supplementary material

Physics Book VIII   DANIEL GRAHAM

Politics Books I and II   TREVOR J. SAUNDERS

Politics Books III and IV   RICHARD ROBINSON
New impression with supplementary material by David Keyt

Politics Books V and VI   DAVID KEYT

Politics Books VII and VIII   RICHARD KRAUT

Posterior Analytics   JONATHAN BARNES
Second edition

Topics Books I and VIII   ROBIN SMITH

Other volumes are in preparation

ARISTOTLE
Nicomachean Ethics

Books II–IV

*Translated
with a Commentary
by*

C. C. W. TAYLOR

CLARENDON PRESS · OXFORD

OXFORD

UNIVERSITY PRESS

Great Clarendon Street, Oxford OX2 6DP

Oxford University Press is a department of the University of Oxford.
It furthers the University's objective of excellence in research, scholarship,
and education by publishing worldwide in

Oxford New York

Auckland Cape Town Dar es Salaam Hong Kong Karachi
Kuala Lumpur Madrid Melbourne Mexico City Nairobi
New Delhi Shanghai Taipei Toronto

With offices in

Argentina Austria Brazil Chile Czech Republic France Greece
Guatemala Hungary Italy Japan Poland Portugal Singapore
South Korea Switzerland Thailand Turkey Ukraine Vietnam

Oxford is a registered trade mark of Oxford University Press
in the UK and in certain other countries

Published in the United States
by Oxford University Press Inc., New York

British Library Cataloguing in Publication Data

Data available

Library of Congress Cataloging in Publication Data
Aristotle
[Nicomachean ethics. Book 2–4. English]
Nicomachean ethics. Books II–IV / translated, with a commentary by
C. C. W. Taylor.
p. cm.–(Clarendon Aristotle series)
Includes bibliographical references and Index.
ISBN-13: 978–0–19–825067–8 (alk. paper)
ISBN-10: 0–19–825067–3 (alk. paper)
ISBN-13: 978–0–19–825066–1 (alk. paper)
ISBN-10: 0–19–825066–5 (alk. paper)
1. Virtue. 2. Aristotle. Nicomachean ethics. Book 2–4 I. Taylor,
C. C. W. (Christopher Charles Whiston), 1936– . II. Title. III. Series.
B430.A5T29 2006 171′.3—dc22 2006011799

Typeset by Laserwords Private Limited, Chennai, India
Printed in Great Britain on acid-free paper by
Biddles Ltd., King's Lynn, Norfolk

ISBN 0–19–825066–5 (Hbk.) 978–0–19–825066–1 (Hbk.)
ISBN 0–19–825067–3 (Pbk.) 978–0–19–825067–8 (Pbk.)

PREFACE

The text translated in this volume is the Oxford Classical Text (hereafter 'OCT'), edited by I. Bywater (Oxford, 1894); any departures from the OCT are indicated in the commentary. In conformity with standard practice, the translation includes the marginal line numeration of I. Bekker's edition of Aristotle (Berlin, 1831), which follows that of the OCT as closely as the differences between Greek and English word order permit.

I am especially indebted to the general editors of the Clarendon Aristotle Series, Professor J. L. Ackrill, who invited me to contribute a volume to the series, and Dr Lindsay Judson, who has read several drafts and mingled warm encouragement with sagacious suggestions for improvement. I am also grateful to Terry Irwin for helpful comments.

The work was considerably advanced during a term spent in 2004 as a Visiting Fellow of the Centre for Ethics, Philosophy, and Public Affairs at St Andrews University. I am most grateful for the facilities provided by the Centre, and especially for the kindness of its director, Professor John Haldane. During my time at St Andrews I presented parts of the work to various seminars and informal groups. It gives me great pleasure to acknowledge the help I received from those who took part in these discussions, and I hope that it will not be invidious to single out Sarah Broadie, Jamie Dow, and Peter Woodward, who all gave me valuable suggestions (including, in the case of the latter, extensive written comments). I spent the spring semester of 2005 at Cornell University, in the course of which I gave a graduate seminar on the *Nicomachean Ethics*, which included some material from the present volume, and gave a talk on a related topic at the Faculty Discussion Club. I am most grateful for the valuable input I received from colleagues and graduate students at both venues, and in particular from Karen Nielsen.

While I have sought as far as possible to avoid the use of gender-specific terminology in the commentary, I have not done so in the translation, since it would be anachronistic to represent Aristotle as sharing modern sensibilities on this point.

C. C. W. T.

CONTENTS

ABBREVIATIONS

Aristotle

An.	*De Anima*
An. Post.	*Posterior Analytics*
Cael.	*De Caelo*
Cat.	*Categories*
EE	*Eudemian Ethics*
HA	*Historia Animalium*
MA	*De Motu Animalium*
Met.	*Metaphysics*
MM	*Magna Moralia*
NE	*Nicomachean Ethics*
PA	*De Partibus Animalium*
Poet.	*Poetics*
Pol.	*Politics*
Rhet.	*Rhetoric*
Sens.	*De Sensu*
Top.	*Topics*

Plato

Grg.	*Gorgias*
Lach.	*Laches*
Leg.	*Laws*
Phlb.	*Philebus*
Prt.	*Protagoras*
Resp.	*Republic*

Other abbreviations

CAG	*Commentaria in Aristotelem Graeca*
DK	H. Diels and W. Kranz, *Die Fragmente der Vorsokratiker*, 3 vols. (Berlin, 1954)
DL	Diogenes Laertius

Il.	*Iliad*
KD	*Kuriai Doxai* (Epicurus)
LSJ	H. G. Liddell and R. Scott, *A Greek–English Lexicon*, rev. H. J. Jones and R. McKenzie (Oxford, 1940)
Lucr.	Lucretius
Men.	*Letter to Menoeceus* (Epicurus)
OCT	Oxford Classical Text
Od.	*Odyssey*
Strom.	*Stromateis* (Clement of Alexandria)
Works	*Works and Days* (Hesiod)

INTRODUCTION

1. THE PLACE OF BOOKS II–IV IN THE *NE*

The topic of NE II–IV is virtue or excellence of character, one of
the two types of excellence which Aristotle takes as constitutive
of the best life for a human being. The examination of excellence
of character is the first stage of the project begun in Book I of
giving an informative specification of that life. Aristotle begins
from the concept of a goal of action, and seeks to show that, as
every rational activity aims to realize some goal which is seen as
good, there is some goal which stands in that relation to human
life as a whole, which can therefore be identified as the good
for humans, or the supreme good. While there is dispute among
commentators as to precisely how Aristotle tries to establish that
conclusion, it is clear that by ch. 4 of Book I he takes himself to
have shown that the supreme good is whatever the art of politics
seeks to realize, so that he is now in a position to try to identify
what that is. Everyone, he says (1095ᵃ17–20), agrees on the name
of the supreme good, viz. *eudaimonia* (i.e. happiness, flourishing,
or well-being), and that what name means is 'living well and
doing well', but people differ on what living well consists in:
e.g. some people think it consists in getting as much enjoyment as
possible, others that it is a life of political achievement, others that
it is the life of the intellect. A possible response to that situation
would be a subjectivist one, according to which living well is
nothing other than getting out of life what you want, whether
that is enjoyment, political achievement, or whatever. Given that
response, there is no question of adjudicating between conflicting
conceptions of the best life, since all the different life-plans satisfy
the only available conception of that life, viz. getting what you
want. Aristotle does not consider that response; he takes it for
granted that the different conceptions which he has identified are
in conflict with one another, and that it is the task of philosophy
to settle that conflict by declaring a winner, whether one of the
suggested candidates or some other still to be identified.

His first step (I. 7) is to confirm the universal belief that the
supreme good is *eudaimonia* by establishing that *eudaimonia* alone

satisfies two conditions which the supreme good must satisfy: first, that it is sought for its own sake and for the sake of nothing else, and secondly, that it is by itself sufficient to make life 'choice-worthy and lacking nothing' (1097^b15). Both conditions have been held to point towards an 'inclusive' conception of *eudaimonia*: i.e. a conception of the supreme good as a life in which the best possible combination of specific goods is achieved. On this view, Aristotle's first claim is that while any specific good such as pleasure or intelligence may be described as sought for its own sake, it is *ipso facto* sought as a constituent of the best life, whereas the best life itself can never be sought for the sake of anything else. And his second claim is that since the best life already includes all constituents sufficient for the best life, nothing needs to be (or indeed can be) added to it to improve it. There has been much dispute among commentators as to whether Aristotle's conception of *eudaimonia* is inclusive as thus specified, or rather 'dominant', i.e. a conception of a life devoted as far as possible to the pursuit of a single specific good.[1] That controversy goes beyond the scope of this Commentary. For our purposes it suffices to point out that even if the formal specification of *eudaimonia* as sought for its own sake and self-sufficient points (as I agree that it does) towards the inclusive conception, that conception is not sufficient for Aristotle's project of adjudicating between the specific claimants to the title of the supreme good. For the formal conception already includes the conception of the best possible combination of specific goods, which commits Aristotle to offering a substantive account of which combination of goods is the best possible.

The first step towards that account is given by the argument from the function (*ergon*) of human beings, which follows immediately. Here again extensive controversy must be bypassed.[2] It suffices to observe that Aristotle's aim is to move towards a substantive account of the best life for humans from consideration in terms of his philosophy of nature of what kind of life human life is. Humans are a kind of animal, specifically rational animals. Hence

---

[1] The terminology of 'inclusive' and 'dominant' was introduced by Hardie (1965). Ackrill (1974) and Kenny (1965–6) offer influential defences of the inclusive and dominant interpretations, respectively. More recent commentators have tended to favour some form of compromise (as I do). For a guide to the controversy see Kraut (1989: 'Introduction'); Kraut himself favours the dominant view.

[2] See e.g. Kraut (1979), Whiting (1988), Lawrence (2001). (The latter contains a comprehensive bibliography of the literature on the topic.)

a distinctively human life is a life of rational activity, and a good human life is one in which rational activity is well employed. But what counts as employing rational activity well? Here a number of complications arise. The first complication arises from Aristotle's view, developed in more detail in I. 13, that the rational element in the human personality is twofold, consisting first in the intellect, which is rational *per se*, and secondarily in the appetites, which are not rational *per se* (since wanting is not as such an exercise of the intellect), but which are derivatively rational in that, unlike the desires of non-rational animals, they are responsive to reason. Hence the notion of employing rationality well is not a simple one, but must find room for the good employment of the intellect on the one hand and of the rationally responsive appetites on the other. Aristotle clearly has this point in mind in the definition of the supreme good which results from the *ergon* argument: 'the human good turns out to be activity of the soul in accordance with excellence, and if there are several kinds of excellence, in accordance with the best and the most *teleion*'[3] (1098ª16–18). The first half of the sentence states that the supreme good for humans is the excellent employment of rationality; the second modifies this claim by considering the consequence of the hypothesis, which Aristotle believes to hold (see above), that there are more ways than one in which rationality is excellently employed. What that consequence is, is disputed between partisans of the inclusive and dominant interpretations (see above); the former interpret it as 'in accordance with the best, i.e. the most complete', understanding the reference to be to the exercise of rationality considered comprehensively as including both the activity of the pure intellect and that of the rationally responsive appetites. The latter interpret as 'in accordance with the best (sc. the best among those just mentioned), i.e. that which is the most final', understanding the reference to be exclusively to the excellent employment of the theoretical intellect, which is described in Book X (1177ᵇ1–15) as the only human activity employed for its own sake alone. While the latter seems to me clearly the more natural reading of this particular sentence, our purpose does not depend on the answer to

---

[3] The word may mean 'complete', 'perfect', or 'final' (i.e. having the character of a final end (*telos*) as defined earlier in the chapter as an end sought for its own sake). I have kept the Greek, since the interpretative dispute mentioned immediately below hinges in part on whether the word in this sentence means 'complete' or 'final'.

that question. We have to note that Aristotle has still taken only the first step towards his goal of a substantive specification of the best life. Whether that consists in the excellent employment of rationality in all its forms, or in one only, or in some compromise between those extreme positions,[4] he has still not told us what are the ways in which rationality is excellently employed. The *ergon* argument still leaves it open for the partisans of the various kinds of lives mentioned earlier to claim that their favoured life-style and it alone constitutes the excellent employment of rationality.

In the succeeding chapters (8–10) Aristotle considers the contribution to *eudaimonia* of external goods such as health and prosperity. His final conclusion is that while the best life must have the excellent employment of rationality as its central goal or goals, since no life can be satisfactory which does not have that aim, nevertheless external goods are necessary for a fully worthwhile life. A full account of *eudaimonia*, then, is that it is a life of excellent rational activity 'sufficiently equipped with the external goods, not for any chance period, but over one's life as a whole' (1101^a14-16). While this may look like a significant modification of the conclusion of the *ergon* argument, that the supreme good is excellent rational activity, there is in fact no real tension between the two accounts. Excellent rational activity, which it is up to the agent to engage in or not, is what one should aim at in one's life, while the external goods, which it is not in the agent's power to guarantee, are the extra conditions which one hopes for in order to make one's life completely worthwhile. The full account of *eudaimonia* thus contains both inclusive and dominant aspects, since its dominant aim is excellent rational activity, but it also includes the external goods. It remains to establish whether that compromise position applies to rational activity itself (see below).

In chapter 13 Aristotle sets out the psychological basis of his distinction of types of excellent rational activity. Since rationality belongs essentially to the intellect, and derivatively to the appetites (see above), the types of excellence are the excellence of the intellect and the excellence of rationally responsive appetite. These types of excellence interpenetrate via the practical function of the intellect. The intellect is employed not merely in speculative thought, but in the direction of conduct, and it performs

---

[4] I state my own view in sect. 2.

its practical role by shaping and directing the appetites. And the appetites are excellently shaped in so far as they respond appropriately to the directions of practical reason. The stage is thus set for Aristotle to expound his account first of the excellence of rationally responsive appetite and then of reason, both theoretical and practical. The first type of excellence is the topic of the books translated and commented on in this volume, and is completed by the account of justice (also counted by Aristotle a virtue of character) in Book V. Excellence of intellect is the topic of Book VI.

This leaves us with the crucial question of why we should identify the excellence of rationally responsive appetite with the virtues of character listed and discussed in Books II–IV. Aristotle attempts no justification of this identification. His implicit strategy relies on the reader's acceptance that, given any specific motivation such as fear or the desire for bodily pleasure, correct responsiveness to that motivation can be seen to be identical with the virtue which he specifies. The familiar criticism that in the last resort Aristotle relies on the evaluative intuitions current in his culture and social milieu, rather than attempting to ground them in any fundamental rational principle or principles,[5] seems to be correct.

This raises two final questions: first, whether Aristotle does in fact attempt any such grounding, and second, whether, if he does not, his failure to do so constitutes a defect in his theory. The first question turns on Aristotle's account of the standard which determines correct practical reasoning. If Aristotle's view is that the ultimate standard of practical reasoning is the promotion of some goal external to that reasoning itself, such as theoretical excellence, then he can be seen as attempting to provide the rational grounding for his theory of virtue which his critics find lacking. I discuss this issue briefly below (pp. 107–10), concluding with the dogmatic assertion (based on the articles of mine referred to in that discussion) that Aristotle's texts are indecisive on this crucial issue. The second question raises general questions about the role of ethical theory which I am certainly not competent to pursue in detail. I must confine myself to observing that some writers sympathetic to Aristotle urge that the attempt to justify or ground a

---

[5] See e.g. Simpson (1991–2).

substantive moral theory from any external standpoint is mistaken in principle, and count it a merit rather than a defect in Aristotle that, as they interpret him, he eschews any such attempt.[6]

2. ARISTOTLE AND VIRTUE ETHICS

In recent years interest in Aristotle's account of virtue of character has been heightened by the development of virtue ethics, which is seen by both adherents and critics as to some degree inspired by, or deriving from, this part of Aristotle's ethical theory. The Aristotelian reference is explicit in Elizabeth Anscombe's seminal 'Modern Moral Philosophy' (1958), generally acknowledged as having given the initial impetus to the development of virtue ethics as a distinctive type of ethical theory, and most writers in this tradition acknowledge some Aristotelian influence.[7]

While there are already different varieties of virtue ethics, and differences between the degrees of significance which individual writers accord to the Aristotelian roots of the theory,[8] virtue ethicists generally agree that the following aspects are central to the theory and broadly Aristotelian in inspiration.

(i) *The primacy of character* The ultimate object of ethical evaluation is the agent, not particular actions or action-types; particular actions and action-types are evaluated as evincing traits of character which are themselves good (virtues) or bad (vices), and traits of character are in turn evaluated as those which a good (virtuous) or bad (vicious) agent would manifest.

(ii) *The primacy of habituation* Following from (i), moral education does not consist in the mastery of moral principles, but in the acquisition of a good character, which is achieved by the development of good habits. An essential element in the development of good habits is the training

---

[6] See esp. McDowell (1979, 1995, 1996); also Wiggins (1975–6, 1995), Woods (1986).

[7] For some instances see Statman's introduction to Statman (1997: 36 n. 148).

[8] An author who particularly emphasizes the Aristotelian aspect is Rosalind Hursthouse, who explicitly designates her type of virtue ethics 'neo-Aristotelianism' (e.g. Hursthouse 1999: 9). It is not coincidental that, like Anscombe, she is a close student of Aristotle's ethical writings.

of the emotions and of likes and dislikes (pleasure and distress), since virtues are not merely reliable behavioural tendencies, but include appropriate attitudes to action-types (e.g. a compassionate person is distressed by the suffering of others and glad to have the opportunity to alleviate it).

(iii) *The centrality of moral sensibility/practical intelligence* Moral judgement consists, not in the application of principles or rules (from (ii)) but in the exercise of a trained sensibility or practical intelligence in virtue of which the agent is responsive to the requirements of particular situations. While there is general agreement among virtue ethicists that these requirements are not codifiable in advance, there is divergence on the role of generalization in the thought of the practically intelligent agent. Some theorists emphasize the primacy of moral sensibility to the extent of eliminating generalization altogether, whereas others regard generalizations as approximations guiding the detailed application of sensibility. (That divergence reflects a difference among Aristotelian commentators as to what his own view was; see below, pp. 109–10.)

(iv) *The centrality of well-being* The value of the virtues is in one way or another grounded in their relation to an overall good life for the virtuous agent, designated by such terms as 'well-being', 'flourishing', 'happiness', or '*eudaimonia*'. This relation is conceived differently by different authors, some seeing the virtues as causal determinants of a life independently identifiable as good overall, others seeing them as constitutive, either wholly or partially, of the value of the overall good life.

It is certainly the case that all the above aspects are to be found in the *NE*:[9] indeed, (i)–(iii) are discussed in the appropriate sections of the commentary in this volume (see below pp. 59–64,

---

[9] This is not to deny that the *NE* also includes elements at least prima facie inconsistent with some of (i)–(iv). Thus Santas (1993) points out that Aristotle defines justice as the disposition which makes us doers of just actions (1129^{a}8–9), and defines just actions as those which accord with law and with principles of fairness which he elucidates in Book V. Hence just actions are definitionally prior to the just agent, which appears inconsistent with (i). Yet at 1105^{b}5–9 Aristotle reverses the priority, saying that actions are called just and temperate when they are the kind of actions that the just and temperate agent would do; but just and temperate agents are not simply those

66–72, 73–7, 94–6, 104–6, 110–12). To that extent the claim that modern virtue ethics is Aristotelian in spirit is perfectly correct. But at the same time we have to recognize a number of differences between Aristotle's conception of the virtues and of ethics more generally and that of modern virtue ethicists, differences which are at the least highly significant and perhaps no less significant than the similarities listed above. Whatever the relative weighting of similarities and differences, it is clear that a balanced picture requires that both be taken into account.

The most obvious difference is to be found in the content of the lists of virtues and vices recognized by Aristotle on the one hand and modern virtue ethicists on the other. The latter typically treat goodness of character as constituted by the possession of recognizably moral virtues, notably courage, justice, moderation or temperance, honesty or integrity, generosity, good temper, and kindness or compassion (closely connected or perhaps identical with charity), and badness of character or wickedness as constituted by opposed moral vices, typically cowardice, injustice, licentiousness, dishonesty, meanness, ill-temper, and unkindness, of which cruelty is the most signal manifestation. Aristotle's list overlaps to a large extent, since it too contains courage, temperance, justice, generosity, and good temper, but it omits kindness and restricts honesty to telling the truth about one's own merits, while including traits typically passed over by modern virtue theorists: namely, greatness of soul, magnificence, and the

---

who do that kind of action, but those who do them in the way that just and temperate agents would do them. So either Aristotle is inconsistent with regard to justice at least, or he is assuming that the kinds of priority in the two passages are not inconsistent with one another. See commentary on 1105^{b}5–9 for further discussion.

In the same article Santas argues that for Aristotle virtuous actions are in general prior in definition to the virtues which they realize, since in terms of his metaphysics the virtues are first actualities of innate human potentialities, and the exercise of the virtues second actualities (as knowing French is the first actualization of the innate capacity to know French, and speaking French the second actualization), and Aristotle holds that second actualities are prior in definition to first actualities (*An.* 415^{a}18–20). That priority certainly holds for the senses, since e.g. sight is defined as the capacity to see, while seeing has an independent specification as the reception by the sense-organ of the visible form of the object. Similarly, knowing French is knowing how to speak and understand sentences of French, which again assumes that what it is to speak and understand such sentences can be specified independently. But the existence of such a specification is precisely what Aristotle denies of virtuous actions at 1105^{b}5–9. I conclude that Aristotle does not intend the thesis enunciated in the *De Anima* passage to apply to all cases of first and second actuality.

social virtues of ready wit (*eutrapelia*) and amiability or friendli-ness (*philia*). Both the omissions and the inclusions point to deep divergences between Aristotle's outlook and that of modern lib-eral thought (including the thought of virtue theorists). Perhaps the most striking omission is that of compassion. Aristotle indeed values some aspects of benevolence, including financial generosity and the avoidance of gratuitous offensiveness in social relations. But his ethical scheme affords no place (much less a central place) for considerations of the good of others as such, and in particular none for the alleviation of the misery or unhappiness of others, not because they happen to have some special relation to us, but just because they are miserable and we are in a position to help. (This is no doubt one area where the influence of Judaeo-Christian thought has produced a major difference between the Greeks and ourselves.) Another aspect of benevolence foreign to Aristotle is the identification of cruelty as a vice, perhaps the worst of all vices. He has simply nothing to say about cruelty *per se*; perhaps he counts it as an aberration peculiar to those at a subhuman level of wickedness, comparable to ripping up pregnant women and eat-ing the foetuses (1148^b19–21), but that is mere conjecture. We are closer to the texts if we take it that his silence on cruelty is the counterpart of his silence on compassion, determined by his failure to take account of benevolence and malevolence in the abstract as possible motivations. (On the significance of that failure for the doctrine of the mean, see commentary, p. 113.)

The modern conception of honesty is a complex one. The core notion is that of trustworthiness, and while contracts and similar relationships constitute a central area of application of the concept, the idea of the honest person as someone true to his or her word puts truthfulness in the central place. Cheating, whether in com-mercial dealings or in games, is a typical instance of dishonesty, but it counts as such insofar as it involves deception of one form or another; a dishonest car salesman lies about the mileage and conceals defects in the bodywork, while a card-sharper relies on unspoken presumptions (e.g. that cards are unmarked) to gain an unfair advantage. But truthfulness has a wider application than to areas which allow of cheating; the word of a truthful person is reliable whatever it is about, since the truthful person values the truth as such, finds it distasteful to lie, and seeks to avoid error of fact, and to correct any misstatements which he or she may inadvertently have made. As in the case of benevolence, the overlap between this concept and Aristotle's concept of truthfulness (*alētheia*) is only partial. He says that truth-telling in agreements and similar transactions falls under justice rather than truthfulness *per se* ($1127^{a}33$–b1), and restricts the application of the latter to truthfulness about one's own merits, as opposed on the one hand to insincere self-aggrandizement and on the other to insincere self-denigration. He does indeed say that the person who is truthful in that restricted sphere regards falsehood as in itself base and blameworthy and truth as fine and praiseworthy ($1127^{a}28$–30), which is the heart of the wider, modern concept, but he still restricts the scope of the virtue to telling the truth about oneself. He may assume that, once truthfulness in agreements has been hived off under justice, statements about one's own merits provide the only scope for truthfulness. But that is to ignore many complexities of the social situations in which truthfulness and untruthfulness figure; for instance, people typically lie to avoid unpleasant confrontations, e.g. by pretending to agree with someone else's strongly expressed opinion, or by pretending to be the sort of person others expect one to be. That of course has some affinities with intentionally exaggerating one's merits, since in each case one's aim is to make others think better of one than the truth warrants, but the types of case just mentioned bring out the connection of truthfulness with moral courage, a connection which is missing from Aristotle's account. Once truthfulness as such is given the central place, phenomena such as avoiding cheating, avoiding boasting and self-denigration, and having the courage to tell the truth as one sees it in the face of hostility, which are unconnected on Aristotle's account, or absent from it altogether, are seen as intelligibly unified.

The presence in Aristotle's list of greatness of soul, magnificence, ready wit, and friendliness distances Aristotle from the modern virtue ethicist in two ways. The first two are more closely tied to ancient Greek values than the virtues of character previously listed as common to Aristotle and the moderns. Traditional Greek morality inherited from its Homeric roots and preserved into the classical period a conception of the good man (*agathos anēr*) as an outstanding individual, superior to others in respect of wisdom, courage, and other admirable traits including personal splendour, and expected the good man to be aware of his superiority and to behave accordingly. The term *megalopsuchia* ('greatness of soul') and its cognates might be applied either to attributes such as courage which were the ground for that sense of superiority or to the sense of superiority itself and to the behaviour expressing it. Aristotle's *megalopsuchia* is the incorporation of that traditional conception into his ethical scheme; his *megalopsuchos* is the agent of complete Aristotelian excellence, whose sense of superiority is grounded in his or her awareness of that excellence, an awareness which expresses itself in detachment from any values other than those of excellence itself. The self-referentiality of the *megalopsuchos* is alien to the modern moral outlook, because, I suggest, that outlook eschews the competitiveness which that self-referentiality presupposes. Consequently, we do not think that it is essential to being a good person that one should be aware of being better than others and of deserving esteem on that account. That is not, of course, to say that we think that a good person should have false beliefs about their merits, e.g. that they are not better than some others and that they do not deserve esteem on that account. Rather, we think that beliefs about one's merits and deserts are not themselves integral to one's ethical outlook, so that someone who, at the extreme, had no such beliefs one way or the other would not be ethically deficient on that account.

Magnificence resembles greatness of soul in its competitive aspect, and is even more closely tied to the life of the Greek *polis*. It is the disposition to engage in major expenditure on projects which are of public benefit and which, through their splendour, reflect credit both on the *polis* for whose benefit they are undertaken and on the individual who undertakes them. It is *par excellence* a virtue of a good citizen, as distinct from a good person, and is necessarily restricted to an élite of wealth and taste. The minor social virtues of ready wit and amiability are, though not restricted to a social élite, none the less closer to social graces than what we consider virtues of character. That is to say, they contribute to making one a good companion or colleague, someone whom it is easy to get along with, rather than a good person in a narrower ethical sense.

This last point raises a central question about the project of virtue ethics, and the extent to which Aristotle should be thought of as engaged in the same project. Historically, virtue ethics was prompted in part by dissatisfaction with the two main systems of modern normative ethics, deontology and consequentialism, and is typically presented as a rival to, and improvement on, those systems. This assumes that all three systems (or 'approaches', if one objects to calling virtue ethics a system) are in the same business, which I take to be that of giving a rational account of how one should live, and thereby providing criteria, or at least general guidance, on what kinds of conduct are good and bad. The rivals to virtue ethics certainly take their task to include the determination of what is right and wrong, which raises the question of whether virtue ethics shares that aspiration too. While some writers in that tradition suggest that the vocabulary of 'right' and 'wrong' is specific to systems in which the notion of moral obligation is fundamental, and should therefore be abandoned when that notion is superseded by those of virtue and the good life, others such as Hursthouse take it that virtue ethics must be able to show that that theory is as well placed as its rivals to show which kinds of actions are right, and seek to demonstrate that it satisfies that requirement. I doubt whether Aristotle shares that ambition. First, he is not reacting to normative theories which purport to specify general criteria of right and wrong. Secondly, as shown above, his scheme of virtues is not compiled from the universalistic perspective which virtue ethics shares with its modern rivals. Virtue ethics aims to specify what constitutes a good human life as such, irrespective of the kind of society in which one lives. Aristotle's scheme of virtues, by contrast, is firmly embedded in the values of the *polis*. On the one hand he takes little account of the abstract notions of benevolence and malevolence, as distinct from their specific manifestations in social situations, and on the other he counts among his virtues of character traits which presuppose the competitive values and social practices of the *polis*. Aristotle does indeed believe that the virtues which make one a good member of the *polis ipso facto* contribute to a good human life as such, but that is because he believes that only in the *polis* are the conditions for a good human life fully realized.

The feature which most distances Aristotle from virtue ethics is the role of intellectual excellence in his theory. Whereas for virtue ethics virtue of character is the primary determinant of the good human life, for Aristotle it is at best a partial determinant, and, on most views, a determinant of secondary importance. While detailed discussion of the relative contributions of intellectual excellence and virtue of character to the best human life falls outside the scope of this work, I take the following theses to be established.

(i) There are two fundamental kinds of human excellence: viz. intellectual excellence and virtue of character.

(ii) This bifurcation is founded in a fundamental distinction between two aspects of the human soul: on the one hand the intellect, which is rational *per se*, and on the other the appetitive, which is derivatively rational in being capable of modification by reason. Intellectual excellence is the excellence of the purely rational element in the soul, whereas virtue of character is the excellence of the appetitive element, consisting in that element's being properly responsive to reason. (See above.)

(iii) Since the purely rational element is the most valuable element in the soul, the excellence of that element is the most valuable human excellence, and the exercise of that excellence is the most valuable activity possible for human beings.

(iv) The best form of human life is a life centred or focused on intellectual excellence. By that should be understood a life in which the exercise of intellectual excellence is the main object of the agent's interests and energies, not a life devoted exclusively to intellectual excellence. (A life of the latter kind is not possible for a human being; see next paragraph.)

(v) Since human beings require a social environment for the satisfaction both of basic bodily needs and of more developed needs, including friendship, the best form of human life must be lived in a social context. Consequently, that life requires the exercise of the social virtues, which are identical with the virtues of character.

(vi) Having specified (a) that intellectual excellence is the focus of the best life and (b) that that life requires the exercise of the virtues of character, Aristotle leaves it indeterminate how these types of excellence combine to make up the ideal life. It does not follow from the centrality of intellectual excellence that the best life is that in which intellectual excellence is maximized; nor does Aristotle assert the latter thesis.

(vii) A life focused not on intellectual excellence, but on virtue of character, is a good life, but less good than one focused on intellectual excellence.

The distance between Aristotle and virtue ethics is summed up in (vii) above; the virtue ethicist's best life is Aristotle's second-best. As in the case of the virtues of character discussed above, the divergence reflects elements specific to Aristotle's culture and remote from the universalistic and egalitarian aspirations of virtue ethics. The priority assigned to intellectual excellence is indeed an expression of intellectual élitism, but that evaluation is itself grounded in Aristotle's psychology and theology. Ultimately, the intellect is the best element in the soul because it is the most god-like, and the intellectual life is the best life in that it most closely approximates to the life of the gods, allowing mortal human beings to 'assimilate to the immortal as far as possible' (*eph' hoson endechetai athanatizein* (1177^b33)).

In pointing out these differences between Aristotle and modern virtue ethics, I do not suggest that we should lose sight of the links between the two which I identified at the beginning, but merely seek to put those links in perspective by setting them against the background of the differences. Virtue ethics has genuine Aristotelian roots, but those roots stretch across an enormous distance of cultural background and theoretical presuppositions. While we can perfectly legitimately call virtue ethics neo-Aristotelian, that should not lead us to think of Aristotle as a proponent of virtue ethics.

TRANSLATION

PRELIMINARY NOTE

Aristotle uses the term *aretē* distributively to designate a feature which contributes towards making the thing which has that feature a good one of its kind, and collectively to designate the set of features which makes the thing which has it a good one of its kind. In the case of humans his doctrine is that there are two basic kinds of features which make human beings good human beings, goodness of intellect and goodness of character, both basic kinds being constituted by a number of specific types. In contexts which discuss these features in general, or which deal explicitly with both kinds, I have translated *aretē* as 'excellence'. In contexts, which predominate in these books, where Aristotle is discussing goodness of character and its specific types, I have translated the singular as 'virtue' and the plural (*aretai*) as 'virtues'. This seems to me justified in view of the following considerations:

(i) Our own conception of goodness of character is of a character constituted by valuable and admirable traits such as honesty and unselfishness which we count as virtues of character; while Aristotle's list extends more widely to include traits such as amiability and ready wit, which we should count rather as social graces than as virtues of character (see Introduction, p. xxi), his central cases—courage, temperance, and justice—are paradigm cases of such virtues.

(ii) A continuous historical tradition of interpretation, beginning from the medieval Latin commentators and continuing to contemporary theorists, regularly refers to this portion of Aristotle's work as his theory of virtue and the virtues. The modern use of the term 'virtue ethics' derives directly from this tradition.

(iii) Aristotle regularly (e.g. 1103ᵇ13–14) refers to the specific types of goodness of character by the abbreviated designation *hai aretai* (abbreviated from *hai ēthikai aretai*), and to goodness of character generically (e.g. 1104ᵇ15) as *aretē* or *hē aretē* (abbreviated from ((*hē*) *ēthikē aretē*)). While these expressions are rendered into perfectly natural English as 'the virtues' and 'virtue' (itself an expression of point (ii) above), 'the excellences' is unnatural, and therefore inferior as a translation, and 'excellence' positively misleading, as it suggests excellence in general, rather than the specific kind of excellence under discussion.

BOOK TWO

CHAPTER I

1103ᵃ Excellence being then twofold, excellence of thought on the one
15 hand and excellence of character on the other, excellence of thought comes into being and develops chiefly through teaching, which is why it requires experience and time, but excellence of character results from habit, whence it has acquired its name (*ēthikē*) by a slight modification of the word *ethos* (habit). Hence it is clear that none of the virtues of character comes to us by nature;
20 for nothing that exists by nature is habituated in a different way, for instance a stone, which naturally falls downwards, could not be habituated to travel upwards, even if one were to try to habituate it by throwing it up ten thousand times, nor fire downwards; nor could anything else that behaves one way by nature be habituated in a different way. So the virtues do not come to us either by nature
25 or contrary to nature, but it is natural to us to be receptive of them, and we are perfected in them through habit. Further, in the case of things that do come to us by nature, we get the capacities for them first, and later we manifest their exercise (which is clear in the case of the senses; for we did not acquire the senses through frequent
30 acts of seeing or hearing, but rather we made use of the senses we already had, but did not come to have them through making use of them); but we acquire the virtues by having previously exercised them, as also in the case of the skills. For what one has to learn to do, we learn by doing, e.g. people become builders by building, and lyre-players by playing the lyre; and so too we
1103ᵇ become just by performing just acts and temperate by temperate acts and courageous by courageous acts. What happens in states bears this out; for legislators make citizens good by habituating

them, and this is the wish of every legislator, and those who do not 5
do this well go wrong, and this is the way in which a good system
of government differs from a bad. Moreover, every excellence is
created and destroyed by the same source and the same means,
and similarly every skill; for it is from playing the lyre that people
become good and bad lyre-players. Similarly with builders and all 10
the rest; for people will be good builders from building well and
bad from building badly. If this were not so, there would have
been no need of a teacher, but everyone would have been born
either good or bad. Now it is the same in the case of the virtues; it
is by their actions in relations with others that some of us become 15
just and others unjust, and by their actions in frightening situations
and by being habituated to be afraid or bold that some become
courageous and others cowardly. It is similar in the case of the
appetites and of anger; some people become temperate and good-
tempered, others intemperate and irascible, because the former 20
behave one way in those situations and the latter the other way.
To sum up, states arise from similar acts. Therefore one must
ensure that one's acts are of such a kind; for one's states follow
according to the differences of the acts. So one's being habituated
one way or another from youth upward makes no small difference,
but an enormous one, or rather it makes all the difference. 25

BOOK TWO

CHAPTER 2

Now since the present enquiry is not undertaken for the sake of theoretical understanding as the others are (for we do not investigate
in order to know what virtue is, but in order to become good, for
otherwise there would have been no profit from it), it is necessary
to investigate the topic of actions, viz. how we are to perform them. 30
For it is they that determine what kind of states we come to have,
as we have said. Now it is agreed that we should act in accordance
with correct reason; let that be our assumption—we shall discuss
it later, considering what is correct reason and how it relates to the
other excellences. And let this also be agreed in advance, that every 1104^a
discussion of practical questions must be expressed in outline and

not precisely, as we said at the outset that discussions should be required to be in accordance with the nature of their subject-matter; practical matters and questions of what is advantageous
5   contain nothing fixed, just like things to do with health. And the discussion of general principles being of that kind, it is even more the case that the discussion of particular cases does not have precision; for it does not fall under any skill or manual of instruction, but those who act must themselves always have regard to the particular circumstances, as is also the case in medicine and
10   steersmanship.

But though the present enquiry is of that kind, we must try to help. So we should first consider that things of that kind are such as to be destroyed by deficiency and excess, as we see in the cases of strength and health (we should apply evidence from
15   clear cases to those which are unclear). For excessive and insufficient exercise destroy one's strength, and similarly excess and deficiency in food and drink destroy one's health, but proportionate amounts produce and increase and maintain it. Now it is similar in the case of temperance and courage and the other virtues; for
20   someone who fears and flees from everything and endures nothing becomes a coward, but the person who fears absolutely nothing and goes to face everything becomes overbold. And similarly the person who enjoys every pleasure and abstains from none becomes intemperate, but the person who avoids every pleasure, as boors
25   do, becomes a sort of insensible person. So temperance and courage are destroyed by excess and deficiency, but preserved by the mean state. But it is not merely the case that dispositions come into being and are increased and destroyed from the same sources and by the same means; besides that, their exercise consists in
30   the same things. For that is the way it is in other, clearer, cases, such as strength; for it comes about from taking a lot of food and undertaking many strenuous activities, and the person best able to do those things is the strong person. So it is in the case of the virtues too; for we become temperate from abstaining from pleasures,
35   and once we have become temperate, we are best able to abstain
1104ᵇ   from them. And similarly in the case of courage too; for it is by being habituated to despise fearful things and endure them that we become courageous, and once we have become courageous, we shall best be able to endure fearful things.

BOOK TWO

CHAPTER 3

One must take as an indication of people's dispositions the pleasure or distress which arises from what they do. For the person who 5
abstains from bodily pleasures and who takes pleasure in doing
just that is temperate, but the person who finds it disagreeable to do
so is intemperate, and the person who endures frightening things
with pleasure, or at least without distress, is courageous, while the
person who feels distress at doing so is cowardly. For virtue of
character has to do with pleasure and distress, since it is because
of pleasure that we do bad things, and because of distress that we 10
fail to do fine things. So from our earliest youth, as Plato says, we
must be brought up to take pleasure in what should please us and
to be distressed by what should distress us; that is correct education. Moreover, if the virtues have to do with actions and feelings,
and every action and every feeling is attended by pleasure and 15
distress, that is a further reason why virtue has to do with pleasure and distress. Punishments, which operate by means of these,
provide another indication of this; for they are sorts of remedies,
and remedies normally operate by means of opposites. Further, as
we have just said, every state of soul is essentially related to and 20
has to do with those things which affect it for better or worse. It is
through pleasure and distress that people become bad, by pursuing
and avoiding those they should not, or when they should not, or
in ways they should not, or however many other features of that
kind are determined by reason. This is why people even define
the virtues as states of absence, i.e. of lack of feeling; they are 25
not correct to do so, because they give that account without qualification, omitting 'as one should, or should not, or when' and the
other additions. So we can take it as laid down that virtue is that
disposition to do with pleasure and distress which leads one to act
so as to achieve the best, and vice is the opposite. It will be clear
also from the following that they are to do with these same things:
since there are three objects of choice, the fine, the advantageous, 30
and the pleasant, and three opposed objects of avoidance, the disgraceful, the harmful, and the unpleasant, the good person is the
one who gets it right in all these respects and the bad the one who

goes wrong, above all with regard to pleasure, which is common
35 to all animals, and characteristic of all objects of choice, since the
1105^a fine and the advantageous seem pleasant. Further, all of us grow
up with these from childhood; that is why it is difficult to rub out
the traces of these feelings, which have soaked into the fabric of
our life. And we measure our actions too, some of us more and
5 some less, by pleasure and distress. That is why our entire activity
must be concerned with them; for doing well or badly in respect of
pleasure and distress has no small effect on our actions. Moreover,
it is more difficult to fight against pleasure than against spirit, as
Heraclitus says, and skill and excellence always have to do with
10 what is more difficult, and doing well in that area is better. So for
this reason too the entire business of virtue and political science
has to do with pleasure and distress; for the person who uses these
well is good, and the one who uses them badly is bad.

This concludes our treatment of the following theses: virtue has
15 to do with pleasure and distress; it is developed and destroyed by
the differential employment of the sources which give rise to it;
and it is exercised in the same kinds of action as give rise to it.

BOOK TWO

CHAPTER 4

Someone might raise the following difficulty over our assertion
that people have to become just by performing just actions, and
temperate by performing temperate ones; if they perform just
20 and temperate actions, they are already just and temperate, as
those who perform literate and musical actions are literate and
musical. But is it not as we say in the cases of technical skills too?
Someone can do something literate by luck, or under the direction
of someone else. So he will only be literate if he both does some-
25 thing literate and does it in a literate way, i.e. in accordance with
the literacy which he possesses.

Moreover the cases of the technical skills and the virtues are not
even alike. The products of technical skills determine in themselves whether their producer has done well; it is enough that
an output of a certain kind is produced. But in the case of the
virtues it is not the case that if the output is of a certain kind, the

action is performed justly or temperately, but also if the agent 30
is in a certain condition when he acts, first if he acts knowingly,
secondly if he acts from choice, and choice of these things for their
own sake, and thirdly if he acts from a stable and unchangeable
state of character. These are not included among the conditions for 1105ᵇ
having the others, i.e. the technical skills, except that of knowing;
but in the case of the virtues knowing has little or no effect, but
the other conditions, which result from frequently performing just
and temperate actions, have no small effect, but are totally deci- 5
sive. So actions are called just and temperate when they are the
sort of actions that the just and temperate person would perform;
but the just and temperate person is not the person who performs
those actions, but in addition the one who acts in the way just and
temperate people do. So it is right to say that one becomes just
from performing just actions and temperate from temperate ones; 10
and no one would ever become good from not performing those
actions. But the majority of people do not perform those actions,
but take refuge in theory, thinking that they are studying philosophy and that thereby they will become good, and so behaving
like sick people who listen carefully to their doctors but do none 15
of the things they are told to do. Now just as people who go in for
that kind of regime will not have a healthy body, similarly people
who study philosophy in that way will not have a healthy soul.

BOOK TWO

CHAPTER 5

Next we must consider what virtue is. Now since the things that 20
come to be in the soul are of three kinds, feelings, capacities,
and states, virtue must be one of these. I call feelings desire,
anger, fear, boldness, spite, joy, love, hatred, longing, envy, pity, in
general what is attended by pleasure and distress; I call capacities
those things in respect of which we are said to be susceptible of
those feelings, for instance in respect of which we are capable 25
of feeling anger or distress or pity, and states those in respect of
which we are in a good or bad condition with respect to feelings.
For instance with regard to feeling anger, if we do so violently or
slackly we are in a bad condition, but if the feeling is in between

we are in a good condition, and similarly for the rest. Now neither
virtues nor vices are feelings, because we are not called good or
30 bad in respect of feelings, but in respect of virtues and vices, and
because we are neither praised nor blamed for our feelings (for it
is not the person who is afraid or angry who is praised, nor is one
1106^a blamed just for being angry, but for being so in a certain way), but
we are praised or blamed for our virtues and vices. Further we are
angry or afraid without choosing to, but the virtues are choices
5 or not without choice. Moreover, we are said to be affected in
respect of feelings, but in respect of virtues and vices we are said
not to be affected but rather disposed in a certain way. And for
these reasons they are not capacities either; for we are not called
good or bad, or praised or blamed, simply for being capable of
feeling. Further we are capable of things by nature, but we do not
10 become good or bad by nature; we spoke about that previously.
So if the virtues are neither feelings nor capacities, it follows by
elimination that they are states. We have now said what kind of
thing virtue is.

BOOK TWO

CHAPTER 6

But one must not say just this, that it is a state, but also what
15 sort of state. Now we should say that every excellence perfects
the good condition of the thing whose excellence it is and makes
it perform its function well; for instance the excellence of the
eye makes the eye and its function good, since it is through the
excellence of the eye that we see well. Similarly the excellence of
20 the horse makes the horse good, i.e. good at running and carrying
its rider and standing firm against enemies. Now if that holds good
in every case, the excellence of a human being would be a state
from which one becomes a good human being and from which
one will perform one's function well. How that will come about
25 we have already said, but in addition it will become clear if we
consider what sort of thing the nature of that excellence is.

In every divisible continuum one can take larger, smaller and
equal quantities, either in respect of the thing itself or in relation to
us; equal quantities are a mean between the larger and the smaller.

The mean in the thing is what I call that which is equidistant 30
from the two extremes, which is one and the same in every case,
and the mean in relation to us is what I call that which is neither
excessive nor deficient; this is not one and the same in every case.
For instance if ten is a lot and two a little, six is taken as the mean
in respect of the thing, since it exceeds and is exceeded by an equal
amount. This is the mean according to arithmetical proportion. But 35
the mean in relation to us is not to be taken in the same way; for
it is not the case that if ten pounds is a lot to eat and two a little, 1106ᵇ
the trainer will prescribe six pounds. For that too is perhaps a
lot or a little for the person who is to take it; it is a little for
Milo, but a lot for someone who is beginning training. Similarly
with running and wrestling. So every expert avoids excess and 5
deficiency and seeks the mean and chooses it, not the mean in
the thing but the mean in relation to us. If, then, every expertise
completes its product well in this way, looking to the mean and
bringing its products into conformity with it (which is why people 10
regularly say of outstanding products that it is impossible to add or
take away anything from them, since excess and deficiency spoil
what is good but the mean preserves it, and good craftsmen, as
we say, work with an eye to this), excellence, which is better and
more precise than any craft, as nature is, is something which aims 15
at and hits the mean.
I am talking of virtue of character; for it has to do with feelings
and actions, and in these there is excess and deficiency and the
mean. For instance, it is possible to feel fear and boldness and
desire and anger and pity and in general pleasure and distress to a 20
greater or lesser extent, and to go wrong in either direction; but to
feel such things when one should, and about the things one should,
and in relation to the people one should, and for the sake of things
one should, and as one should, is the mean and the best, which
belongs to virtue. And similarly there is excess and deficiency and
the mean in the case of actions too. Virtue has to do with feelings
and actions, in which excess and deficiency are wrong and are 25
subject to blame, but the mean is praised and is right, both of
which belong to virtue. So virtue is a kind of middle state, in that
it is something which aims at and hits the mean. Further, it is
possible to go wrong in many ways (for what is bad comes within
the sphere of the indefinite, as the Pythagoreans conjectured, but 30
what is good within the definite) but to be correct in only one way

(which is why the former is easy and the latter hard, since it is easy to miss the mark but hard to hit it); so for these reasons excess and deficiency belong to vice, and the middle state to virtue;

35　　　　　　noble in one simple way, bad in all sorts of ways.

1107ᵃ Virtue, then, is a state concerned with choice, in a mean in relation to us, a mean determined by reason, namely the reason by which the person of practical wisdom would determine it. It is a mean between two vices, one of excess and the other of deficiency; further, it is a mean in that some states fall short of and others 5 exceed what should be in feelings and in actions, but virtue finds and chooses the mean. Therefore virtue is a mean in its nature and according to the formula which says what its essence is, but an extreme in point of value, in that it is the best.

Not every action or every feeling admits of the mean; for the 10 names of some of them of themselves include badness, e.g. joy in misfortune, shamelessness, and spite, and in the case of actions adultery, theft, and murder. For all of these and things like these are said as such to be bad, and not the excesses or the deficiencies 15 of them. Now one can never be right in regard to these, but must always go wrong; nor is there such a thing as doing well or not in such cases, in questions of whom one should commit adultery with, or when or how, but without qualification doing any of these is doing wrong. Now it is like looking for a mean and excess and deficiency in the cases of injustice and cowardice 20 and intemperance; that way there would be a mean in excess and deficiency and excess of excess and deficiency of deficiency. And just as there is no excess and deficiency in temperance and courage, since the mean is in a sense an extreme, so there is no 25 mean or excess or deficiency in those, but they are wrong in so far as they are done. For in general there is no mean in excess or deficiency, nor excess or deficiency in a mean.

BOOK TWO

CHAPTER 7

This account should not merely be stated universally, but should 30 also be applied to the particulars. For in practical discussions uni-versal statements have wider application, but specific ones are truer. Actions are concerned with particulars, and one must agree about these. Now one can get these from the table. Concerning fear and boldness courage is the mean; of those who are exces- **1107^b** sive the one who is excessive in lack of fear has no name (there are many which have no names), but the one who is excessive in boldness is overbold, and the one who is excessive in being afraid and deficient in being bold is cowardly. Concerning pleasure and distress—not all, and to a lesser extent concerning distress—the 5 mean is temperance and the excess is intemperance. There is simply no one who is deficient concerning pleasures, which is why people of that kind have not acquired a name, but let them be called insensible. Concerning giving and acquiring wealth the mean is generosity, and the excess and deficiency extravagance 10 and ungenerosity. In these matters they are excessive and deficient in opposite ways; the extravagant person exceeds in spending and is deficient in acquiring, but the ungenerous person exceeds in acquiring and is deficient in spending. Now for the present we are speaking in outline and by headings, which is sufficient 15 for the purpose; more precise discussion will come later. There are other dispositions to do with wealth; the mean is magnificence (the magnificent person differs from the generous, since the former has to do with large sums, the latter with small), the excess is bad taste and vulgarity, the deficiency shabbiness. These differ from 20 the subject-matter of generosity; how they differ will be explained later. Concerning honour and dishonour the mean is greatness of soul, the excess is what is called a sort of vanity and the deficiency is small-mindedness. And in the way we said that generosity differs from magnificence, in that it deals with small sums, there is 25 one that differs in the same way from greatness of soul (which deals with great honour), in that it deals with small-scale honour; for one can desire honour as one should and more and less than that, and the person who is excessive in these desires is ambitious, and the person who is deficient unambitious and the one who is in the middle has no name. The dispositions too have no 30 names, except the ambition of the ambitious person. This is why the extremes contest the middle ground; and sometimes we too call the person in the middle ambitious and sometimes unambitious, and sometimes we praise the ambitious and sometimes the **1108^a** unambitious. Why we do this will be explained in what follows; now let us speak of the rest in the way we have indicated.

There is excess and deficiency and a mean in respect of anger
5 too, and while these are more or less nameless, let us call the
person in the middle good-tempered and the mean good temper;
of the extremes let the excessive person be called irascible and
the vice irascibility, and the deficient a sort of 'unangry' person
and the deficiency 'unanger'. There are three other means which
10 have a certain similarity to one another, which none the less differ
from one another; they all have to do with social relations in
words and actions, but differ in that one has to do with the truth
in these matters, and the others with what is pleasant, the one in
amusement and the other in all the affairs of life. So let us treat
15 of these too, so as to see even more clearly that in all cases the
mean is praiseworthy but the extremes are neither praiseworthy
nor correct but blameworthy. Here too most of these have no
name, but we should try, as in the other cases, to coin names
ourselves for the sake of clarity, to make the exposition easier to
20 follow. Concerning the truth let the person in the middle be called
a truthful sort of person and the mean truthfulness, and let pretence
which exaggerates be called boastfulness and the person who goes
in for it a boaster, and pretence which minimizes dissembling
and the person who goes in for it a dissembler. Concerning what
is pleasant in amusement, the person in the middle is witty and
25 the disposition is wit, the excess is buffoonery and its possessor
a buffoon, while the deficient person is a kind of boor and the
disposition is boorishness. Concerning the rest of what is pleasant,
in life as a whole, the person who is pleasant as one should be is
friendly and the mean is friendliness, while the excessive person,
if it is not for any particular purpose, is ingratiating, or, if it is for
personal advantage, a flatterer, while the person who is deficient
30 and unpleasant in everything is quarrelsome and disagreeable.

There are also means in episodes and kinds of feeling; for
shame is not a virtue, but yet the modest person too is praised. In
these cases that kind of person is said to be in the middle, while
another is called excessive, i.e. the bashful one who is ashamed
35 of everything; the one who is deficient, or who is ashamed of
absolutely nothing, is shameless, and the one in the middle mod-
1108ᵇ est. Indignation is a mean between spite and joy in misfortune,
and they are concerned with pleasure and distress at what happens to others; the indignant person is distressed at those who
do well undeservedly, but the spiteful person exceeds him in

being distressed at everyone's good fortune, while the person who 5
rejoices in misfortune falls so far short of being distressed as actually to rejoice.

There will, however, be a further opportunity to discuss these
topics later; after that we shall consider justice, and since that term
is not applied in a single sense, we shall distinguish both its kinds
and show in what way each is a mean. And similarly with the
intellectual excellences.   10

BOOK TWO

CHAPTER 8

As there are three dispositions, two of them vices, one of excess
and the other of deficiency, and one a virtue, the mean, all of
them are in a way opposed to each other. For the extremes are
opposite both to the mean and to one another, and the mean to the 15
extremes; as the equal is larger than the smaller and smaller than
the larger, so the mean states exceed the deficiencies and fall short
of the excesses in feelings and actions. For the courageous person
appears overbold in comparison with the coward and cowardly in 20
comparison with the overbold, and similarly the temperate person
appears intemperate in comparison with the insensible and insensible in comparison with the intemperate, and the generous person
extravagant in comparison with the ungenerous, and ungenerous in
comparison with the extravagant. This is why each of the extremes
pushes the person in the middle in the direction of the other, and
the coward calls the courageous overbold and the overbold calls 25
him a coward, and analogously in the other cases.

While they are opposed to each other in this way, the greatest
opposition is that of the extremes towards one another, rather than
to the mean; for they are further from one another than from the
mean, as the large is further from the small and the small further 30
from the large than both are from the equal. Moreover, in the case
of some extremes a certain similarity is apparent when they are
related to the mean, e.g. in overboldness in relation to courage and
in extravagance in relation to generosity; but the greatest unlike-
ness is that of extremes in relation to one another. Those which
are furthest from one another are defined as opposites, so that the

35　further apart things are, the more opposite they are. In relation
1109ᵃ　to the mean, in some cases the deficiency is more opposed and
in others the excess, for instance in the case of courage it is not
the excess, overboldness, but the deficiency, cowardice, but in the
case of temperance it is not the deficiency, insensibility, but the
5　excess, intemperance. This comes about for two reasons, the first
intrinsic to the thing itself; it is because one extreme is closer to
the mean and more like it that we regard not it but its opposite
as more opposed to the mean. For instance, since overboldness
10　seems more like courage and closer to it, but cowardice less like,
we regard the latter as more opposed; for the things further from
the mean seem to be more opposite. This is one reason, intrinsic
to the thing itself. The other is due to us; the things we ourselves
15　are naturally more prone to, seem more opposite to the mean.
For instance we ourselves are naturally more prone to pleasures,
and so we are more readily inclined towards intemperance than
towards moderation. So we call those things more opposite, to
which we are more given; that is why the excess, intemperance,
is more opposite to temperance.

BOOK TWO

CHAPTER 9

20　We have, then, done enough to show that virtue of character is a
mean, and how it is, namely a mean between two vices, one of
excess and the other of deficiency, and that it has that character in
so far as it aims at and hits the mean in feelings and actions. This
is why it is a hard task to be good. For in each case it is a hard
25　task to find the mean, as finding the centre of a circle is a task
not for anyone, but for the expert. Similarly it is easy to be angry
and to give and spend money, and anyone can do those things;
but to whom and how much and when and for the sake of what
and how, that is no longer a matter for anyone, nor easy. That is
why doing well is something rare and praiseworthy and fine.
30　　　Therefore the person who is aiming at the mean must first of
all keep away from what is more opposite, as Calypso advises

　　　Keep your ship well off from that surge and spray.

For of the extremes it is a greater error to be in one, a lesser to be in the other. So since it is difficult to hit the mean exactly, the next best course, they say, is to choose the least of the evils; 35 and the best way to do that is to follow this advice. And we must **1109^b** keep an eye on what we are ourselves inclined to, since some of us are naturally prone to one thing, others to another; that will be clear to us from the pleasure and distress we feel. We must force ourselves in the opposite direction; for it is by keeping well away 5 from wrongdoing that we shall attain the mean, as people do who straighten warped planks. Above all we must beware of pleasure and what is pleasant; for our judgement of it is not unbiased. So we should feel about pleasure as the elders of the people felt about Helen, and we should always repeat their maxim; in that 10 way we shall dismiss it and do less wrong. So, to sum up, if we do these things, we shall best be able to hit the mean. But that is perhaps difficult, especially in particular cases; for it is not easy to 15 determine how and with whom and about what and how long one should be angry. Sometimes we praise people who are deficient in this respect and say that they are good-tempered, and sometimes those who are angry, calling them manly. The person who deviates from doing well to a small extent, either too much or too little, is not blamed, but the person who deviates more is, for such a 20 person does not escape notice. But up to what point and to what extent one's deviation is blameworthy is not easy to determine by reason, nor is any other instance of what is perceptible; for these things are in the sphere of particulars, and the judgement lies in the perception of them.

So much then to show that the mean state is praiseworthy in all cases, but that one should sometimes incline towards excess and 25 sometimes towards deficiency; that way we shall most easily hit the mean and do well.

1109ᵇ Since virtue is concerned with feelings and actions, and since praise and blame are accorded to those that are voluntary and excuse, and sometimes pity as well, to those that are involuntary, it is presumably necessary for those who are investigating the topic of virtue to define the voluntary and the involuntary, and it is also

35 useful for legislators with a view to honours and punishments.

1110ᵃ Now things that occur by force or through error appear to be involuntary; something that occurs by force is something whose origin is external, so that the agent (or rather the person to whom the thing happens) contributes nothing—for instance, if one is carried away somewhere by the wind or by men who have one in their power.

Things done for the fear of greater evils or for the sake of some-
5 thing fine—for instance if a tyrant who had one's parents and children in his power were to order one to do something shameful, and if they would be saved if one did it but killed if one did not—give rise to dispute whether they are involuntary or voluntary. Something similar arises in cases of jettisoning in a storm;
10 no one jettisons voluntarily without qualification, but to save oneself and the others every sensible person does. So actions of that kind are mixed, but they more closely resemble voluntary actions; for they are choiceworthy at the time when they are done, and an action is complete according to the circumstances prevailing at the time. So the terms 'voluntary' and 'involuntary' are applied to
15 the action when it is done. And one acts voluntarily, because in such actions the origin of one's moving one's limbs is in oneself; and where the origin is in oneself, it is also up to one to act or not. So such things are voluntary, though perhaps they are, taken without qualification, involuntary; for no one would choose any such thing for itself.

20 People are sometimes even praised for such actions, when they endure something shameful or distressing for the sake of something great and fine; but if it is the reverse, they are censured, since

enduring the most shameful things for the sake of nothing fine, or a small thing of that kind, is the mark of a bad person. In some cases praise is not accorded, but excuse, when one does something one should not because of things that overstrain human nature and which no one would endure. But there are some things which perhaps one cannot be necessitated to do, but one should rather die having suffered the most terrible things; and indeed the things that 'necessitated' Euripides' Alcmaeon to commit matricide appear absurd. And it is sometimes difficult to determine what one should choose in preference to what and what one should endure in preference to what, and more difficult still to stick to what one has decided, since usually the things one expects to occur are distressing and the things one is necessitated to do are shameful, whence praise and blame are accorded to those who are necessitated or not.

What sorts of things, then, are to be described as occurring by force? Should we say that the term applies without qualification to those things where the cause is external and the agent contributes nothing? But those which are in themselves involuntary, but which are chosen in the present circumstances and for the sake of such-and-such ends, and whose origin is in the agent, are in themselves involuntary, but in the present circumstances and for the sake of such-and-such ends voluntary. And they are more like voluntary actions; for actions are determined by the particular circumstances, and those are voluntary. It is not easy to pronounce on what should be chosen in preference to what; for there are many variations in the particular circumstances.

If one were to say that pleasant and fine things are forcible, on the ground that they are external things which necessitate, one would have to count everything as occurring by force; for everyone does everything for the sake of those ends. And people who act under forcible compulsion and involuntarily find it distressing, but those who act for the sake of the pleasant and the fine do so with pleasure. It is absurd to count external things as the cause of what one does, rather than oneself for being readily ensnared by such things, and to count oneself as the cause of one's fine actions, but pleasant things as the cause of one's shameful ones. Hence, it seems that what occurs by force is that whose origin is external, the person who is forced contributing nothing.

Everything done through error is non-voluntary, while things done through error which one regrets and is distressed to have done

are involuntary; the person who has done something through error
20 who is not at all displeased at the action has not acted voluntarily,
in that he did not know what it was that he was doing, but has
not acted involuntarily either, since he is not distressed. Of those
who act through error, the person who regrets doing so seems to
have acted involuntarily, but let the person who does not regret
doing so (who is a different case) be said to have acted non-
voluntarily; since he is different, it is better that he should have a
specific name.

25   Acting through error appears different from acting in error;
someone who is drunk or angry does not seem to act through
error but through one of those conditions, and not to act knowingly but in error. Now every wicked person is in error about what
one should do and what one should abstain from, and it is because
they go wrong in that way that they become unjust and in general
30 bad people; but the term 'involuntary' is not applied if one is in
error about what it is appropriate to do. Error in one's choice is
a cause, not of involuntariness, but of wickedness, nor is universal error (people are censured for this); involuntariness is caused
1111ᵃ by error about particular circumstances in which and about which
one's action occurs. Pity and excuse are accorded on the basis of
them, since it is the person who is in error about one or other of
them who acts involuntarily.

Perhaps it is not out of place to determine what they are and of
how many kinds: who did something and what they did and to do
with what and in what circumstances, and sometimes with what,
5 e.g. with what instrument, and with a view to what, e.g. saving
someone, and how, e.g. gently or violently. Now no one but a
madman could be in error about all of these, and it is clear that
one could not be in error about the agent; for how could one be in
error about oneself? But someone could be in error about what he
is doing, e.g. people say that things slipped out while they were
10 talking, or they did not know that they were secret, like Aeschylus
about the mysteries, or they wanted to demonstrate it but let it off,
like the man with the catapult. And one might think that one's
son was an enemy, like Merope, or that a sharpened spear had a
button on the end, or that the stone was pumice. And one might
give someone a drink to save them, but kill them; and one might
15 want to touch someone lightly, as in sparring, but strike them hard.
Now error arises about all these circumstances of the action, and

[margin notes in handwriting: "ERROR ∠ OF action? Knowledge?"; "In error about what is appropriate to do"; "having to do w/ particulars"]

the person who is in error about any one of them appears to have acted involuntarily, and particularly as regards the most important, which are the circumstances of the action and its aim. If anything is counted involuntary because of this kind of error, the action 20
must also be distressing and be regretted.

Since the involuntary consists of what occurs by force and through error, the voluntary would appear to be that of which the origin is in oneself, when one knows the particular circumstances of one's action.

Now presumably it is not correct to say that things done from 25
spirit or desire are involuntary. First of all, in that case none of the other animals, or children, will act voluntarily. Then, is it the case that we do voluntarily none of the things we do from desire and spirit, or that we do the fine ones voluntarily and the shameful ones involuntarily? Surely that is ridiculous, since they have a single cause. And presumably it is absurd to call involuntary things one 30
should want; and indeed one should get angry at some things and desire some things, such as health and learning. And it seems that things that occur involuntarily are distressing, but things that occur in accordance with our desire are pleasant. Further, how do cases where we go wrong in calculation differ in respect of being involuntary from those where we go wrong through spirit? Both are to be avoided, and the non-rational feelings appear no less 1111ᵇ
proper to humans, so that actions from spirit and desire are no less human actions. So it is absurd to class them as involuntary.

BOOK THREE

CHAPTER 2

Now that the voluntary and the involuntary have been defined, the next topic for discussion is choice, as it seems most intimately 5
bound up with virtue and seems to distinguish types of character more than actions do.

Choice seems to be something voluntary, but not identical with it, since the voluntary extends more widely; children and the other animals have a share in the voluntary, but not in choice, and we call sudden actions voluntary, but not in accordance with choice. 10
Those who say that it is desire or spirit or wish or some kind of

belief do not appear to be correct; for choice is not common to the non-rational creatures too, but desire and spirit are. And the uncontrolled person acts from desire, but not from choice; whereas the
15 self-controlled person, on the contrary, acts from choice, not from desire. And desire is opposed to choice, but desire is not opposed to desire. And desire is for what is pleasant and what is distressing, but choice is neither of the unpleasant nor of the pleasant. Even less is it spirit; things done from spirit seem least of all in
20 accordance with choice. Then again, it is not wish either, though it appears closely related; for one cannot choose impossible things, and someone who said that he chose such things would seem silly, but one can wish for impossible things too, such as immortality. And one can also wish for things which could never be brought about through one's own efforts, e.g. that a certain actor or athlete should win; but no one chooses things like that, but rather things
25 that one thinks would come about through one's own agency. And wish is rather for the end, but choice is of the things which contribute to the end, for instance we wish to be healthy and choose the things that will make us healthy, and we wish to be happy and say we do, but it is not appropriate to say we choose to be
30 happy; in general choice is concerned with the things that are up to us. Nor would it seem to be belief; belief seems to be concerned with everything, eternal and impossible things no less than what is up to us. And it is differentiated into the true and the false, not the bad and good, but choice is differentiated rather by
1112ᵃ the latter. Perhaps no one identifies it with belief as such; but it is not identical with any specific kind of belief either, since our characters are differentiated by our choice of good or bad, but not by our beliefs. We choose to have or to avoid such things, but our beliefs are about what something is or whom it is good for
5 or how; we simply do not believe to have or to avoid something. Our choices are praised for being of the right thing rather than for being made in the right way, but our beliefs for being true. And we choose what we most assuredly know to be good, but we have beliefs about what we do not at all know; and the same people do not always seem to choose the best things and to believe that
10 they are the best, but some people believe that something is better, but through vice choose what they should not. It makes no difference if belief precedes or follows choice; that is not what we are considering, but whether it is the same as some kind of

belief. So what is it, or what kind of thing, since it is none of the things we have mentioned? It seems to be voluntary, but not everything voluntary is an object of choice. Is it then what has been deliberated before? <u>For choice is accompanied by reasoning and thought.</u> <u>The name too seems to indicate that it is something chosen before other things.</u> 15

BOOK THREE

CHAPTER 3

Do people deliberate about everything, and is everything an object of deliberation, or are there some things about which there is no deliberation? Perhaps we should call an object of deliberation not what a silly person or a madman would deliberate about, but what a sensible person would. Now no one deliberates about things that are eternally so, such as about the cosmos or the incommensurability of the side and the diagonal. Nor about things which involve change, but which always happen in the same way, whether by necessity or by nature or from some other cause, such as the solstices and the risings of the heavenly bodies. Nor about variable events, such as droughts and rains. Nor about things that happen by chance, such as finding treasure. Nor about all human affairs, e.g. no Spartan deliberates about the best form of government for the Scythians. <u>For none of these things would come about through our agency, but we deliberate about things that are up to us and can be done</u>: that is, the remainder when those are excluded. For the causes of things seem to be nature and necessity and chance, and then intelligence and every kind of human agency. And among humans, each kind of people deliberate about the things that are to be done though their agency. 20 25 30

There is no deliberation about the precise and self-standing sciences, e.g. writing (for we do not differ about how one should write); but <u>we deliberate about things that come about through our agency, but not always in the same way</u>, for instance about medicine and money-making, and about steersmanship more than about athletics, in so far as it has been less precisely worked out, and similarly about the rest, and more about the practical crafts than about the sciences, since we differ more about those. Deliberation occurs in the sphere of things which hold for the most part, 1112^b 5

where it is unclear how they will turn out, and in which there is
10 an indefinite element. We call in advisers on important matters,
since we are distrustful of our own ability to decide.

And we deliberate not about our ends but about the things which
contribute to our ends; a doctor does not deliberate whether to heal,
or an orator whether to persuade, or a statesman whether to create
15 good order in society, nor do any of the rest deliberate about their
end; rather, having posited their end, they consider how and by
what means they can achieve it. And if it appears that it can come
about in several ways, they consider by which it will be best and
most easily achieved, and if it can be achieved by only one, how
it will come about by means of that and by what means that in
turn will come about, until they reach the first cause, which is the
20 last thing to be discovered. The deliberator seems to investigate
and analyse in this way as one does a geometrical problem (it
seems that not every investigation is deliberation, e.g. mathematical investigations, but all deliberation is a sort of investigation),
and the last step in the analysis is the first in bringing about the
25 result. If they come on something which is impossible, they give
up; for instance, if one needs money, but none is to be had; but if
it seems possible, they set about doing it. Things which are possible are those which could come about through our own agency;
and things which come about through the agency of our friends
do so in a way through our own agency, since their origin is in
us. Sometimes we seek to find instruments and sometimes how to
30 use them; and similarly in the other cases we seek a means or a
method or someone through whose agency it could come about.
As we have said, it seems that it is the human being who is the
origin of his actions; deliberation is about things to be done by
oneself, but one's actions are for the sake of other things. It is
not one's end which is an object of deliberation, but the things
1113ᵃ which contribute to one's end. Nor is it particular things, e.g. if
this is bread or if it is properly baked; those are matters for perception. If one never stops deliberating, one will go on to infinity.
The object of deliberation and the object of choice are the same,
except that the object of choice is what has already been determined; for it is what has been judged as the result of deliberation
5 that is the object of choice. Each person stops investigating what
to do when he brings the origin back to himself, and specifically
to the controlling element in himself; for that is what makes the

[margin note:] Not the end that delib is concerned w/

[bottom handwritten note:] So some decisions are (NOT) the products of deliberation since some must end delib.

choice. This is clear also from the ancient forms of government which Homer described; for the kings announced to the people what they had chosen to do. Since the object of choice is one of the things which are up to us, something which is an object of deliberation and desire, choice is deliberative desire of the things which are up to us; having judged as a result of deliberation, we desire in accordance with our deliberation. This may suffice as an outline account of choice and its objects, including its being concerned with the things that contribute to our ends. 10

[margin note: DELIB. ↕ DESIRE ↓ DELIBERATIVE DESIRE]

BOOK THREE

CHAPTER 4

We have said that wish is for the end; some people think that it is for the good, others that it is for the apparent good. A consequence for those who say that the object of wish is the good is that what the person who chooses incorrectly wishes for is not an object of wish (for if it is an object of wish, it will also be good; but it was, as it happened, bad); and for those who say on the other hand that the apparent good is the object of wish, it is a consequence that there is nothing which is by nature an object of wish, but what seems so to each individual; different things seem so to different people, including opposites, in some cases. Now if neither view is satisfactory, should we say that what is really and without qualification an object of wish is the good, but for each person what appears so to him? So for the good person it is what is really so, but for the bad it is whatever it happens to be, just as the things which are really healthy are healthy for those in good bodily condition, but other things for those who are diseased, and similarly bitter and sweet and hot and heavy and all the rest. For the good person judges each of these things correctly, and in each thing the truth appears so to him. For each type of character has kinds of fine and pleasant things which are specific to it, and perhaps the good person differs the most by seeing the truth in each, being as it were the standard and measure of them. But the deception to which most people are subject seems to be effected by pleasure, which appears good but is not. So they choose what is pleasant as a good, and avoid distress as an evil. 15 20 25 30 1113^b

BOOK THREE

CHAPTER 5

Since the end is something which we wish for, and the things
which contribute to the end are things which we deliberate about
5 and choose, actions concerned with those things are in accordance with choice and voluntary. And the exercise of the virtues
is concerned with those things. So virtue is up to us, and vice as
well; where acting is up to us, not acting is up to us too, and where
one can say No, one can also say Yes; so that if doing something
fine by acting is up to us, then equally, doing something disgrace-
10 ful by not acting will be up to us, and if doing something fine by
not acting is up to us, so is doing something disgraceful by acting.
And if doing fine and disgraceful things is up to us, the same is
true of not doing them, and since that is what being good and bad
is, being worthy or unworthy people is therefore up to us.

15 Saying that no one is voluntarily wicked or involuntarily blessed
seems to be partly true, partly false; no one is blessed involuntarily,
but wickedness is voluntary. Or should we dispute what has been
said, and say that a person is not the origin and begetter of his
actions as of his children? But if that does seem to be so, and we
20 cannot take our actions back to any other origins than those in us,
then those things whose origins are in us are themselves up to us
and voluntary.

This seems to be confirmed both by our individual behaviour and
by the practice of legislators; for they chastise and punish those
who do wicked things, provided it is not by force or through error
25 for which they are not themselves responsible, and they honour
those who do fine things, with a view to promoting the one and
preventing the other. But no one is encouraged to do what is not
up to us or voluntary, since there would be no point in being
persuaded not to get warm or suffer pain or be hungry or anything
30 else like that; we shall suffer them none the less. And indeed they
punish people for error itself, if one seems to be responsible for
one's error; for instance, in cases of drunkenness the penalties are
doubled, for the origin was in the person himself; he was capable
of not getting drunk, and that was what was responsible for his
error. And they punish people for being in error about things in
the laws which one ought to know and which are not difficult to

find out, and similarly in other cases where people seem to be in error through carelessness, since they were capable of taking care.

But perhaps someone is of such a nature as not to take care. But people are themselves responsible for becoming like that through living slackly, and of being unjust or intemperate through acting 5 unjustly or spending their life in drinking bouts and so on; it is their practice in each kind of case which makes them that sort of person. That is clear from people who train for any kind of contest or activity; they practise continually. Now not to know that states 10 of character develop from practice in every kind of case is the mark of someone totally lacking in sense.

Moreover, it is absurd to say that the person who is behaving unjustly does not wish to be unjust, or that the person who is behaving intemperately does not wish to be intemperate. If someone not in error does things as a result of which he will be unjust, he will be unjust voluntarily, but that does not mean if he wishes to he will stop being unjust and will be just instead, any more than a sick person will be healthy. But if the circumstances 15 are such, he is ill voluntarily, through living in an uncontrolled way and disobeying his doctors. Then it was possible for him not to be ill, but when things have gone on it is no longer so, just as someone who has thrown a stone is no longer able to bring it back. But all the same, throwing it was up to him; for the origin was in him. In the same way it was possible from the start for the unjust and the intemperate not to become that sort of people, 20 so they are so voluntarily; but once they have become so it is no longer possible for them not to be.

It is not only defects of the soul which are voluntary, but in some cases those of the body too, which we also censure; for no one criticizes people who are naturally ugly, but we do those who are so through lack of training and carelessness. Similarly with 25 those who are weak or crippled; no one would reproach someone congenitally blind, or blind from illness or as a result of a blow, but would rather pity them; but everyone would criticize someone blind through heavy drinking or some other kind of intemperance. It is, then, bodily defects which are up to us which are censured, and those not up to us which are not; and if that is so, those defects 30 of other kinds which are censured are up to us.

Now suppose someone were to say that everyone pursues the apparent good, and we are not in control of how things appear to

1114ᵇ us, but the end appears to each person corresponding to the sort of person he is. Now if each individual is in a way responsible for his state of character, he will be himself responsible for the way things appear to him as well. If not, no one is responsible for evil-doing,

5 but does these things through error about the end, in the belief that he will achieve what is best by doing those things; no one's pursuit of the end is self-chosen, but it must develop naturally like sight, enabling one to judge well and choose what is really good, and the person in whom this has developed well will be someone who has natural goodness. The greatest and finest thing

10 is something which one cannot pick up or learn from someone else, but it will result from natural development, and having developed well and finely in this respect is complete and genuine natural goodness.

Now if that is true, why will virtue be more voluntary than vice? To good and bad alike the end appears and is established by nature

15 or however else, and for the rest they act however they do with reference to that. Now if it is not by nature that the end appears however it does to each person, but there is something which they contribute themselves, or if the end is natural, but virtue is voluntary in view of the fact that the good person does the other

20 things voluntarily, vice in its turn would be no less voluntary. For in the case of the bad person too there is something which comes about through him, in his actions even if not in the end. So if, as is said, our virtues are voluntary (for we are in a way ourselves jointly responsible for our states, and it is by being people of such and such a kind that we set up such-and-such an end for ourselves),

25 our vices too would be voluntary; for the cases are alike.

We have, then, spoken about the virtues collectively and outlined the kind of thing they are: namely, means and states, pointing out that they are in themselves productive of the very things which give rise to them, and that they are up to us and volun-

30 tary, and that they are as correct reason prescribes. Actions and states are not voluntary in the same way; for we are in control of our actions from beginning to end, since we know the particular

1115ᵃ circumstances, but as far as states are concerned we are in control of their origin, but their detailed development is not known to us, as is the case with diseases. But as it is up to us make use of them or not in any particular way, for that reason they are voluntary.

Let us resume and, taking the virtues individually, say which each one is, and what its objects are and how it relates to them;   5 at the same time that will make it clear how many they are.

BOOK THREE

CHAPTER 6

First, courage. It has already been made clear that it is a mean concerned with fear and boldness; it is clear that we fear fearful things, and that these are, speaking without qualification, evils. That is why people define fear as expectation of evil. Now we   10 fear all evils, such as ill-fame, poverty, illness, lack of friends, and death, but the courageous person does not seem to be concerned with all of them. For there are some things which one should fear, and which it is fine to fear and disgraceful not to, such as ill-fame; the person who fears that is good and modest, but the person who does not fear it is shameless. Such a person is said by some   15 to be courageous in a transferred sense, since he has something in common with the courageous person, since the latter is also a fearless sort of person. Perhaps one should not fear poverty or illness, or in general evils which are not the result of wickedness or one's own fault. But in any case the person who is fearless about those is not courageous. That person too we call courageous in virtue of similarity; for some who are cowardly in the perils of   20 war are generous and endure financial loss in a cheerful spirit. Nor if someone fears outrages against his wife and children, or spite or anything like that, is he cowardly, nor if he is undaunted when he is about to be flogged is he courageous. So what fearful things is the courageous person concerned with? Surely the most fearful.   25 For no one is more enduring of frightening things. And death is the most fearful thing; for it is the end, and it seems that for the dead nothing is good or bad any more. But the courageous person would not seem to be concerned with death in every circumstance, e.g. at sea or from illness. In which, then? Surely in the finest   30 circumstances. Death in battle is of that kind; for it occurs amid the greatest and the finest danger. The honours accorded by states and monarchs bear this out. Now the person who is called courageous in the primary sense is the one who is fearless in the face of a

noble death and its imminent causes, and these are above all the
35 circumstances of battle. The courageous person is indeed fearless
1115^b at sea and in illness, but not in the way that sailors are; courageous
people have given up hope of survival and despise a death of that
kind, while sailors are confident through experience. Then, people
show courage in circumstances in which one can resist the danger
5 or in which it is fine to die, neither of which is the case in those
kinds of death.

BOOK THREE

CHAPTER 7

What is fearful is not the same for everyone, but we say that
some fearful things are beyond human capacity. These are fearful
to every sensible person; but things that are fearful for a human
10 being differ in magnitude and degree, and similarly with things
that inspire boldness. The courageous person is undisturbed as
appropriate to a human being. So he will fear such things, but
will endure them as he should and as reason prescribes for the
sake of the fine; for that is the goal proper to virtue. Now one
can fear these things to a greater or lesser degree and can also
15 fear things which are not fearful as if they were such. One way of
going wrong is fearing what one should not, another as one should
not, another when one should not, and so on; and similarly with
boldness. The person who endures and fears what one should for
the sake of what one should, as and when one should, and is bold
in the same way, is courageous; for the courageous person feels
20 and acts as is appropriate and as reason prescribes. The goal of
every activity is what is in accordance with the state; and to the
courageous person courage is something fine. So that is the nature
of the goal; for each thing is determined by its goal. So it is for
the sake of the fine that the courageous person endures and does
courageous actions.

Of those in excessive states the person who is excessive in
25 lack of fear has no name (we said previously that there are many
which have no name), but would be some sort of madman or
insensate person if he feared nothing, not even an earthquake or
the waves, as they say the Celts do; but the person who is excessive

in boldness about fearful things is overbold. The overbold person
seems to be a boaster who puts on a pretence of courage; at any rate   30
he wants to appear the way the courageous person is with regard to
fearful things, so he imitates him in circumstances in which he can.
That is why many of them are 'bold cowards'; though they are
bold in those circumstances, they do not endure fearful things. The
person who is excessive in fearing is a coward; for he fears what
he should not and as he should not, and all the rest follows in his   35
case. He is also deficient in boldness, but is more obvious for his   1116^a
excess of distress. The coward is someone who lacks hope, since
he fears everything. But the courageous person is the opposite;
for boldness is the mark of the confident person. So the coward
and the overbold and the courageous are concerned with the same
things, but are in different conditions with respect to them; for the   5
first two are excessive and deficient, but the third is in a mean
state and as one should be. And the overbold are impetuous, eager
before danger occurs but avoiding it when it comes, while the
courageous are keen in action but quiet beforehand.

As we have said, courage is a mean with regard to things which   10
inspire boldness and fearful things; the term is applied in those
circumstances, and the courageous person chooses and endures
them because it is fine to do so or disgraceful not to. Dying to
avoid poverty or love or something distressing is not appropriate
to a courageous person, but rather to a coward; for it is softness
to flee from what is unpleasant, and one does not endure death   15
because it is fine, but as a way of fleeing from an evil.

BOOK THREE

CHAPTER 8

That is the sort of thing which courage is, but there are five other
states which are called sorts of courage. First comes civic courage,
since it has the closest resemblance. Citizens seem to face dangers
because of the penalties of the law and public disgrace and honour,
and therefore the most courageous seem to be those among whom   20
the cowardly are disgraced and the courageous honoured. Homer
depicts people of that kind, such as Diomede and Hector, who say

Polydamas will be the first to heap reproach on me

and

25
>   Hector will say when he speaks to the Trojans
>   'The son of Tydeus has fled from me.'

This sort most closely resembles the one previously discussed,
because it comes about from virtue, i.e. from shame and the desire
for the fine (namely honour) and the avoidance of disgrace, as
30 something shameful. Someone might class under the same heading
those who are compelled by their leaders; but they are inferior,
inasmuch as they do this not from shame but from fear, and what
they avoid is not disgrace but suffering. For those in command
compel them, as Hector does when he says

>   If I see anyone shrinking from the battle
35   He will not be able to avoid the dogs,

1116ᵇ and their officers, who beat them if they retreat, do the same, as
do those who make them stand in front of trenches and things
like that; all of these are forms of compulsion. But one should be
courageous not from compulsion, but because it is fine.

Every sort of experience also seems to be a sort of courage;
5 hence Socrates thought that courage was knowledge. Different
sorts of people are experienced in different areas, and in military matters it is professional soldiers. For there are many aspects
of war where there is no danger, which they in particular have
become familiar with; so they seem courageous, because the others do not know how these things are. Further, as a result of
their experience they are particularly capable of performing feats
10 without being harmed, because they can use their weapons and are
best equipped to perform and to avoid harm. They are like armed
men fighting against unarmed or athletes against the untrained; for
in conflicts of those kinds it is not the most courageous who are
15 the most capable, but the strongest, who are in the best physical
condition. But professional soldiers become cowardly when the
danger overreaches them, and they are let down by their numbers
and their preparations; they are the first to run away, but the citizen
soldiers hold their ground and are killed, as happened in the battle
at the shrine of Hermes. For to them running away is disgraceful
20 and death preferable to survival by such means; but the others ven-
tured from the start on the assumption that they were the stronger,
but when they realize the truth, they run away, fearing death more
than disgrace. But the courageous person is not like that.

People also bring spirit under the heading of courage. Those who from spirit rush like wild beasts against those who have injured 25 them also seem courageous, since for their part courageous people are spirited. For spirit is something which especially spurs people on to face dangers; hence we have in Homer 'he cast strength into his spirit' and 'he stirred up rage and spirit' and 'fierce rage breathed through his nostrils' and 'his blood boiled'. All such expressions seem to stand for impetus and the rousing of spirit. 30 Now courageous people act for the sake of the fine, and spirit helps them; but animals do it from pain, because they have been struck or are frightened, since if they are in a wood they do not attack. Now rushing into danger because one is driven on by pain and spirit without any sense in advance of the frightening things one has to face is not courage, because on that score even donkeys 35 would be courageous when hungry, since they don't stop grazing **1117ᵃ** even when they are beaten; and adulterers do lots of daring things from lust. Now courage prompted by spirit seems to be something purely natural, but it is when in addition it includes choice and 5 the goal that it is courage. And people feel distress when they are roused to anger, and pleasure when they retaliate; people who fight for these reasons are combative, but not courageous; for they do not do it for the sake of the fine or as reason prescribes, but from feeling. And so they have something similar to courage.

Nor indeed are the confident courageous. They are bold amid 10 dangers because they have often won and beaten many opponents. They are similar, because both kinds of people are bold; but the courageous are bold for the reasons stated, whereas these people are bold because they think they are extremely strong and will come to no harm. People in drink behave the same way; they 15 become confident, but when things do not turn out that way, they run away. But it was, we saw, the mark of the courageous person to endure things which are and appear fearful for a human being because it is fine to do so and disgraceful not to. That is why it appears to be the mark of a more courageous person to be fearless and undismayed in sudden alarms than in those which are expected. Acting that way springs more from one's state of 20 character, because less from preparation; when things are apparent in advance, one can choose what to do from calculation and reasoning, but in sudden cases one acts in accordance with one's state of character.

The ignorant also appear courageous; they are not far removed from the confident, but are inferior in so far as they do not have any self-esteem, whereas the confident do. That is why the latter stand firm for a time; but once those who have made a mistake
25 know that things are other than they supposed, they run away, as the Argives did when they attacked the Spartans, taking them for Sicyonians.

We have now said what sort of people the courageous are, and those who merely seem courageous.

BOOK THREE

CHAPTER 9

While courage is concerned with boldness and fear, it is not con-
30 cerned with both equally, but more with fearful things. For the person who is undisturbed amid them and in the right condition about them is courageous, rather than the person who is that way with things that inspire boldness. It is from enduring distressing things, as we have said, that people are called courageous. That is why courage is itself unpleasant, and is rightly praised; for it
35 is more difficult to endure distressing things than to abstain from
1117^b pleasant. But for all that, the goal in cases of courage seems to be pleasant, but to be obscured by the circumstances, as is also the case in sporting contests. For boxers the goal for which they fight,
5   the crown and the honours, is pleasant, but since they are made of flesh and blood, being punched and all the trouble involved is painful and distressing. And because there is a great deal of that, the goal seems something small, with nothing pleasant about it. Now if the case of courage is like that, death and wounds will be distressing to the courageous person, who will suffer them unwillingly, but he will endure them because it is fine to do so or because
10 it is disgraceful not to. And the more complete his virtue is and the happier he is, the more he will be distressed at the prospect of death; for to someone like that life is most worth living, and he will knowingly be deprived of the greatest goods, and that is distressing. But he will be no less courageous, and perhaps even
15 more so, in that he chooses the fine in battle in preference to those things. So it is not the case that in all the virtues the exercise of them is pleasant, except in so far as it achieves the goal.

Perhaps there is nothing to prevent the best soldiers being not people like that, but those who are less courageous, but have no other good in their lives; they are ready for dangers, and give their lives in exchange for modest gains.   20

That concludes our discussion of courage; it is not difficult to get an outline of it from what has been said.

BOOK THREE

CHAPTER 10

Next let us discuss temperance; for these seem to be the virtues of the non-rational parts.

Now we have said that temperance is a mean concerned with   25
pleasures; it is concerned with distress to a lesser extent and not in the same way. Intemperance appears to have the same sphere. So let us now demarcate which pleasures it is concerned with. Let us distinguish bodily pleasures from those of the mind, such as love of honour and love of learning; in either of those cases the   30
person enjoys the thing he is a lover of, without the body being affected in any way, but rather the intellect, but people are not called temperate or intemperate with reference to pleasures of that kind. It is the same with people who go in for the other non-bodily pleasures; we call people who love stories and news and like spending their time on trivial matters gossips, not intemperate,   35
nor do we apply that term to people who are distressed by money   1118^a
matters, or by what happens to their friends. But temperance would seem to be concerned with bodily pleasures, but not even all of those; for people who enjoy objects of sight, such as colours and shapes and drawings, are called neither temperate nor intemperate.   5
Yet it would seem possible to enjoy such things as one should, too much, and too little. And similarly with objects of hearing; no one calls people who excessively enjoy music or plays intemperate, nor temperate those who enjoy them as one should. Nor people who enjoy smells, except incidentally; we do not call people who enjoy   10
the smell of apples or roses or incense intemperate, but rather those who enjoy the smells of perfumes or dainties, because intemperate people enjoy those things, since they arouse memory of the things they desire. One can indeed see other people too enjoying the

15 smell of food, when they are hungry; but enjoying such things
is the mark of the intemperate person, for it is he who has those
desires. Other animals do not have pleasure in these senses except
incidentally; dogs take pleasure, not in the smell of hares, but in
20 eating them; smell enabled them to perceive their prey. Nor does
the lion take pleasure in the lowing of the cow, but in eating it; but
it perceived by the sound that it was nearby, and so seems to take
pleasure in the sound. And similarly it does not take pleasure in
seeing 'a deer or a wild goat', but in the fact that it will have food.

Temperance and intemperance are concerned with such pleas-
25 ures as are common to the other animals too, whence they seem
slavish and bestial; these are touch and taste. But they seem to
make little or no use of taste; for to taste belongs the judgement of flavours, the sort of thing wine-tasters do, and people
preparing fancy dishes. But they do not at all enjoy those, or at
30 any rate intemperate people do not; what they enjoy is indulging,
which arises wholly from touch in food and drink and what are
called 'the pleasures of Aphrodite'. That is why a certain glut-
ton wished that his throat were longer than a crane's, since he
1118ᵇ enjoyed the touch. So the sense which intemperance is concerned
with is the most common, and it would rightly appear reprehensible, since it belongs to us not in so far as we are human, but in
so far as we are animals. Now enjoying such things and loving
5 them above all is appropriate to beasts. For the most reputable of
the pleasures of touch are in a separate category, e.g. those which
occur in the gymnasium when one has a massage or gets warm;
the touch which the intemperate person enjoys does not affect the
whole body, but certain parts only.

BOOK THREE

CHAPTER 11

Some bodily desires appear to be common, but others peculiar
to certain people and acquired. For instance, the desire for nour-
10 ishment is natural; everyone who is lacking solid or liquid nour-
ishment desires it, and sometimes both, and, as Homer says, the
young man in his prime desires sex; but not everyone desires this
particular kind, or that, nor do they all desire the same. That is

why that seems something peculiar to each of us. But all the same it has a certain natural element; different things are pleasant to different people, and some things are pleasanter to everyone than 15 merely whatever comes to hand.

Now few people go wrong in their natural desires, and they go wrong in one direction, that of excess; eating whatever comes along or drinking till one is overfull is quantitative excess over what is natural, since natural desire is the filling up of a deficiency. That is why those people are called 'belly-mad', since they fill it up contrary 20 to need. It is very slavish people who turn out like that. But many people go wrong with regard to individual desires, and go wrong often. For people are called lovers of such-and-such from enjoying things they should not, or enjoying things more than most people, or not as they should, and the intemperate are excessive in all respects; they enjoy some things which one should not (since they are hateful), 25 and if one should enjoy any such things, they do so more than one should and more than most people do.

It is clear that excess in respect of pleasures is intemperance and something blameworthy. In respect of distress it is not the case that, as with courage, one is called temperate for enduring it 30 and intemperate for not doing so; rather, the intemperate person is so from being more distressed than one should be at not getting pleasant things (pleasure brings him distress as well), and the temperate person from not being distressed by their absence or by abstaining from what is pleasant.

Now the intemperate person desires all pleasant things or the 1119^a pleasantest, and is driven by the desire for these to choose them in preference to the rest. That is why he is distressed both when he desires them and when he fails to get them; for desire is accompanied by distress, but it seems absurd to be distressed by pleasure. 5 People who are deficient with respect to pleasures and enjoy them less than one should are simply not found; insensibility of that sort is just not human. For even the other animals discriminate in their food, and enjoy some sorts and not others, and if there is someone to whom nothing is pleasant and there no difference between one thing and another, he would be far from human; such a person has 10 not acquired a name because they are simply not found. The temperate person is in a mean condition with respect to these things; he does not enjoy the things the intemperate person especially enjoys, but rather disdains them; nor in general does he enjoy what one

should not, nor does he enjoy anything like that intensely, nor is he distressed by their absence or desires them, except moderately, nor
15 more than one should, nor when one should not, nor in general in any of those ways. But he will desire moderately and as one should those pleasant things which promote health or good condition, and other pleasant things which do not interfere with them or are discreditable or beyond his means. The person who is like that
20 loves such pleasures more than they are worth; but the temperate person is not like that, but is as correct reason prescribes.

BOOK THREE

CHAPTER 12

Intemperance seems closer to the voluntary than cowardice, since the former arises from pleasure, the latter from distress, of which the former is something to be chosen, the latter something to be avoided. Further, distress disturbs and corrupts the nature of the person who suffers it, but pleasure does nothing like that. So it is
25 more voluntary. That is why it is more reprehensible; it is easier to be habituated to those things, for many such things occur during one's life, and habituation involves no danger, but the opposite is true of fearful things. And when we consider particular circumstances, cowardice would not seem to be equally voluntary; cowardice itself causes no distress, but the circumstances disturb
30 people through distress, making them throw away their arms and behave shamefully in other ways; that is why they seem to be done under compulsion. In the case of the intemperate person, on the contrary, the particular instances are voluntary (for they happen to someone who desires and wants them), but intemperance as such less so; for no one desires to be intemperate.

Now we also apply the term *akolasia* to the naughtinesses of
1119ᵇ children, as they have a certain resemblance. It makes no difference for the present purpose which is called after the other, but it is clear that the posterior is called after the prior. The transferred application seems not a bad one; for something which has an appetite for shameful things and a capacity for considerable
5 growth requires to be disciplined, and bodily desire on the one hand and children on the other seem particularly to be things of

that kind. Children live in accordance with bodily desire, and the appetite for pleasure is particularly strong in them; so if it is not made submissive and subject to some control, it will grow to a large extent. The appetite for pleasure is insatiable and attacks the thoughtless person from all sides, and the actual occurrence of bodily desires increases that aspect of our nature, especially if 10 they are strong and intense, and if they drive out rational thought. So they ought to be moderate and few, and ought not to oppose reason in any way—we call something like that submissive and disciplined. Just as the child ought to live in accordance with the instructions of its tutor, so the desiderative part ought to be in accordance with reason. That is why the desiderative part of the 15 temperate person ought to be in agreement with his reason; for the goal of both is the fine, and the temperate person desires the things he should and as he should and when; and that is what reason prescribes for its part.

That concludes our discussion of temperance.

BOOK FOUR

CHAPTER I

1119ᵇ

25

30

1120ᵃ

5

10

15

Next let us discuss generosity. It seems to be the mean concerned with wealth; for the generous person is praised not in military matters, nor in those things which concern the temperate person, nor in judicial decisions, but concerning the giving and acquiring of wealth, and particularly in giving. We call wealth everything whose value is measured in money. Extravagance and ungenerosity are excesses and deficiencies concerning wealth; we always apply the term 'ungenerosity' to people who care about wealth more than they ought, but sometimes when we accuse people of extravagance we combine different ideas, for we call people who lack self-control and who spend money on intemperance extravagant. That is why they seem to be the worst sort of people, as they have many vices simultaneously. Now that is not the strict application of the term, for being extravagant means being guilty of a single fault, that of destroying one's substance; the self-destructive person is unsparing of himself, and the destruction of one's substance is a sort of self-destruction, since it is from that that one lives. That is how we understand extravagance.

Things that have a use can be used well or badly. Riches are something useful, and everything is put to the best use by the person with the appropriate excellence. Now riches will be put to the best use by the person who has the excellence to do with wealth, and that is the generous person. The use of wealth appears to be spending and giving; acquiring and keeping amount rather to getting it. That is why it is more appropriate to the generous person to give to whom he should than to acquire from where he should and not acquire from where he should not. For it is more characteristic of virtue to do well than to be well treated, and to do fine things than not to do disgraceful things; it is not in doubt that doing well and doing fine things are associated with giving, and being well treated and not doing disgraceful things with acquiring. And thanks and praise are accorded rather to someone who gives than to someone who does not acquire. And not acquiring is easier than giving; for people part with what belongs to them less readily than they refrain from taking what belongs to someone else. It is those who give who are called generous; those who do not acquire are not praised for generosity (but they are praised for justice none 20 the less), while those who do acquire are not praised at all. Of all virtuous people the generous are pretty well the best liked; for they are useful, and that from their giving.

Virtuous actions are fine and are done because they are fine; so the generous person will give because it is fine and will do so 25 correctly, to whom he should and as much as he should and when he should, and the other features of correct giving; he will do so gladly or without distress, for virtuous action is pleasant or done without distress, it is not distressing in any way. The person who gives to those to whom he should not, or not because it is fine but for some other reason, will not be called generous but something else. Nor will the person who feels distress at giving; he prefers 30 wealth to fine actions, and that is not the mark of the generous person. Nor will he acquire from where he should not; acquisition of that sort is not the mark of someone who does not care about wealth. Nor would he be the sort of person to ask for money; someone who does good is not readily a recipient of favours. He will take from where he should, e.g. from his own property, not **1120^b** because it is something fine but because it is necessary, in order to have the means of giving. Nor will he be careless of his own possessions, since he wants to use them to be of service to others. Nor will he give to people indiscriminately, in order to be able to give to whom he should, when he should, and where it is fine to do so. It is highly characteristic of the generous person even to 5 be excessive in giving, so as to leave less for himself, since not considering oneself is a mark of the generous person. Generosity is ascribed relative to one's means. The generosity of the act does not consist in the amount that is given, but in the state of the giver, and that consists in giving relative to one's means; there is nothing to prevent someone who has given less from being more 10 generous, if he gave it from a smaller amount.

The more generous people seem to be those who have not made their own fortune, but have inherited it; for they have no experience of want, and everybody loves their own creation more, e.g. parents love their children and poets their works. It is not easy for the generous person to be rich, for he is neither acquisitive of 15

wealth nor keen to preserve it, but gives it away and values it not
for its own sake but for the sake of giving. That is why people
reproach fortune, saying that those who most deserve riches have
the least. But that is not surprising, since one cannot have wealth
20 if one does not take trouble over having it, as with other things.
But all the same he will not give to people to whom he should
not, nor when he should not, and so on; for then he would no
longer be acting generously, and having spent on those cases he
would not have anything left for what he should spend on. As we
said, the generous person is the one who spends according to his
means and on what he should; the person who spends excessively
25 is extravagant. That is why we do not call tyrants extravagant;
it does not seem easy for them to exceed the amount of their
possessions in gifts and expenditure.

   Now since generosity is a mean to do with giving and acquiring
wealth, the generous person will give and spend as much as he
30 should on the things he should, alike on a large and on a small
scale, and do so gladly; and he will acquire from where he should
and as much as he should. For the virtue being a mean to do with
both, he will do both as he should. Correct giving is associated
with the same sort of acquiring, but acquiring which is not of
that kind is opposed to it. Giving and acquiring which are associated coincide, which is clearly not the case with opposed giving
1121^a and acquiring. If it happens that the generous person incurs some
expense which is inappropriate and not as it should be, he will be
distressed, but moderately and as he should; for it is a mark of
virtue to be pleased and distressed as one should and about the
things one should. The generous person shares his wealth readily;
5 he is open to being treated unjustly, since he does not care about
money, and is more upset at not having spent what he should than
distressed at having spent what he should not; in that respect he
does not agree with Simonides. But the extravagant person goes
wrong in these respects also; he is neither pleased nor distressed
as he should be, nor at the things he should be. This will become
clearer as we proceed.
10   Now we have said that extravagance and ungenerosity are kinds
of excess and deficiency, and that they occur in two respects, in
giving and in acquiring; we include spending in giving. Extravagance exceeds in giving and in not acquiring, but is deficient
15 in acquiring, while ungenerosity is deficient in giving and exces-

sive in acquiring, but on a small scale. The two aspects of extravagance are not totally combined, for it is not easy to give to
everyone while not acquiring from anywhere. Private individuals
who give soon find their means giving out, and they are the people
who appear extravagant. Yet someone like that would seem to be
much better than the ungenerous person; he is easily cured by the   20
passage of time and experience of want, and so is able to reach
the mean point. He has some of the characteristics of the generous
person, in that he gives and does not acquire, but he does neither
of those well nor as he should. But if he were habituated in that
respect, or changed in some other way, he would be generous,
in that he will give to those he ought, and will not acquire from   25
where he ought not. That is why he seems not to be of a bad
character; excess in giving and not acquiring is characteristic of
someone who is not wicked or ignoble, but foolish. The person
who is extravagant in this way seems to be much better than the
ungenerous person, for the reasons stated and because the former
helps many people but the latter helps no one, not even himself.   30
But most extravagant people, as we have said, also acquire from
where they ought not, and are in that respect ungenerous. They
become grasping through wanting to spend, but not being able to
do so easily, because their means soon give out, and so they are
forced to provide from elsewhere. And at the same time, because   1121^b
they do not care about what is fine, they acquire from all sources
without thinking, since they want to give, and it makes no difference to them how or from what source they do it. That is why their
acts of giving are not in fact generous; they are not fine, nor are
they done for that reason, or as they should be. But sometimes they 5
enrich people who ought to be poor, and they would give nothing
to people of good character, but a lot to flatterers and people who
provide other kinds of pleasure. That is why the majority of them
are intemperate; since they spend readily they are willing to pay
for their indulgences, and because they do not live with an eye to
what is fine they incline toward those pleasures. The extravagant   10
person who is not properly brought up ends up like that, but if he
were taken care of, he would arrive at the mean and the right point.
But ungenerosity is irremediable (for age and every kind of
incapacity seem to make people ungenerous), and it is more natural
for people than extravagance; for the majority are money-lovers   15
rather than prone to giving. It is very widespread, and varied;

there are many kinds of ungenerosity. As it consists of two things,
deficiency in giving and excess in acquiring, it is not in every
20 case present as a whole, but sometimes they are separate, some
people being excessive in acquiring and others deficient in giving.
People who are called things like sparing, grasping, or tight-fisted
are all deficient in giving, but do not go for what belongs to others or try to get it, sometimes because of a certain honesty and
25 avoidance of anything disgraceful (some people seem to take care
of their money for this reason, that they should not be obliged
to do anything disgraceful, or at least that is what they say; such
are the cheese-parer and everyone like that, who are so called
from their excessive avoidance of giving anything). But others
hold off from what belongs to other people out of fear, since it
is not easy for someone to take what belongs to someone else
30 without others taking from him; so they are content neither to
take nor to give. Others again are excessive in acquiring in that
they acquire everything from whatever source, such as people
who engage in discreditable trades, brothel-keepers and everyone like that, and people who lend small sums at high interest.
1122^a All these people acquire from sources one should not, and in
amounts one should not. What seems common to them is dishon-
est gain; they all put up with reproach for the sake of gain, even
a small one. We do not call ungenerous people who acquire great
amounts from sources they should not, and things they should
5 not, e.g. tyrants who sack cities and pillage temples, but rather
we call them wicked and irreligious and unjust. But the gambler,
footpad, and robber count as ungenerous, since they make dishonest gains. Both kinds of people act and put up with reproach
10 for the sake of gain, and thieves undergo the greatest dangers
for the sake of profit, while gamblers gain from their friends,
whom they ought to give to. Both kinds of people make dishonest
gains, in that they are willing to gain from sources from which
one should not; all acquiring of that kind is discreditable. It is
reasonable that ungenerosity is said to be the opposite of gener-
15 osity; it is a greater evil than extravagance, and people go more
wrong in that direction than in respect of what is called extravagance.

That concludes our discussion of generosity and its opposed
vices.

BOOK FOUR

CHAPTER 2

The next topic in order would appear to be magnificence, as it too
is a virtue to do with wealth, but it does not extend to all activities 20
involving wealth as generosity does, but only to those involving
expenditure. There it exceeds generosity in grandeur; as the name
itself implies, it is fitting expenditure on a grand scale. Grandeur is
relative; equipping a warship does not involve the same expenditure as providing for a sacred embassy. What is fitting is relative 25
to the agent, the circumstances, and the object. Someone who
spends appropriately on a small or a moderate scale is not called
magnificent, nor someone who 'often gave to the wanderer', but
someone who does so on a large scale. Now the magnificent person is generous, but it does not follow that the generous person
is magnificent. The deficiency of this state is called shabbiness, 30
the excess vulgarity and bad taste etc.; the latter do not consist
in an excess of grandeur on appropriate objects, but when people
make themselves conspicuous in the wrong circumstances and in
the wrong way. We shall discuss these points later.

The magnificent person is like an expert; he is able to discern 35
what is fitting and expend large sums appropriately. As we said at   **1122^{b}**
the outset, states are defined by the activities they give rise to, and
by their objects. Now the expenditure of the magnificent person is
grand and fitting, and so are its objects. That is how the expenditure
will be great and befitting its object; the object must be in keeping 5
with the expenditure, and the expenditure in keeping with the
object or even exceeding it. The magnificent person will undertake
such expenditure because it is fine; that is common to the virtues.
Further, he will do so gladly and open-handedly; taking precise
account of expense is shabby. And he will be more concerned with
its being most splendid and fitting than with how much it costs
and how it can be done most cheaply. Necessarily, the magnificent 10
person is generous; for the generous person too will spend what he
should and as he should. In these matters it is scale, grandeur so to
speak, which is the mark of the magnificent person; generosity has
the same subject matter, but it is scale which creates something
more magnificent from the same outlay.

Possessions and the products of magnificence do not have the 15
same criteria of excellence. In the case of possessions what is most

valuable is what is most costly (gold, for example), but in the case
of products it is what is grand and fine (for that is what arouses
admiration in those who see it, and the magnificent is what arouses
admiration); the excellence of something wealth is spent on, its
magnificence, is in its grandeur. This belongs to expenditure on
20 what we call honourable things, such as things to do with the gods,
votive offerings and ritual objects and sacrifices, and similarly with
all religious matters, and things where there is proper competition
in public benefactions, for instance when people think that they
should equip a chorus or a warship splendidly, or feast their fellow
citizens. Now in all these cases, as we have said, people have
25 regard to the agent, who he is and what resources he has; what is
done must be in keeping with them, and fit not only the object but
also the person providing it. That is why a poor person could not
be magnificent; he does not have the resources to spend a great
deal in a fitting manner. The poor person who tries to do so is silly,
since it is not in accordance with his means or with what should be
done, while it is in accordance with virtue to do things properly.
30 That is appropriate for those who already have such resources
either as a result of their own efforts or by inheritance or from
rich associates, and who are people of good birth and reputation
and so forth; all of those things are sources of grandeur and credit.

So that, above all, is the sort of person that the magnificent
person is, and that is the sort of expenditure in which magnificence
35 consists, as we have said: namely, the grandest, which brings the
greatest honour. In the private sphere these are things which occur
1123^a once only, such as a wedding or something like that; there are
also things about which the whole city and the most prominent
people compete, such as the reception and sending-off of guests,
and giving and returning gifts. The magnificent person does not
5 spend on himself, but for the common good, and his gifts have
something of the same character as votive offerings. It is also
appropriate for the magnificent person to provide himself with a
house befitting his wealth (for this too is an ornament), and in this
regard to spend particularly on objects which last, since they are
the finest, and in every case on what is fitting; the same things
10 are not appropriate for gods and men, nor is what befits a temple
appropriate for a tomb. For every kind of thing there is an amount
which is a great amount to spend on a thing of that kind; the most
magnificent expenditure without qualification is great expenditure

on a great object, while magnificent expenditure in a particular
sphere is great expenditure on things of that kind, and there is a
difference between the greatness of the object and the greatness
of the expenditure; the finest ball or oil-flask makes a magnificent   15
gift for a child, but the value of such things is small and mean.
That is why it is appropriate for the magnificent person to do
magnificently whatever kind of thing he does (since that kind of
thing is not easily surpassed), and to do things in keeping with the
amount of his expenditure.

That, then, is the magnificent person; but the excessive, vulgar person is excessive in spending inappropriately, as we have   20
said. He spends a great deal on small items and makes himself
inappropriately conspicuous; for instance, he entertains the members of his dining club on a scale suitable for a wedding, or when
he provides a chorus for a comedy, he brings them on to the stage
dressed in purple, like the people at Megara. He does all that
sort of thing not because it is fine, but to display his wealth and   25
because he thinks he will be admired for it, and where he should
pay out a lot, he spends little, and where it should be a little, he
spends a lot. The shabby person will be deficient in everything
and despite spending a great deal will spoil what is fine by faults
of detail, and will put off doing what he should because he is   30
considering how to do it for the least expense, and even that he
does grudgingly, thinking that he is doing everything on a larger
scale than he should. Now these states are defects, but they do
not incur reproach because they are neither harmful to others nor
excessively unseemly.

BOOK FOUR

CHAPTER 3

Greatness of soul seems, as the word itself indicates, to have to do
with great things; what these are should be our first question. (It   35
makes no difference whether we investigate the state itself or the   **1123ᵇ**
person who has it.) Now the great-souled person seems to be the
person who thinks himself worthy of great things and actually is
worthy of them; the person who does the same but is not worthy is
silly, and no virtuous person is silly or thoughtless. So the great-
souled person is the one we have said. The person who is worthy

5   of small things and regards himself as such is sound-minded, but
not great-souled; for greatness of soul belongs to greatness, just
as beauty belongs to large stature, while small people are neat and
well-proportioned, but not beautiful. The person who thinks himself worthy of great things when he is unworthy is vain; but not
everyone who overvalues himself is vain. The person who under-
10 values himself is small-minded, whether he is worthy of great
things or moderate things, or if he is worthy of small things but
thinks himself worthy of even less. The most small-minded are
those who are in fact worthy of great things; what would they
do if they were not worthy of so much? Now the great-souled
person is at the extreme in greatness, but at the mean in being as
15 he should, since he values himself according to his worth, while
those others are respectively excessive and deficient. Now if he
thinks himself worthy of great things and is worthy of them, and
especially the greatest, he would be concerned especially with
one thing. What one is worthy of is expressed in terms of external
goods; the greatest such good we would consider to be what we
accord to the gods, and what prominent people seek above all, and
20 what is the reward of the finest deeds; and that is honour. So that
is the greatest of the external goods, and so the great-souled person is as he should be with respect to honour and dishonour. Even
without the benefit of theory it is apparent that great-souled people
are concerned about honour, for they think themselves worthy of
honour above all, and are so. The small-minded person is deficient
both relative to his own worth and relative to that of the great-
25 souled person, while the vain is excessive relative to himself, but
not relative to the great-souled.

The great-souled person, since he is worthy of the greatest
things, is the best person; for the better is always worthy of the
greater, and the best of the greatest; so the truly great-souled per-
30 son must be good. It would seem appropriate to the great-souled
person to achieve greatness in every virtue; and so it would never
be fitting for a great-souled person to run away headlong or to
act unjustly, for what could induce someone who holds nothing
of importance to behave disgracefully? When one considers particular instances, it is apparent that the great-souled person would
be totally ridiculous if he were not good; nor would he be worthy
35 of honour if he were base, for honour is the reward of virtue, and
1124ᵃ is accorded to the good. So it seems that greatness of soul is as

it were an ornament of the virtues; it makes them greater, and does not occur without them. That is why it is difficult to be truly great-souled; it is not possible without complete virtue.

So the great-souled person is concerned above all with honour 5 and dishonour. He will be moderately pleased by great honours conferred by good people, thinking them appropriate to him, or even less than he deserves; for there is no honour that could match complete virtue, but nevertheless he will accept them as the best that they can bestow on him. He will be totally indifferent to 10 honour from all and sundry, or honour for small achievements, since they do not match his worth, and similarly with dishonour, which he will never deserve. So the great-souled person will, as we have said, be concerned above all with honour, but he will also have a moderate attitude to riches and power and all good and ill fortune, however it turns out, not being overjoyed in good fortune 15 or especially cast down by ill fortune. For he will not even have those attitudes to honour, as if it were the greatest thing. Power and riches are choiceworthy for the sake of honour; at any rate those who have them want to be honoured for them, but someone who cares little even about honour will care little about the rest as well. That is why such people appear arrogant. 20

Good fortune is thought to contribute to greatness of soul, since people of good birth and the powerful and the rich are regarded as worthy of honour; they are in a position of superiority, and whatever is superior in respect of a good is more worthy of honour. That is why such things make people more great-souled; they are honoured by some people. In reality it is only the good person who is 25 worthy of honour; but the person who has both is regarded as more worthy of honour. People who possess such goods without virtue are not entitled to think themselves worthy of great things, nor are they correctly called great-souled, for that is impossible without complete virtue. People who possess such goods are among those who become arrogant and insolent, since as they lack virtue they 30 do not handle their good fortune properly; and since they cannot handle it and think themselves superior to other people, they look **1124ᵇ** down on them and behave in any way they like. Though they are not like the great-souled person, they imitate him in so far as they can; they do not act virtuously, but they look down on others. 5

The great-souled person is entitled to look down on people (for his judgement is true), but most people do so arbitrarily. Because

he values few things, he neither takes risks in small matters, nor is
he fond of taking risks, but he takes risks over great matters, and
when he does so he is unsparing of his life, since he does not hold it
worth saving one's life by any means whatever. He is happy to be
10 a benefactor, but ashamed to receive benefits, since the former is
the mark of the superior, the latter of the inferior. When he returns
a favour, he gives more than he received; that way the person who
did the favour in the first place will be in receipt of a benefit and
will still be in his debt. They seem to remember the benefits they
have conferred but not those they have received (for the recipient
is inferior to the benefactor, and he wishes to be superior), and
15 to like hearing about the former, but to dislike hearing about the
latter; that is why Thetis did not tell of her services to Zeus, nor
the Spartans of theirs to the Athenians, but of the benefits they
had received. It is characteristic of the great-souled person to ask
for nothing, or very little, but to be eager to be of service, and to
be haughty to prominent people and those who are enjoying good
20 fortune, but modest towards those of middle rank; for it is difficult
and noble to be superior to the former, but easy in the case of the
latter, and it is not ignoble to behave proudly to those people, but
contemptible to do so towards the humble, as it is to exercise one's
strength against the weak. And it is characteristic of him not to go
for things which confer honour, or where other people are in first
place, and to be inactive and put off acting except where there
25 is great honour or a great task to be done, and to undertake few
things, but great and notable things. And necessarily he is open in
his likes and dislikes (for concealment, and neglecting the truth for
the sake of one's reputation, are appropriate for someone who is
fearful) and he speaks and acts openly (he speaks freely because he
30 looks down on people, and is truthful except in so far as he speaks
by way of dissembling to ordinary people) and is incapable of
1125ᵃ living at the disposal of anyone except a friend, for that is slavish.
That is why all flatterers are servile and all humble people are
flatterers. Nor is he given to admiration, for nothing is great in
his eyes. Nor does he bear grudges, for it is not appropriate for a
great-souled person to keep things, especially bad things, in mind,
5 but rather to overlook them. Nor does he gossip about people; he
will speak neither about himself nor about someone else, since it
does not matter to him whether he is praised or others are blamed.
Nor again is he given to praise; hence he is not malicious either,

even about his enemies, unless to insult them. Least of all is he
prone to make a fuss and ask for help about small, unavoidable   10
things; behaving like that is the mark of someone who cares a lot
about such things. And he is apt to acquire fine but unprofitable
things in preference to profitable and useful; that is more the mark
of a self-sufficient person. The movements of the great-souled
person seem to be slow, his voice deep, and his speech measured;
for someone who cares about few things is not always in a hurry,
nor is someone who thinks nothing of great importance tense, and   15
a shrill voice and quick movements arise from those traits.

Such, then is the great-souled person; the deficient person is
small-minded, and the excessive person vain. Those people too
do not seem to be bad exactly, for they are not evil-doers, but
they have gone wrong. For the small-minded person will deprive   20
himself of the goods which he deserves, and seems to suffer some
harm from not thinking himself worthy of good things and being
mistaken about himself; for he would have wanted the good things
he deserved. Yet people like that do not seem to be silly, but
rather hesitant. That sort of belief seems to make people worse;
for each person wants what they deserve, and they hold back from   25
fine actions and activities, as well as from external goods, on
the grounds that they do not deserve them. Vain people are silly
and mistaken about themselves, and obviously so; they attempt
things which confer honour though they do not deserve it, and
are then shown up. They are elaborate in their style of dress,   30
etc., and they want their good fortune to be manifest, and they
talk of those things as if they would bring them honour. Small-
mindedness is more opposed to greatness of soul than vanity is;
it is more frequent and worse. So greatness of soul is concerned   35
with great honour, as we have said.

BOOK FOUR

CHAPTER 4

Here too, as we said in our preliminary remarks, there seems to be   1125^b
a virtue which would appear to stand to greatness of soul pretty
much as generosity does to magnificence; both are removed from
the element of greatness, and dispose us properly with regard to   5

what is moderate and what is small in scale. And just as there is a
mean and excess and deficiency in acquiring and giving wealth, so
too we can desire honour more or less than we should, or from the
things that we should and as we should. We blame the ambitious
person for wanting honour more than one should and from things
10 one should not, and the unambitious for not choosing even to
be honoured for fine things. Sometimes we praise the ambitious
person as manly and as a lover of the fine, and sometimes the
unambitious as moderate and sound-minded, as we said in our
preliminary remarks. It is clear that, since the expression 'lover
of such-and-such' is applied in a number of ways, we do not
15 always apply the term 'honour-loving' to the same thing; when
we use it as a term of praise, we apply it to wanting honour more
than most people do, but when it is a term of blame, we apply
it to wanting honour more than one should. And since the mean
lacks a name, the extremes contest the middle ground as if it were
empty. But where there is excess and deficiency, there is a mean
20 as well; and people want honour more than they should and less;
so it is possible to want it as one should. That, then, is the state
which is praised, the mean with respect to honour which lacks a
name. In comparison with ambition it looks like lack of ambition,
and in comparison with lack of ambition it looks like ambition,
and in comparison with both it looks like both in a way. The
25 same seems to be true for the other virtues as well; but here the
extremes seem opposed to one another because the mean has not
been given a name.

BOOK FOUR

CHAPTER 5

Good temper is a mean to do with anger; since the middle state
lacks a name, and the extremes pretty much as well, we apply
the term 'good temper' to the middle. (It inclines towards the
deficiency, which lacks a name.) But the excess might be termed
30 a sort of irascibility. Now the feeling is anger, and its causes are
many and various. Someone who gets angry about the things one
should and with the people one should, and also as and when and
for as long as one should, is praised. That is the sort of person

we would count as good-tempered, since good temper is praised.
Being good-tempered means being untroubled and not being carried away by the feeling, but being angry about the things reason 35
says one should, and for as long as it says. It seems to err rather **1126**[a]
in the direction of the deficiency; for the good-tempered person
is not vengeful, but rather forgiving. The deficiency, whether it
is called unanger or whatever, incurs blame; for people who do
not get angry over what they should seem silly, as do those who 5
do not get angry as or when they should or with the people they
should. They seem not to notice those things nor to be distressed
by them, and as they do not get angry, they are not apt to defend
themselves; but putting up with being dragged through the mud
oneself and standing by watching it happen to people who belong
to one is slavish.

The excess occurs in all these respects, getting angry with people
one should not, about things one should not, more than one should, 10
and more quickly, and for longer, but not all these happen to the
same person at once. That would be impossible; the defect cancels
itself out, and if it is total in all respects, it becomes impossible to
sustain. Now irascible people get angry quickly, and with people
they should not and about things they should not and more than
they should, but they calm down quickly; that is the best thing 15
about them. This happens because they do not bottle up their
anger, but retaliate openly because of their sharp temper, and then
they calm down. People who are extreme in anger are sharp to
excess, irascible in everything and about everything; hence the
name. Bitter people are hard to be reconciled and are angry for 20
a long time; for they bottle up their fury. That ceases when they
retaliate; for vengeance brings their anger to an end, by causing
them pleasure in place of distress. But if that does not happen, they
retain the burden of their anger; for since it is not apparent, no
one gives them any advice, and it takes a long time to digest one's 25
anger on one's own. People like that are the most burdensome to
themselves and to their closest friends.

We call difficult those who are angry about things they should
not be and more than they should be and for longer, and do not
stop without getting their own back or exacting punishment. And
we count the excess as more opposed to good temper; it happens 30
more often, for retaliation is a more natural human characteristic,
and difficult people are worse at living together. What we said

previously is clear also from these observations; it is not easy to determine how and with whom and about what and how long one should be angry, and to specify what extent is right and what is
35 wrong. Someone who deviates slightly in the direction of either
1126ᵇ too much or of too little is not blamed; sometimes we praise those who are deficient and call them good-tempered, and sometimes those who are angry, calling them manly, since they are capable of being in control. But how big a deviation, and what kind, is blameworthy is not easy to specify by reason; for that is in the sphere of particular cases, and the judgement lies in the perception
5 of them. But this much is clear, that the mean state is praiseworthy, in virtue of which we get angry with the people we should and about the things we should and as we should and all that, while the excesses and the deficiencies are blameworthy, to a lesser extent if they are small, and more if they are bigger, and very much if they are really large. So it is clear that one should stick to the mean
10 state. That concludes our discussion of the states to do with anger.

QUESTION:
How are the
(MEAN) & the
doing things according
to (PARTICULARS)

reconciled
?

‖
∨

seem
like
2
diff.
approaches

BOOK FOUR

CHAPTER 6

In the sphere of personal relations, of social life and associations in words and actions, some people seem ingratiating; these are people who approve of everything to please others and never oppose them, thinking that one should avoid offending the people one meets. But
15 people of the opposite kind, who oppose others in everything and do not care at all about causing offence, are called disagreeable and quarrelsome. Now it is clear that the states just mentioned are blameworthy, and that the one in between them is praiseworthy, in which one will agree or refuse to do what one should and as one
20 should. It has not been assigned a name, but it seems most like friendliness. For that is the sort of person, the person in the mean state, whom we are apt to call a good friend, with the addition in the latter case of emotional attachment. It differs from friendliness in the absence of feeling and emotional attachment to those to whom one relates; it is not from liking or disliking that such a person takes everything as one should, but from being that sort

of person. He will do this alike to those he knows and those he 25
does not know, to those he is intimate with and those he is not,
except to the extent that in each case he behaves appropriately,
for it is not proper to care equally for one's intimates and for
strangers, or to offend them equally. Now we have said in general
that he will relate to them as he should, and with a view to what
is fine and advantageous he will aim at pleasing them, or avoiding 30
offence. It seems that he will be concerned with pleasing and
displeasing people in personal relations; to the extent that it is
ignoble or harmful for him to please others in such cases, he will
refuse to do so, preferring to offend them. If pleasing someone
brings no little discredit or harm to the person who does it, while
opposing their wishes causes only small offence, he will not agree 35
to do what they want, but will refuse. He will relate differently to
prominent and to ordinary people, and to those who are better or **1127**^{a}
less known to him, and similarly with other differences; he will
treat everyone appropriately, and in his actions themselves will
seek to please others and avoid offending them, subject to the
promotion of more significant consequences, I mean what is fine 5
and advantageous. He will cause a small offence for the sake of a
great amount of pleasure to come.

   The person in the middle is like that, but he has not been given
a name. Of those who please others, the person who aims at being
pleasant for its own sake is ingratiating, while the person who
does so to gain some monetary advantage, or something money
can buy, is a flatterer; and we have said that the person who refuses 10
everyone is disagreeable and quarrelsome. It is because the mean
lacks a name that the extremes seem to be opposed to one another.

BOOK FOUR

CHAPTER 7

The mean between boastfulness and dissembling has to do with
pretty much the same things, and it too has no name. It will not
be a bad idea to investigate states of that kind too; for we will 15
acquire a fuller knowledge of the topic of character by considering
it case by case, and will be more firmly convinced that the virtues
are mean states when we see that that is so in every case.

20 In regard to social life, relations involving pleasure and distress have been discussed; let us now consider truth and falsehood alike in words and deeds, especially in the claims people make. Now the boaster seems to be someone who claims merits which he does not have and greater merits than he actually has, and the dissembler on the contrary seems to deny those that he has or to make them less than they are, while the person in the middle seems to be straightforward, truthful in what he does and what he

25 says, acknowledging his actual merits and making them neither greater nor less. It is possible to do each of these things either for the sake of some advantage, or for none. Each type speaks and acts and lives in accordance with his own character, unless he is acting for the sake of some advantage. In itself falsehood is base

30 and blameworthy, truth fine and praiseworthy. Hence the truthful person, who is in the middle, is praiseworthy, while both types who utter falsehoods are blameworthy, but the boaster more so. Let us discuss both, but first the truthful person.

We are not talking about people who tell the truth in agreements, or in matters to do with justice and injustice (these belong to
1127ᵇ another virtue), but about someone truthful in word and deed when nothing hangs on it, simply in virtue of his state of character. That kind of person seems to be good. For the truth-lover, who tells

5 the truth when nothing hangs on it, will tell the truth yet more when it does matter; he will avoid it as something disgraceful, since he was used to avoid falsehood as such. Someone like that is praiseworthy. He will veer away from the truth rather in the direction of understatement; that seems more appropriate because of the unpleasant character of exaggeration.

10 The person who claims greater merits than he has, but not for the sake of any advantage, is like someone base (otherwise he would not enjoy telling lies), but seems stupid rather than bad. If it is for some advantage, the person who does it for the sake of reputation or honour is not very blameworthy, but the one who does it for money, or for things that he can sell for money, is more contemptible. (One is a boaster not through one's abilities,

15 but through one's choice; it is in virtue of one's state of character and of being that type of person that one is a boaster.) Similarly, some people are liars because they enjoy the very act of telling lies, others because they are seeking reputation or gain. People who boast for the sake of reputation pretend to what attracts praise

or congratulation, but those who do it for gain pretend to things
which are useful to others, where it is possible to pretend to be   20
what you are not, e.g. an expert seer or doctor. That is why most
pretenders and boasters are found in those areas; it is there that
one finds the things just mentioned.

    Dissemblers, who play down the truth, seem more stylish in
character; they do not seem to say what they do for gain, but to
avoid pomposity, and above all they disclaim what is meritori-   25
ous, as Socrates used to do. Those who do this over small and
obvious things are called humbugs and are more despicable; and
sometimes this seems to be a form of boasting, like the clothes the
Spartans wear, as both exaggeration and excessive down-playing
are boastful. But people who practise dissembling to a moderate   30
extent about things which are not too manifest and obvious are
regarded as stylish. The boastful person seems to be opposed to
the truthful; he is worse.

BOOK FOUR

CHAPTER 8

Since relaxation is a part of life which includes passing the time
in amusement, there too there seems to be an appropriate style of   **1128^a**
personal relations, to do with the content and manner of speaking
and listening. (The sort of people one speaks to or listens to also
makes a difference.) It is clear that here too it is possible to exceed
and to fall short of the mean. People who make jokes to excess are
regarded as vulgar buffoons, always on the look-out for what is   5
funny and trying to raise a laugh rather than to speak decorously
and to avoid offending the person who is being made fun of.
But people who never make a joke themselves and disapprove of
those who do are regarded as boorish and harsh. Those who joke
appropriately are called witty, since they have their wits about   10
them; things of this kind seem to be movements of the character,
and just as people's bodies are assessed by their movements, so
are their characters. Since occasions for humour are frequent, and
most people like amusement and making fun of people more than
they should, even buffoons are called witty, on the ground that   15
they are stylish; but it is clear from what has been said that they
are different, and in no small measure.

Cleverness belongs to the mean state; it is characteristic of the clever person to say what is appropriate to the good and respectable person, and to listen in the same way. There are some things
20 which are suitable for such a person to say and hear by way of amusement, and the amusement of a respectable person differs from that of a slavish person, and that of an educated person from an uneducated. One can see this from the old-style comedies and the new; in the former the humour consisted in vulgar language, while in the latter it is rather a matter of innuendo, which makes
25 it much more seemly.

Should the person who makes fun properly be defined by his saying things which are not unfitting for a respectable person, or by his not offending his hearers, or even pleasing them? Or is that sort of thing indefinable, since different things are pleasant and displeasing to different people? He will also listen to the same sort of thing; for what people sit and listen to, it seems that they
30 will do as well. Now he will not do absolutely anything; making fun of people is a sort of abuse, and some kinds of abuse are forbidden by legislators, and perhaps it ought to be the same with making fun of people. Now the stylish and respectable person is like that, as it were a law for himself. Now the person in the middle is that sort of person, whether he is called clever or witty.

The buffoon is a slave to what is funny, sparing neither himself
35 nor anyone else if he can raise a laugh; he says things none of which a stylish person would say, and some things that he would
1128ᵇ not even listen to. The boor is useless in such relations; he contributes nothing and disapproves of everything. But relaxation and amusement seem to be necessary in life.
5 So the social mean states which we have discussed are three in number, all having to do with social relations in words and actions; they differ in that one has to do with truth and the others with what is pleasant. And of those to do with pleasure one is in amusements and the other in relations concerning the rest of life.

BOOK FOUR

CHAPTER 9

10 It is not proper to speak of shame as a virtue, since it is more like a feeling than a state. At any rate it is defined as fear of

disgrace, and has effects similar to those of the fear of evils; people
blush when they are ashamed and turn pale when they fear death.
Both of these appear to be a sort of physical effect, which seems
to belong rather to a feeling than to a state. The feeling is not   15
appropriate to every age, but to the young. We think that people
of that age should be modest because they go wrong in many ways
through living by their feelings, but are prevented by shame. And
we praise those young people who are modest, but no one would   20
praise an older person for being given to shame, since we think
he should not do anything which is a source of shame. Shame is
not appropriate for the good person, since it is base deeds which
are sources of shame. (One should not do things of that sort. It
makes no difference whether they are really base or only thought
to be so; neither kind of thing should be done, so one ought not to   25
be ashamed.) It is a base person who is such as to do something
disgraceful. But being the sort of person who feels ashamed at
doing something of that sort, and thinking oneself good on the
strength of that is absurd; one is ashamed of what is voluntary,
but the good person will never voluntarily do base things. Shame
would be conditionally good, in that one would feel ashamed were   30
one to do such things; but that is not appropriate to the virtues. And
even if shamelessness and not being ashamed of doing disgraceful
things is base, it does not follow that the person who is ashamed
of doing such things is good. Nor is self-control a virtue, but a
sort of mixed state; that will be discussed later.   35

Now let us consider justice.

COMMENTARY

BOOK TWO

CHAPTER I

1103ᵃ14–15 The twofold character of human excellence was asserted at the end of I. 13, at 1103ᵃ3–7. There the distinction of the two kinds of excellence was said to be determined by (*kata*, lit. 'according to') the division of the soul into intellect and 'the appetitive and in general the desiderative' which was established in I. 13. Intellectual excellence is specific to the former, and excellence of character to the latter, being the perfection of that 'part' or aspect of the soul. But since that part is derivatively rational, in that it is responsive to the direction of the intellect (1102ᵇ30–1103ᵃ3), its perfection consists in its being properly attuned to the intellect. There is therefore an intellectual aspect to excellence of character, and conversely there is an activity of the intellect, and an excellence appropriate to that activity, whose function is the direction of the appetitive personality, and specifically of the conduct which expresses that personality. This interpenetration of character and intellect pervades Aristotle's ethical works, and is specifically mentioned at a number of places in Books II–IV; see 1105ᵃ28–ᵇ5, 1106ᵇ36–1107ᵃ2.

1103ᵃ15–17 Aristotle does not elucidate the distinction between teaching and habit, presumably taking it as familiar without further elucidation. The heart of the distinction is no doubt that between purely theoretical instruction on the one hand and the acquisition of good and bad habits of behaviour (in which the development of likes and dislikes is crucial; see 1104ᵇ3–24) on the other. But the distinction is not quite as clear-cut as Aristotle suggests; mastery of even the most abstract disciplines, such as the various branches of mathematics, requires the acquisition of good habits, e.g. of rigour in proof. Aristotle might wish to emphasize 'chiefly', suggesting that whereas the acquisition of such habits is central to the development of character, it is subordinate to theoretical instruction in the acquisition of theoretical excellence. But that must be rather a matter of degree than of kind, since Aristotle counts technical skill (*technē*) among intellectual excellences (1139ᵇ16), and in the case of certain such skills, e.g. those in the performing and productive arts, the acquisition of good habits, and of the appropriate likes and dislikes, is at least as central as the acquisition of information via formal instruction.

1103ᵃ16–17 'which is why it requires experience and time'. Contrast 1142ᵃ11–16, where Aristotle says that the reason why young people can be skilled in mathematics and similar sciences, but not possessed of practical wisdom (*phronēsis*), is that the latter requires a lot of experience of particular cases (of what to do and not to do), whereas the young lack experience. Experience and time are not, then, strictly necessary for the achievement of theoretical excellence. Aristotle is presumably here speaking of what is true for the most part (*hōs epi to polu*); there can indeed be mathematical prodigies, but for the most part mastering a theoretical discipline requires a long period of instruction.

1103ᵃ17–18 Aristotle takes it (i) that the Greek word for 'character' (*ēthos*) and the adjective *ēthikē* formed from it (rendered 'of character') are morphologically derived from the word for 'habit' (*ethos*) by the 'slight modification' of lengthening the initial vowel from epsilon to eta, and (ii) that this morphological dependency reflects the causal dependency of the development of character on the acquisition of habits. The theory that the morphology (including morphological derivation) of words reflects the nature of the things the words stand for has its fullest expression in Plato's *Cratylus*.[1]

1103ᵃ18–26 Aristotle argues in this section that the dependence of character on habit shows that character is neither a natural endowment nor contrary to nature. The argument is somewhat confused. He begins (ᵃ18–19) by asserting that it is clear from the dependence of character on habit that none of the excellences of character is a natural endowment; but the only evidence which he cites (ᵃ19–23) is the impossibility of habituating any natural substance to behave in an unnatural way, e.g. it is impossible

---

[1] See Sedley (2003).

to train stones to move upwards when released, or fire to move downwards. That is at best evidence in favour of the thesis that excellence of character is not contrary to nature, but at ª23–4 he draws the conclusion that excellence of character is neither natural nor contrary to nature. He must be assuming a conception of a natural endowment according to which no such endowment can be dependent on the acquisition of habits.

That conception is clarified by Aristotle's claims (ª23–6) that excellences of character are not natural endowments, but it is natural for us to acquire them, and that we are perfected in them by habit. A natural endowment, then, is a perfection which belongs to a thing of a certain kind just in virtue of being a thing of that kind, e.g. the keen sight of a bird of prey. Any normal member of the kind possesses that attribute, which is not developed by practice or training. Excellence of character is not like that; we are not good by nature, as an eagle is naturally keen-sighted. By nature we are capable of becoming good, and the process of becoming good is the acquisition of good habits.

1103ª26–ᵇ2 The above is presumably the point which Aristotle is aiming at in his contrast between the senses (which are examples of natural endowments) and excellence of character, but the point is slightly obscured by the introduction of the contrast between a capacity and its exercise. The essential point is that seeing, hearing, etc. are not acquired skills, whereas the virtues of character, in common with technical excellences, are skills which we develop through practice of the acts which express them. Hence we become skilled builders by practice in building, and we become just and temperate people through practice in behaving justly and temperately, but we do not acquire the senses of sight or hearing by practice in seeing or hearing. In those cases, Aristotle says (ª26–31), we have the capacities (*dunameis*) first, and then exercise them, whereas in the case of the virtues and technical skills we acquire them by exercising them (ª31–ᵇ2). But the notion of capacity now seems to obscure the contrast. In the case of the senses, what we have first is the ability to see (= the sense of sight) which we then exercise in acts of seeing. But the ability to build (corresponding to the ability to see) surely cannot be acquired by the performance of acts of building, since one could not perform those very acts unless one already had the ability to build. As in the case of seeing, we have first the ability to build, which we then exercise in acts of building. So the contrast seems to disappear.

The problem of how one acquires a skill by exercising it will be discussed more fully below (see ch. 4). For the present it is sufficient to say that Aristotle's discussion requires a more nuanced treatment of capacity than he employs here. In the case of the senses we have the simple contrast between the possession of a capacity and its exercise. The normal animal, according to Aristotle, is born with the capacity to exercise a sense and at the appropriate time (allowing for e.g. kittens which are blind at birth) it exercises that capacity completely; there is no room for a process of getting better at seeing etc. through practice. (Whether this is a true account of the development of sensory capacities is another matter.) In the case of technical skills we start with certain rudimentary capacities, e.g. the capacity to put bricks on top of one another and to follow instructions as to how to make things by putting bricks on top of one another. By exercising those capacities we gradually acquire higher-level skills in building; the developed expertise which is the end-product is not identical with the primitive capacities from which we started, but has developed from them via a process of adaptation, varied application, and extension. Yet the subject-matter of both levels of skill is building; so we start with a low-level capacity to build and via the exercise of that acquire a further, higher-level capacity to build. And to that process nothing corresponds in the case of the senses.

In this section Aristotle gives his answer to the question which opens Plato's *Meno* (70a1–4); is excellence (1) imparted by teaching (*didakton*) or (2) acquired by practice (*askēton*) or (3) a natural endowment or (4) acquired in some other way? In so far as the question refers to excellence of character, Aristotle accepts alternative (2); for intellectual excellence he accepts (1).

1103ᵃ32–ᵇ3 In making the point that we acquire virtues of character and technical skills by performing the actions which manifest them, Aristotle first gives two instances of technical skills, building and lyre-playing, and then three instances of virtues of character. In this context he distinguishes the latter from natural capacities (exemplified by the senses) by indicating features which differentiate both virtues and skills from capacities. He does not at this stage explicitly distinguish virtues from skills; that distinction is first drawn at 1105ᵃ26–ᵇ5 (see notes on ᵃ26–30, ᵃ30–3, and ᵃ33–ᵇ1).

ᵃ32:   'as also in the case of the skills': lit. 'as in the case of the other skills'. See note on 1105ᵃ33–ᵇ1.

There may be a hint of the distinction in the fact that in the technical examples the verb employed is *poiein* (translated 'do') whereas in the case of the virtues it is *prattein* (translated 'perform'). In Book VI, chapters 2–5, Aristotle distinguishes *poiēsis* from *praxis*, defining the former as the production of an end (e.g. an object such as a house or a pot, or a state such as the health of a patient) distinct from the activity by which that end is produced, whereas *praxis* is activity directed towards no good apart from its own excellent performance (1139ᵇ1–4, 1140ᵃ1–23, 1140ᵇ1–7). In the same section he defines *technē* (skill) specifically as a productive disposition with a true conception (sc. of what is to be produced) (1140ᵃ9–10), and asserts explicitly that since production (*poiēsis*) differs from action (*praxis*), *technē* belongs to the sphere of the former, not to that of the latter (ᵃ16–17). I.e. *technē* is skill in production exclusively; the corresponding skill in action belongs to practical wisdom (*phronēsis*), the comprehensive ability to organize one's life well as a whole (1140ᵃ25–32, ᵇ4–6).

Here Aristotle apparently classes musical performance together with building as a productive activity, contrasted with the examples of action (*praxis*) provided by the virtues of character. The latter count as cases of *praxis* because they are performed for their own sake (1105ᵃ31–2; see note on 1105ᵃ30–3). But the classification of musical performance under *poiēsis* requires that Aristotle should view it as having as its aim not (as we might expect) simply its own excellence, but the production of an independent end which stands to it as the finished house stands to house-building. What that end is Aristotle does not tell us. Perhaps we are to think of the sound itself as the product,[2] or possibly, as suggested by *Pol.* VIII. 5–6, Aristotle regards music and the performing arts generally not as autonomous activities with their own internal standards of excellence, but as educational influences whose function in the promotion of good character is analogous to the productive role of medicine in promoting good health.

---

[2] As suggested by Müller (1982: 219–20).

1103ᵇ6–12   'Moreover . . . badly.' The meaning is that every skill is acquired and developed (or spoiled) by the performance of the same activities as manifest the skill. Those activities are both the source of the skill (i.e. the starting-point from which we begin to acquire it) and the means by which we develop it (for good or ill). The claim is repeated at ᵇ21–3.

'by the same source and the same means'. The Greek is literally 'from (*ek*) the same things and by means of (*dia*) the same things'. In ᵇ8–12 'for it is from playing . . . building badly' the only preposition used is *ek*. The argument should concern not merely the source of the acquisition of skills but also the process; hence it seems that from application specifically to the source of acquisition in ᵇ7 the preposition is applied in ᵇ8–12 alike to the source and to the process. (Alternatively, *ek* has the wider application throughout the passage, in which case 'by means of the same things' merely repeats 'from the same things' presumably for emphasis. The former interpretation, which avoids the repetition, is adopted in the translation.)

1103ᵇ12–13   The conception of teaching here is the broad one of training in the acquisition of good habits, in contrast to the more restricted notion of theoretical instruction which was employed at 1103ᵃ15–16.

1103ᵇ21–3   'states': specifically states of character. Also ᵇ31. See notes on 1105ᵇ20–1 and ᵇ25–6.

While normally rendering *hexis* as 'state', I have preferred 'state of character' in some passages (e.g. 1117ᵃ18–22) where the fact that the state in question is a state of character is not immediately indicated by the context.

BOOK TWO

CHAPTER 2

1103ᵇ27   'as the others are'. The contrast is with enquiries such as geometry or astronomy which are undertaken with no aim other than the achievement of theoretical understanding (*EE* 1216ᵇ11–16). Aristotle acknowledges that the latter may have practical applications, e.g. to land-surveying or navigation, but maintains that such applications are accidental to the enquiry, whereas it is apparently essential to practical enquiries such as ethics or medicine to have as their ultimate aim the achievement of their respective good. The contrast cannot be a matter of historical origin; Aristotle's point would hold even if it were true that e.g. geometry originally developed from Egyptian techniques of mensuration. It must be a point about the nature of the developed activity; the point of pursuing the science of geometry is geometrical understanding, whereas the point of studying ethics is not to understand what goodness is, but to become a good person. (That is of course compatible with its being the case that one can't become a good person without understanding what goodness is; the claim is about the ultimate aim of the enquiry.) But what assures us that that claim about the ultimate aim of the enquiry is true? How might Aristotle seek to refute someone who maintained that the ultimate point of studying ethics is as a branch of psychology, as part of understanding what it is to be human? Similarly, one might suggest that the point of studying aesthetics is not to become better at producing or appreciating works of art, but to understand what the nature of artistic production and appreciation is.

1103ᵇ28–9 'no profit from it'. In the light of the above, this must be understood as 'no ultimate profit from it'.

1103ᵇ31 'as we have said'. In the preceding chapter, summed up at 1103ᵇ21–3.

1103ᵇ32–4 '[I]n accordance with correct reason' renders *kata ton orthon logon*. The basic meaning of *logos* is 'thing said', from which it extends to a wide range of connected applications, including 'statement', 'formula', 'definition', 'proportion', 'argument', 'rationality', 'reason', and 'reasoning'. Fundamental to Aristotle's account of correct action is the thesis that actions should be correctly responsive to reason. That thesis leads to a systematic connection between two senses of *logos*, viz. 'principle' and 'reason', since Aristotle assumes that the task of reason is to formulate principles, and that correct principles are arrived at by the application of reason. Hence a possible alternative translation is 'in accordance with the correct principle'. Translators divide on whether Aristotle is referring (a) to the result (a principle, rule, formula, etc.) which reason arrives at, or (b) to the reason (or reasoning) which arrives at that result: (a) Ross rev. Ackrill/Urmson has 'according to the right rule', Gauthier/Jolif 'selon la droite règle', Rowe 'in accordance with the correct prescription'; (b) Dirlmeier 'nach der richtigen Planung', Crisp 'in accordance with right reason', Ross rev. Urmson (in Barnes 1984) 'according to right reason', Natali 'in conformita alla retta ragione'. Irwin's rendering 'accord with the correct reason' deliberately leaves it open whether Aristotle intends (a), (b), or both.

Renderings such as 'principle' which take the reference to be to the output of reasoning do not imply that that output must be fully specific. Any such principle will be to some degree indeterminate, requiring to be supplemented by perception of the particular circumstances of action; see note on 1104^{a}5–10.

The question of what correct reason is will be discussed in the context of the definition of virtue of character in II. 6; see note on 1106^{b}36–1107^{a}2.

'[T]he other excellences' suggests that Aristotle here treats *ho orthos logos* as itself an excellence, whereas it normally appears in contexts which suggest that it is not itself an excellence, but a constituent of excellences of character and intellect. (Hence this may be a further example of the idiomatic use of 'other' noted at 1103^{a}32 and 1105^{b}1.) On the other hand, at 1144^{b}26–8 he says that virtue of character is not only in accordance with the correct *logos* but with (i.e. involving) the correct *logos*, and that practical wisdom (*phronēsis*) is the correct *logos* in such matters. In that context *ho orthos logos* must be understood as 'correct reason' (as Aspasius takes it), and we can see how Aristotle can class the correct exercise of practical reason as itself an excellence, and consider its relation to the other excellences.

1103^{b}34–1104^{a}5   The reference to what was 'said at the outset' is to I. 3, 1094^{b}11–27.

1104^{a}1–7:   '[D]iscussion(s)' in this passage renders *logos* and its plural *logoi*.

The question of exactly what Aristotle is maintaining about the inexact character of ethical theory needs careful examination. The claim that every account of practical questions should be stated in outline and not precisely repeats the assertion of 1094^{b}19–21 that in matters of that kind we should be content that the truth should be demonstrated 'coarsely' (*pachulōs*) (perhaps best rendered by 'with a broad brush') and in outline. (I take it that 'coarsely' and 'not precisely' are interchangeable.) 1094^{b}21–2 adds 'and as we are speaking about things which hold for the most part and reasoning from premises of that kind our conclusions should be of that kind too'. That sentence suggests that Aristotle might think that all propositions of ethical theory belong to the class of truths which hold 'for the most part', i.e. usually but not without exception, a class represented by many generalizations of natural science, e.g. 'It is hot in summer', 'Dogs have four legs', 'People go grey as they age'. And if that were his view, it would be natural to suppose that that is the reason why ethical propositions hold 'coarsely and in outline', viz. that all propositions which hold for the most part can be stated only coarsely and in outline. Such propositions state only broad generalizations, not the precise truth.[3]

In our present passage there is no explicit mention of truths which hold only for the most part (though the reference back to the earlier passage may be held to imply it). More significant is the fact that Aristotle clearly does not believe that literally all propositions of ethical theory hold only for the most part. For instance, the definition of human good as 'activity of the soul in accordance with excellence' (1098^{a}16–17) does not state a truth which holds only for the most part; Aristotle does not believe that while it is true of most human beings that that is what their good consists in, there are some exceptional humans whose good consists in something else. That is a universal truth about human beings, derived from the equally unqualified universal truth that the *ergon* (function, or distinctive activity) of humans is rational activity of the soul (1098^{a}7). Yet the definition stated above is explicitly described as stated in outline only, it being the task of further investigation to fill in the detail (1098^{a}20–2). It is clear from this that it is not Aristotle's view that in every case ethical propositions state the truth in outline and without precision *because* they hold only for the most part. While it may be that some propositions state the

---

[3] For useful discussions of the role of that type of proposition in Aristotle's scientific theory see Mignucci (1981) and Judson (1991). Winter (1997) provides a detailed comparison of the roles of such propositions in Aristotle's ethics and in his general scientific theory.

truth in outline and without precision for that reason, there are
certainly some, as in the instance cited, in which the reason for
the lack of precision is something different.

In the case cited Aristotle's point is simply that the definition
specifies the human good in outline only, without filling in all
the detail. It tells us that human good is activity of the soul in
accordance with excellence, but doesn't itself specify what kind
or kinds of activity are in question, nor what kinds of excellence
or specific excellences must characterize that activity/those activities in order to achieve the good. Those specifications are the
subject-matter of the rest of the treatise. To give another instance,
the definition of virtue of character as 'a state concerned with
choice, in a mean in relation to us, a mean determined by reason,
namely the reason by which the person of practical wisdom would
determine it' ($1106^{b}36$–$1107^{a}2$; see below) holds universally, not
only for the most part, but is in itself unspecific, requiring to be
filled in by the detailed specification of the mean relative to us and
the reason employed by the person of practical wisdom. There is,
then, a class of ethical propositions, including some of the fundamental propositions of the system, whose lack of precision is
explained, not by their holding only for the most part, since they
do not hold in that way, but for the quite different reason that their
subject-matter is schematic. It is precisely because they state the
fundamentals of the system that their expression is abstract and
general, requiring to be filled in by the data of experience in order
to be applicable to specific kinds of case and particular instances
of those kinds.

But that is not the whole truth, since Aristotle continues
'practical matters and questions of what is advantageous contain
nothing fixed, just like things to do with health'. Here too, he
cannot be claiming that there are literally no exceptionless truths
in medicine. No doubt 'Health consists in the proper constitution
of the bodily organism' and (more specifically) 'Health arises from
the proper balance of the bodily humours' would be instances of
such exceptionless truths. But as in the ethical cases, these are
entirely schematic. When it comes to specification of the various
causes and symptoms of health and disease, Aristotle's claim is
that all generalizations hold for the most part. Thus 'such and
such a quantity of rhubarb is an effective purgative' and 'Anyone
with a temperature of $106°$ will die within 24 hours' are sound

generalizations, but there will sooner or later be exceptional cases. The situation in ethics is similar. 'Stand your ground in the face of the enemy' and 'Pay back what you have borrowed' are sound maxims, but counter-examples provided by exceptional cases are familiar from Plato (respectively *Lach.* 191a–c; *Resp.* 331c). It is tempting, then, to attribute to Aristotle the view that practical generalizations which are specific enough to contain substantive prescriptions as to what one should do hold only for the most part.

But it is clear that that view is itself one which Aristotle could have believed to hold only for the most part. He holds that some kinds of act—matricide (1110^{a}26–9), adultery, theft, and murder (1107^{a}11–12)—should never be done, and some kinds of motives—*schadenfreude*, shamelessness, and spite (1107^{a}10–11)—should never be felt or acted on. So 'Never under any circumstances commit matricide' and 'Never oppose the promotion of a deserving candidate out of spite' are substantive, but exceptionless generalizations. Such cases are indeed the minority, but Aristotle is committed to admitting them. So his claim about the lack of 'fixity' in practical matters is itself to be treated as a generalization with exceptions.

1104^{a}5–10 Aristotle now says that, even more than generalizations, particular practical judgements lack precision. Since the claim that generalizations lack precision appears to mean either that they lack the detail which makes them applicable to particular cases, or that they do not hold of all particular cases without exception it is hard to see how judgements about those very cases could lack precision in either sense. 'One should always show courage in the face of the enemy' lacks precision in the first sense, and 'The courageous thing to do is stand your ground' lacks precision in the other; but in what sense does 'At the battle of Delium Socrates behaved courageously by retreating in an orderly way' lack precision? Aristotle's explanation, that such cases do not fall under any skill or instruction manual, but those who act must always have regard to the particular circumstances, is hardly perspicuous. The point appears to be that it is not possible to specify exhaustively the circumstances in which exceptions to a generalization about conduct are warranted; so there can be no manual which reads 'Always stand firm in the face of the enemy, except in circumstances x, y or z'. (At best the manual could read 'Always stand fast, except in circumstances x, y, z, etc., etc.') But that is merely to repeat the point that generalizations about conduct lack precision; it is not clear how that lack of precision is supposed to be transferred to the particular judgement that in this case, having regard to the particular circumstances, the courageous thing to do is to retreat.

At $1109^{b}20$–3 and $1126^{b}2$–6 Aristotle says that judgements on particular questions of ethics are not determined or made specific by reason (*logos*) but by perception. The negative assertion is presumably a restatement of the point that particular judgements cannot be entailed by any general formulae. Such formulae (*logoi*) give at best indeterminate specifications: e.g. 'for the typical patient the correct dose of this drug will be between x and y mg'. But the correct dose for this particular patient must be decided by the doctor in the light of his or her best assessment of all the relevant particular circumstances.

It is not clear how much illumination is cast by the description of that decision as based on perception. If the correct dose for the typical patient is between 2 and 2.5 mg, is it plausible that in this particular case the doctor 'just sees' that the correct dose is precisely 2.36 mg? It is more likely that the particular decision is itself based on certain rough generalizations: e.g. 'I've noticed that patients above a certain height and weight tend to require a larger dose, whereas those with certain allergies need a smaller one. This patient is just above that height and weight, and he also suffers from such-and-such an allergy. But his allergy is a mild one, so taking everything into account it seems better to go for a dose nearer the upper limit, though not so near as it would be if he had no allergy.' Here the crucial notion is that of experience rather than strictly that of perception. Experience is of course grounded in perception; the experienced doctor has seen lots of similar cases. But that experience is typically summed up in general considerations of the kind instanced, which guide, without wholly determining, the eventual decision.

What does, then, determine that decision? In some cases experience yields the result 'Somewhere in the range 2.35–2.37 is right, but we can't hope to identify the figure more precisely'; in that case the final decision 'Let's make it 2.36' may be avowedly arbitrary. In others the decision may itself be based on the rule of thumb 'Best go for the mid-point of the range unless there are contrary indications', while perception, guided by experience, reveals the absence of contrary indications, leading to the final choice of 2.36. In others again the final decision may be precisely to administer a dose anywhere between 2.35 and 2.37 since the (precisely) correct answer to the question 'How big is the right dose?' specifies, not any single point on a numerical scale, but a range on a scale. In such a case the actual dosage given (2.36) may, once again, be chosen arbitrarily, but alternatively it may not be chosen at all, but (a) produced by the mechanical procedure of administration (e.g. pouring a liquid) and (b) accepted as falling within the required limits.

Medicine is an example of a kind of practice where experience is formulable in fairly rich generalizations which guide decisions without fully determining them. In other practices, such as steering a boat or playing an instrument, the role of generalizations is more attenuated and 'getting a feel for it' correspondingly more important. Typically in such cases the right result is not specifiable except as the result which the skilled practitioner and observer can recognize as right. The flautist must indeed be guided by the general rule of blowing neither too hard nor too gently, but the precise breath pressure required to produce the perfect pianissimo can be recognized only ostensively; 'That's it exactly'. Here it seems literally the case that 'the judgement lies in the perception' (1109^b24, 1126^b4), as does not seem to be the case in medicine. Aristotle may accept this conception of experience as providing the dominant model for ethics; but his citing steersmanship and medicine together at 1104^a9-10 suggests that he may not have differentiated the two. He may simply take it for granted that 'hav[ing] regard to the particular circumstances' (1104^a8-9; literally *looking* to the occasion') is a sort of perception, without considering the different roles of generalization and perception in different kinds of practice.

The thesis that ethics lacks precision thus embodies the following:

1. The fundamental principles of ethics are schematic, requiring to be fleshed out by detailed specifications of their component concepts.
2. Many (but not all) substantive ethical generalizations hold only 'for the most part'.

3. Particular ethical judgements cannot be read off from rules given in advance, but must be based on assessment of the relevant circumstances of their application. In that assessment perception plays a central role (though there are some indications that Aristotle's conception of the nature of the perception involved may itself be somewhat imprecise).

For fuller discussions see Devereux (1985–6), Sherman (1997: ch. 6), Irwin (2000), and London (2000–1).

1104ᵃ11–27 The common-sense observation of the effects of excess and deficiency, enunciated first in the spheres of health and strength (ᵃ14–18) and then applied to the virtues of character, specifically courage and temperance (ᵃ18–27), introduces the technical account of virtue of character as a mean, without itself presupposing any technical detail. Aristotle simply points out that it is characteristic of someone prescribing a diet or a fitness programme to avoid too much or too little of e.g. any food or type of exercise, and thereby to go for what is in between those extremes, i.e. what is appropriate or 'proportionate' (*ta summetra*, ᵃ17–18). He then points out that an analogous principle governs the acquisition of good or bad dispositions of character with respect to pleasure and fear (and their opposed motivations). These are two areas where the basic impulses of liking (and hence going for) and disliking (and hence shunning) are liable to be distorted by excess and deficiency. Going for absolutely every kind of pleasure and going for none whatever are opposed forms of distortion, as are being afraid of (and hence avoiding) every kind of danger and being afraid of none. For fuller discussion of the account of virtue of character as a mean, see commentary on ch. 6.

1104ᵃ12 'things of that kind': i.e. the subject-matter of practices characterized by the kinds of imprecision which Aristotle has just been discussing.

1104ᵃ22–5 At 1107ᵇ6–8 Aristotle says that the state of being insufficiently appreciative of bodily pleasures lacks a name in ordinary usage, because it is never found. The application to it of the word rendered 'insensible' (*anaisthētos*, i.e. 'lacking sense') is, as the later passage makes explicit, his own.

1104ᵃ25–9 As Aspasius points out, 'destroyed' must be understood as 'prevented from developing' (also in 1105ᵃ15); see 1105ᵃ33 and the concluding paragraph of the note on 1105ᵃ30–3.

1104ᵃ26 The notion of 'the mean state' (*tēs mesotētos*) is introduced purely negatively, by reference to the principle of the acquisition of virtues and vices which has just been enunciated. As one's character is in these respects spoiled by excess or deficiency in the ways described, it is preserved by the avoidance of both. It is taken for granted that avoiding both excess and deficiency is in some way being in between the two; hence 'mean' (= 'middle'). The precise sense in which virtue of character is 'in between' opposed vices will be elucidated in ch. 6.

1104ᵃ27–ᵇ3 This repeats the substance of 1103ᵇ6–12. '[B]esides that … same things' (ᵃ28–9) suggests that Aristotle is adding a further point, but the appearance is illusory, since the point of the earlier passage was that skills and virtues of character are developed by means of the very activities in which their exercise consists. What is new in this passage is the identification of a feedback loop; not only is it the case that we acquire a skill or virtue by doing the very acts in which the exercise of that skill or virtue consists, but having acquired the skill or virtue makes us better at doing those very acts.

BOOK TWO

CHAPTER 3

1104ᵇ3–5 Since character is the state of one's personality with respect to action and motivation, the agent's motivational attitudes are the primary ground of differentiation of types of character. The primary motivational attitudes are pleasure (*hēdonē*) and distress (*lupē*). Both these terms are generic, designating a family of attitudes, respectively positive and negative, towards action, whether past, present, or future. Thus pleasure in an action may consist in enjoyment of the action, or in being pleased to do it, or eager anticipation of it, or being glad to have done it, and so on. Similarly, distress in or at an action may consist in doing it reluctantly, finding it irksome, unpleasant, troublesome (either actually to do, or in prospect), being sorry that one has done it, etc. In any particular passage it is a matter for investigation which type or types of pleasure or distress are in question, or whether either term is being used more or less generically.

In a number of places in this chapter (1104ᵇ8–9, ᵇ15–16, ᵇ21, ᵇ27–8, 1105ᵃ13–14) Aristotle asserts that virtue (or the virtues) is (are) concerned with *hēdonai* and *lupai*, using the Greek terms in the plural, a usage which is ambiguous between 'instances of pleasure and distress' and 'kinds of pleasure and distress'. (Since Aristotle believes that virtue is concerned with both, there is no need for him to resolve the ambiguity.) Since the plural 'distresses' has no idiomatic English use, it is undesirable to make Aristotle assert that virtue has to do with pleasures and distresses, and it is unwarranted to resolve the ambiguity pointed out above by rendering uniformly 'instances of pleasure and distress' or 'kinds of pleasure and distress'. The more traditional translation of *lupē* as 'pain' allows the idiomatically contrasted pair 'pleasures and pains'. But although 'pain' has a well-established philosophical use in the wide range of applications corresponding to those of *lupē* (exemplified e.g. in Mill's dictum (*Utilitarianism*, ch. 2) that 'pleasure, and freedom from pain, are the only things desirable as ends'), its predominant connotation, particularly to the modern reader, is that of physical pain, and consequently its systematic use to render Aristotle's *lupē* is liable to mislead. I have therefore avoided the plural forms of 'pleasure' and 'distress' in the translation, while pointing out in the notes the places where the terms are used in the plural.

'which arises from what they do'. It is made clear by the next sentence that Aristotle is thinking exclusively of the pleasure or distress which agents take in their own actions; pleasure or distress caused to others is not in question.

1104ᵇ5–8   (a) It is unclear just what Aristotle has in mind by 'tak[ing] pleasure in doing just that' (i.e. in abstaining from bodily pleasures). Is the claim that the temperate person enjoys abstaining from bodily pleasures, or merely that he or she does so gladly, or is pleased to do so? (I might be glad to help out a sick friend by doing her shopping without actually enjoying the shopping. Nor does that imply that I have in any sense changed my mind between taking on the task and actually doing it. I can be keen or eager to do something, and count myself fortunate in having the opportunity to do it, without enjoying doing it (without, indeed, having the smallest expectation that I shall enjoy doing it). Think of a martyr going eagerly to the stake; see further commentary on 1117^{a}33–^{b}16, with n. 28.) In the case of facing danger, doing it 'with pleasure' (*chairōn*) is a more positive attitude than doing it 'without distress' (*mē lupoumenos*). Aristotle is clear that facing danger readily or without reluctance is sufficient to count as courage, and does not demand in addition that the courageous person does it 'with pleasure'. But it is still indeterminate how much more is implied by the stronger description.

Aristotle here shows no sign of recognizing that in some cases finding it unpleasant to do what it is right to do is a sign not of deficiency in virtue, but of virtue itself. It may be the right thing to switch off the ventilator which is keeping a brain-dead patient breathing, but the doctor who does so enthusiastically is to that extent callous and insensitive, while the one who does so with repugnance is to that extent humane. The general form of such cases is that doing the right thing involves the sacrifice of some good which it is appropriate for the virtuous person to cherish. Aristotle recognizes a particular instance of this general form in the case of courage, which is unpleasant for the virtuous person in that it involves facing up to the loss of the value residing in his or her good life (see commentary on 1117^{a}33–^{b}16), but does not generalize to other cases of conflict of values. The importance of regret for the psychology of virtue is emphasized by Hursthouse (1999: chs. 2–3).

(b) Aristotle contrasts the temperate person, who abstains from bodily pleasures (i.e. from bad bodily pleasures) and takes pleasure in doing so, with the person who abstains from that sort of pleasures but dislikes doing so. The latter is called 'intemperate' (*akolastos*), and similarly the person who faces danger but is distressed by doing so is called a coward (*deilos*). I.e. each of those persons is characterized by a vice opposed to the respective virtue. In VII. 1 Aristotle refines his moral psychology by introducing the states of self-control (*enkrateia*) and lack of control (*akrasia*) as intermediate between virtue and vice; the virtuous agent does the right thing effortlessly and gladly, the self-controlled does the same thing but with an effort, struggling against contrary impulses,

the person lacking control acts against his or her better judgement through giving in to those contrary impulses, and the vicious
person acts viciously from considered choice. In terms of that
developed psychology the persons whom Aristotle here characterizes as vicious count, not as vicious, but as self-controlled.

The above comment takes literally Aristotle's descriptions of the
person who abstains from pleasures while finding it disagreeable
and of the person who endures dangers while being distressed,
as implying that those people do actually abstain, and endure the
dangers, respectively. But the fluidity of the notion of distress (see
above) at least makes it possible that, in addition (or possibly even
alternatively) Aristotle has in mind people who do not abstain,
because they would find it disagreeable to do so, and who do not
endure dangers because the prospect of doing so distresses them
too much. If that is so, then, rather than characterizing as vicious
types of agent whom the more developed psychology counts as
self-controlled, Aristotle should here be seen as making no distinction between the vicious and the self-controlled. Indeed, since
the pejorative descriptions can also apply to those who think that
they ought to abstain, etc., but give way to their distaste for doing
so, he can fairly be seen as making no distinction between any of
the types of non-virtuous person distinguished in Book VII.

1104^b8–9 'has to do with pleasure and distress'. The nouns are
plural in the Greek.

1104^b9–11 'it is because of pleasure ... fine things'. For pleasure as the primary motive see 1104^b35–1105^a1. We fail to do fine
things because of distress in that we are deterred from the pursuit
of noble aims by reluctance to undergo the troubles necessary to
achieve them.

1104^b12 'as Plato says': *Leg.* 653a–c.

1104^b13–14 'the virtues have to do with actions and feelings'.
See ch. 5.

1104^b14–15 'every action ... and distress'. For the role of pleasure and distress in the account of feelings see 1105^b19–23. It is
not clear how sweeping a claim Aristotle intends to make about

actions. At its widest it would be the claim that every individual action (e.g. my brushing my teeth now) is in some way pleasant or unpleasant. I am not clear whether anything in Aristotle's theory requires so sweeping a claim. More plausibly the claim is looser: viz. that our choice of kinds of action undertaken as good is motivated by our likes and dislikes, and thus determined by the kinds of thing we find pleasant and unpleasant (in the wide connotation of those terms described above).

1104^{b}14–16 'every feeling is attended by pleasure and distress, that is a further reason ... pleasure and distress'. At the first occurrence of 'pleasure and distress' the nouns are singular, at the second plural.

'[I]s attended by' renders *hepetai*, lit. 'follows'. The meaning is that pleasure and pain are dependent on feelings; for discussion of the ways in which they are so dependent, see note on 1105^{b}20–3.

1104^{b}16–18 This sentence relies on (a) a remedial theory of punishment, (b) the medical theory that cures work through the application of opposite factors, e.g. a fever caused by excess of heat in the body is cured by the application of cold compresses. For (a) see Plato, *Grg.* 479a–c; *Resp.* 409e; *Leg.* 735d–e, 854d–e, 862d–863a. The latter was a commonplace of much ancient (as of much modern) medical theory; see e.g. the Hippocratic treatise *On Breaths* 1. Bad actions are thought of (loosely) as resulting from an excess of pleasure in the soul (cf. ^{b}9–10), which is counteracted by deprivation of pleasure or infliction of pain.

As Anon. remarks, the theory of cure by opposites assumes that the best state is intermediate; the application of cold compresses to a fevered patient is intended to bring the patient into a state of being neither too hot nor too cold. See note on 1104^{a}11–27.

1104^{b}18–21 Virtue and vice are essentially related to pleasure and distress for the reason stated at ^{b}3–8: viz. that the agent's pleasure and distress in his or her actions is partly constitutive of those dispositions. '[A]nd has to do with [them]' (^{b}20) appears simply to repeat 'is essentially related to ... those things'. 'which affect it'; i.e. which affect the soul.

1104^{b}21–4 This sentence explains the preceding one. Aristotle specifies a number of ways in which one's pursuit of pleasure or avoidance of distress (plural in the Greek) may go wrong, indicating in the concluding formula 'or however ... reason' that the specification is not exhaustive. At 1106ᵇ21–3 (see below) he employs a similar, but more extended list of conditions which have to be satisfied if one's disposition is to be virtuous. That later list does not contain a concluding formula similar to the one here (having the force of 'or in any other relevant way'), which leaves it open that the later specification is intended to be exhaustive.

ᵇ23–4: 'determined by reason': alternatively, 'determined by one's rational principle'. Cf. note on 1103ᵇ32–4; see also 1107ᵃ1–2 and note.

1104ᵇ24–6 Aristotle does not attribute the definition of virtue as lack of feeling to anyone in particular (the verb lacks a subject in Greek, hence the most literal rendering is 'they (unspecified) define', which I have tried to capture by 'people define'). He may simply intend to characterize it as a common misconception. At *EE* 1222ᵃ3–5, the concluding sentence of a chapter which corresponds closely to the present chapter, he says that everyone readily (or perhaps 'rashly' (*procheirōs*)) defines the virtues in that way. Some editors propose deleting 'everyone' from that passage to assimilate it to our present sentence, but, assuming that Aristotle does intend to point to a widespread error, emendation is unnecessary.

The doctrine that well-being or happiness consists in a state of freedom from disturbance, including disturbance by emotions, goes back to Democritus (DL IX. 45), from whom it descended to the Epicureans in the form of the doctrine that the good is *ataraxia*. Speusippus is also reported as holding that the good is *aochlēsia*, lack of trouble (Clement, *Strom.* II. 22. 133). But these sources do not refer specifically to accounts of the virtues.

Rather than look for a specific theorist or theorists as Aristotle's target, it fits his programme best if we see him as aiming at what he takes to be a widespread misconception. So far he has concentrated on the examples of courage and temperance, arguing that they are a matter of the proper disposition of the impulses towards pleasure and self-preservation. Since the intemperate person is overcome by bodily desire and the coward by fear, it is obviously tempting to suppose that the opposed virtues are simply lack of desire and of fear respectively. Aristotle points out that this is wrong; being virtuous consists, not in absence of feeling, but in having proper feeling and lacking improper ones; i.e. it is a matter of having and lacking feeling as one should, when one should, etc. This will be spelled out in more detail in subsequent chapters.

1104^{b}27–8 'so as to achieve the best'. The construction of the sentence suggests that 'pleasure and distress' (plural in the Greek) should be supplied after 'the best'. Another obvious possibility is 'actions'. But since Aristotle is here arguing that the best actions are precisely those in which the agent experiences and is motivated by the right (= the best) pleasure and distress, the doctrine is the same in either case.

In *EE* II. 5 Aristotle begins with the very similar assertion (1222^{a}6–8) that virtue is the disposition by which we are such as to achieve the best, and then proceeds to define the best as a mean defined in terms of pleasure and distress (^{a}8–17).

1104^{b}30–1105^{a}1 Aristotle treats the tripartition of objects of desire as a commonplace.[4] He treats pleasure as the most fundamental, in that things desired for either of the other reasons present themselves to us as pleasant. That seems to be true, at least in the sense that if we want them, we believe that we shall be pleased to achieve them.

Aristotle here treats the universality of the pleasure instinct (^{b}34–5) in all animals as confirming the status of pleasure as the most fundamental object of desire. Elsewhere he reports different theorists as drawing opposed conclusions from this phenomenon. In X, 1172^{b}9–11, he reports that Eudoxus argued that pleasure is the supreme good from the fact that all creatures, rational and non-rational alike, pursue it; in VII, 1152^{b}19–20, on the other hand, he cites unnamed theorists as arguing that pleasure is not a good at all from the fact that children and animals pursue it.

1105^{a}3–5 'And we measure ... distress.' It is not easy to see what Aristotle is saying in this sentence. On a literal construal he is saying that the assessment of actions in terms of pleasure and distress varies from person to person. Assessing (lit. measuring)

---

[4] See *Top.* 105^{a}28, 118^{b}28, and Cooper (1996b/1999: 264–6 (page refs. to (1999))).

actions in terms of pleasure and distress presumably means evaluating them, using pleasure and distress as the measure of value. But if the point is that some people rely more on a hedonistic scheme of evaluation, and others less, how is that supposed to show that, as he asserts in the next sentence, our *entire* activity (*pragmateia*, rendered 'business' in ª11) must be concerned with pleasure and distress? That claim surely needs to be supported by some statement to the effect that hedonistic evaluation is universal, and thereby fundamental.

I am therefore inclined to suggest that we should take the sentence as elliptical, construing the phrase 'some of us more and some less' as modifying, not the verb 'measure' (which is what the syntax of the sentence undeniably requires) but the verbs which are to be understood as expanding the expression 'pleasure and distress'. I.e. we all measure our actions by pleasure and distress, but we measure them differentially, depending on whether they cause us more or less pleasure and distress. (The more we enjoy some kinds of actions, the more favourably we tend to evaluate them, and the more we find them unpleasant, the less favourably we evaluate them.)

If that is correct, then the Greek sentence must be construed, not as a full expression of Aristotle's meaning, but as a cryptic note, whose meaning has to be reconstructed by an expansion designed to fit the argumentative context.

1105ª7–8 'Moreover ... Heraclitus says'. Spirit (*thumos*) is the instinct of self-assertion, which manifests itself in ambition, anger when thwarted, resentment of injuries or insults, etc.

Existing collections of the fragments of Heraclitus do not include a saying to the effect that it is more difficult to fight against pleasure than against spirit. One fragment (DK 22B85, preserved by Aristotle and Plutarch) runs: 'It is difficult to fight against spirit; for what it wants, it buys at the price of soul' (which presumably means 'spirit makes people risk their lives to get what they want'). Some commentators (including most recently Irwin (1999*a*)) take it that Aristotle is here referring to that passage, interpreting 'it is more difficult to fight against pleasure than against spirit—and Heraclitus tells us how difficult it is to fight **that**'. Others, including Gauthier/Jolif, take him to be citing that passage inaccurately, which is puzzling in view of the fact that he cites it correctly in two other places. It seems to me easier to suppose that Aristotle is referring to another saying of Heraclitus, otherwise lost. (The question as to whether this sentence should be accepted as itself preserving a genuine fragment of Heraclitus should be pursued elsewhere.)

1105ᵃ11, ᵃ13–14 'pleasure and distress': plural in the Greek.

1105ᵃ12 'political science' (*hē politikē* (sc. *epistēmē*)): i.e. ethics. Since human good has to be achieved by humans in a social context, of which in Aristotle's view the *polis* (city-state) is the most developed form, *politikē* is his regular term for the enquiry which studies that good. Typical passages are 1094ᵇ14–15: 'The fine and the just, which are investigated by *politikē*, contain much divergence and room for dispute', and 1095ᵃ15–16: 'What is it that we say *politikē* investigates, i.e. which is supreme among all the goods to be achieved by action?'

On Aristotle's account of the acquisition of virtue of character see Burnyeat (1980),[5] Kosman (1980), Sherman (1989: ch. 5), Vasiliou (1996), McDowell (1996), Kraut (1998).

BOOK TWO

CHAPTER 4

1105ᵃ17–21 Aristotle returns to the thesis enunciated in chapter 1, that we acquire the virtues of character by exercising them, and raises the difficulty mentioned in the commentary (on 1103ᵃ26–ᵇ2), that in the case of virtues and of technical skills alike the exercise of the skill or virtue apparently presupposes that one already has it, whence it is impossible that one comes to have it by exercising it.

---

[5] Burnyeat's influential discussion is extensively criticized by Curzer (2002). One of Curzer's targets is Burnyeat's thesis that pleasure has a central role in the training of character; in opposition to that view Curzer stresses the importance of negative conditioning through shame and punishment. While the details of the controversy go beyond the scope of the present discussion, it is clear that Aristotle's insistence that correct education proceeds via pleasure and distress (1104ᵇ9–16) stresses the importance both of positive reinforcement of desirable character traits via pleasure and negative reinforcement of undesirable traits via distress; at its simplest, we have to learn to like acting well and to dislike acting badly.

1105ᵃ21−6   Aristotle's reply assumes at the outset the parallelism of skills and virtues on which he relies in chapter 1. He distinguishes between doing something which a certain skill prescribes and doing it in the special way characteristic of the person who possesses the skill. His example is that of *grammatikē*, literally skill in writing, which, including as it does spelling and the correct formation of written sentences, is rendered 'literacy'. One can 'do something literate' (e.g. spell a word correctly) without actually being literate, since one might spell it correctly purely by chance, or copy down the letters correctly from a teacher's dictation. That is contrasted with doing something literate 'in a literate way', e.g. spelling a particular word correctly in virtue of knowing how to spell. Aristotle says that only the person who gets things right in a literate way is literate, and that that person does so 'in accordance with the literacy which he possesses'; clearly the person who gets things right otherwise does not exercise the skill of literacy, since that person does not possess that skill, and no-one can exercise a skill which he or she does not possess.

But now Aristotle seems to have slipped away from addressing the crucial problem, at least as it arises from the formulation in chapter 1. There he explicitly asserts (1103ᵃ31−2) that we acquire the virtues and other skills by having previously exercised them, and treats examples such as 'we become builders by building' (ᵃ33−4) as satisfying that general description. If that is still his problem in this chapter, he does not solve it by distinguishing between exercising a skill and doing the things prescribed by that skill without possessing it. For the latter is not exercising the skill; hence the distinction contributes nothing to answering the question 'How is it possible to acquire a skill by exercising it?'

One might suggest that Aristotle's conception of the problem has changed between chapters 1 and 4; he no longer counts the apprentice's acts of building as exercises of skill in building, and now conceives the problem as that of explaining how we acquire skills by performing unskilled acts of the type prescribed by the skill. But, first, he gives no signal that his conception of the problem has changed in this way, and more importantly the suggested later conception of the problem is inferior to the earlier one. For the later conception loses sight of Aristotle's central insight that the acquisition of skills is cumulative, so that we do acquire fully mature skills via a process of development in which the exercise of those very skills at a more primitive level is progressively refined and elaborated (see above). Even the apprentice builder builds 'in accordance with the building skill which is in him'. The crucial point is that building skill is in the apprentice in a less developed form than that in which it is in the master, just as the nature of an animal species is in an immature member of the species in a less developed form than that in which it is in an adult.

1105ª26–30 Aristotle now abandons the parallelism between virtues and technical skills. Whether an act is an instance of excellence in technical skill is determined purely by its output, whereas in the case of virtues production of the right output is necessary but not sufficient for an act to be an instance of a virtue. In addition, certain internal conditions of the agent's intellect and motivation must be satisfied, which are detailed at ª31–3 (see below). This distinction enables Aristotle to offer in the case of virtue a solution of his problem; an essential part of the process of learning to act while satisfying those further conditions consists in acting without satisfying them.

As Irwin (1999*a*: 195) observes, he is not contradicting the point he has just made, that a good product may be produced by luck. That type of case does not involve the exercise of skill at all; here his claim is that when skill is exercised, its being exercised well is determined purely by the excellence of the product, whereas in the case of the virtues extra conditions concerning the agent must be satisfied for the act to be virtuous. It is hard to see the force of this distinction. Consider a potter. To exercise skill in pottery well, it is not sufficient that on some particular occasion the potter should have used his or her skill in potting to make what is in fact a good pot. Suppose he or she intends to make a pottery duck, but fails to keep his or her mind on the job and slips into an ingrained routine for making a pot, with the result that the end-product is an excellent pot. While the product is a good pot, the act by which it was produced, though a skilled act, is not a good piece of potting. To have done well as a potter, the artist must have intended to produce a certain sort of artefact, the resultant object of that sort must in fact be a good one, and the artist must have been able, through his or her skill at pottery to realize his or her intention to produce an artefact of that sort, and must have had the further intention to realize his or her primary intention by the exercise of that very skill. The distinction between virtues and skills cannot then consist in what Aristotle says it consists in, viz. that in the latter case doing well is determined wholly by the nature of the product, whereas in the former various conditions of the agent have to be satisfied as well.

The conditions for exercise of skill and for virtuous action are indeed different from one another; as Heliodorus points out, one may exercise skill in acting under duress, whereas virtuous actions must be chosen for their own sake (see below). But the point remains that the exercise of skill requires the appropriate agent-conditions (as specified above) in addition to the excellence of the product. Consideration of Aristotle's account of the agent-conditions required for virtuous action will reveal how far those conditions diverge from those we have found necessary for the exercise of technical skill.

1105ᵃ30–3 The agent-conditions required for virtuous actions are threefold:

    (i) the agent acts knowingly;
    (ii) the agent acts from reasoned choice of the action for its own sake;
    (iii) the agent acts from a stable and unchangeable state of character.

Each of the three conditions presents problems.

    (i) '[K]nowingly' translates the Greek *eidōs*, lit. 'knowing'. So the first requirement is that the agent acts in the possession of some knowledge. Plainly, this knowledge cannot be incidental to the action: e.g. if someone acts temperately while (as it happens) possessing the knowledge that Paris is the capital of France. The knowledge in question must be knowledge about the action, and it is clearly implied that the agent acts not merely *while* possessing it, but *in virtue of* possessing it; i.e. this knowledge is part of the explanation of the action. What is it, then, that the virtuous agent must know about his or her action if that action is to be an instance of virtuous action?

It is clearly a necessary condition of an action's instantiating a virtue that the agent should know what he or she is doing in performing that action. This condition excludes the kinds of case discussed in III. 1 under the heading of 'ignorance' or 'error' (*agnoia*), i.e. things done in one way or another unintentionally (including things done by mistake, under a misapprehension, by accident, etc. (see later discussion)). Thus if I hand over £10 to Jones, thereby discharging a debt, while believing that I am handing a note to a servant to deliver, I pay the debt inadvertently, and hence my act is not an instance of just conduct. But even here I knew what I was doing, *under some description*; e.g. I knew that I was handing the man a piece of paper. The knowledge condition must, then, be more precisely specified if it is not to be entirely trivial, i.e. to be a condition of the agent's having *acted* at all, as opposed to having made a reflex movement, etc. How precise must the specification be? Do I satisfy the condition if I know that I am handing over money, or handing over £10? But in either case I might have mistaken my creditor for someone I intended to bribe, and so still have paid the debt inadvertently. If, as we assume, this first condition is intended to exclude cases of unintentional action, the knowledge in question must be knowledge that the action is of a certain type T, and it must further be the case that it is in virtue of belonging to type T that the action is an instance of the virtue in question. So in our present example, it must be in virtue of being a payment of a debt that the handing over of £10 is an instance of just conduct, and the agent must know that what he or she is doing is paying a debt.

Does Aristotle's knowledge condition also require that the agent knows that in paying a debt he or she is acting justly? It is clear that Aristotle's general theory of virtue requires virtuous agents to be aware of their reasons for acting, and also clear that those reasons relate essentially to the virtues. But first there is some unclarity as to how explicitly specification of the virtues enters into the agent's consciousness of his or her reasons for acting (see below), and secondly it is problematic how sharply Aristotle distinguishes the knowledge condition (i) above from the choice condition (ii). Both points will be elucidated via consideration of the choice condition.

(ii) The choice condition is stated in terms of *prohairesis*. While *prohairesis* will be discussed in detail below (see III. 2–3), it will suffice to say here that it requires the agent to act for reasons, to be aware of those reasons and to choose or decide on the action as a result of deliberation in which those reasons are decisive. Hence to the extent to which the just agent's reasons for paying a debt include its being just to do so, the knowledge that it is just to do so is itself a constituent of the agent's reasoned choice to pay the debt. So if the knowledge condition is not to be subsumed under the choice condition, it would seem preferable to restrict the former to some more basic kind of knowledge presupposed by, rather than constitutive of the agent's reasoned choice. That suggestion may be supported by the statement at 1105ᵇ2–3 that in the case of the virtues knowing has little or no effect; since the knowledge that e.g. paying a debt is just is essential to the virtuous agent's reasoned choice to pay, it is hard to see what might be meant by the assertion that that knowledge has little or no effect. If that knowledge is partly constitutive of my reasons for acting, then my having those reasons has the effect of making me a virtuous person. On the other hand, the knowledge that I am paying a debt could figure as readily in a chain of reasons leading to a wicked decision as to a virtuous one: e.g. if paying a debt is part of a plot to enmesh my creditor in a dishonest scheme. Hence the knowledge that I am paying a debt has a more remote link to my having a virtuous character than the knowledge that paying a debt is just.

The choice condition specifies that the virtuous agent makes a reasoned choice of virtuous actions 'for their own sake' (*di' auta*). We should expect that to mean that the virtuous agent chooses to perform acts which fall under the various virtues precisely because they are instances of those virtues: e.g. to do just actions because they are just, and temperate actions because they are temperate. While that is broadly correct, there are problems of detail.

One difficulty is apparent only. This is presented by Aristotle's repeated assertion that the virtuous agent acts 'for the sake of the fine' (*tou kalou heneka*, 1115ᵇ12–13, 23, 1120ᵃ23–4, 1122ᵇ6–7, 1123ᵃ24–5; *EE* 1230ᵃ27–9, 1248ᵇ36–7).[6] One might read these passages as claiming that every virtuous act, of whatever kind, is directed to the attainment of a single common goal, the achievement of 'the fine', and construe that claim as inconsistent with the claim that the virtuous agent does just acts because they are just, temperate acts because they are temperate, etc. But clearly there is no incompatibility. Even if the virtuous agent always has the

---

[6] Verbal variants occur at 1116ᵃ11, ᵇ3, ᵇ31, 1117ᵃ8, ᵇ9. See also *MM* 1190ᵃ28–34, 1191ᵃ20–4, ᵇ15.

achievement of 'the fine' in mind (an assumption to be considered below), his or her doing so allows that just acts are seen as fine in virtue of being just, temperate acts as fine in virtue of being temperate, and so on. Being instances of this virtue or that are different ways of being fine; hence the claim that all virtuous acts are done for the sake of the fine is not in tension with the claim that instances of the different virtues are chosen for their own sake.[7]

There is, however, tension between the latter claim and the fact that certain kinds of virtuous action are necessarily instrumental in character, in that they are necessarily directed to the attainment of goals which are distinct from the performance of the acts themselves. Thus Aristotle's paradigm of courageous action is facing death in battle in defence of one's city, an act which has as its goal the city's future state of freedom and flourishing life. Again, benevolent actions are done for the sake of the benefit to the recipient. In what sense, then, can courageous or benevolent actions be done for their own sake? Here we have to distinguish between internal goals of actions of certain types and external reasons for performing actions of those types. An act's being directed toward the goal of the preservation of one's city counts towards its being an act of courage, and an act's being directed toward one's neighbour's good counts towards its being benevolent. In that sense those goals are internal to acts of those kinds. But there is the further question 'Why does one (or 'why should one') perform actions which have those internal goals?'; this is a question about what does or should motivate one to pursue those goals. And to that question Aristotle offers the answer that what motivates the virtuous person to pursue those goals is that it is fine to do so, the fineness of doing so being modulated by the specific character of the particular virtue in question (as described above).[8]

---

[7] See Mele (1981: 412): ' "The noble" is practiced for its own sake; and insofar as particular actions that proceed from the virtues are noble, *they* are done for their own sakes. But this is not to say that they are *not* done for the sake of the noble; indeed it is precisely because they *are* done for the sake of the noble ... that they are said to be done for their own sakes' (author's emphases).

[8] So Korsgaard (1996: 216): 'When we say that the courageous person sacrifices himself in battle for its own sake, we need not be denying that he sacrifices himself for the sake of his country. It is the whole package—the action along with its purpose, sacrificing your life for the sake of your country—that is chosen for its own sake.'

Other illuminating discussions of doing something for its own sake are those by Kraut (1976) and Ackrill (1978*b*).

How is this motivation to be conceived? We are not obliged
to attribute to Aristotle the supposition that, on every occasion of
acting, the thought 'That would be a/the fine thing to do (in so
far as courageous, etc.)' must be in the virtuous agent's mind. At
$1117^a17–22$ he says that one's behaviour in unexpected situations
of danger is more indicative of courage than one's behaviour in
situations one has had time to prepare for, since 'when things are
apparent in advance' one can choose what to do from calculation
and reasoning, but in sudden cases one acts in accordance with
one's state of character'. While he is in the first instance pointing
out that immediate, unreflective response to sudden danger is a
better indication of character than actions which result from prior
deliberation, it is clear that he has in mind such cases as that of the
bodyguard who, at the first sound of gunfire, hurls the President
to the ground and covers him with his own body. Clearly he had
no time to deliberate, but equally clearly the thought 'Covering
the President's body with mine would be a fine thing to do' need
not have crossed his mind. What is 'in the agent's mind' at the
moment of action is not the central issue, since Aristotle is explicit
that not every item in an agent's set of reasons for acting need
be consciously rehearsed (*MA* $701^a26–31$). But that still leaves it
open for Aristotle to maintain that the heroic bodyguard's reason
for throwing himself on the President was his belief that it would
be a (or the) fine thing to do.

The belief that such and such would be a fine (*kalon*) thing to do
allows for a range of nuances which make that belief more or less
self-regarding. At one extreme, 'fine' is glossed by terms such as
'admirable' or 'creditable' (even more strongly, 'glorious, magnificent') where the predominant sense is that the action is such as
to deserve or attract the admiration of others for the agent. Here
the ultimate motivation is that characteristic of the Homeric hero,
who wants above all to be admired and praised, by contemporaries
certainly, but even more by posterity. We may contrast with this a
use where the focus is less on the agent than on the action itself;
an action may be seen as embodying an ideal of human behaviour which the agent has the opportunity to embody. The famous
last words of Sydney Carton in Dickens's *A Tale of Two Cities*,
spoken before he goes to the guillotine in place of another man
whose identity he has assumed, illustrate this well: 'It is a far, far

better thing that I do than I have ever done.'⁹ While the key word is 'better', not 'finer' or 'nobler', the thought is appropriate to the Greek *kalon* (and would, I suspect, more naturally be rendered in Greek by *kallion* than by *kreitton*); it is the thought that for once in his life he has the opportunity to do something unqualifiedly good (and thereby to make up for the meanness and selfishness of his previous life). While there is still a self-regarding content to this thought, it is not 'How justly shall I be admired for this' but 'How fortunate I am to have had this opportunity'.¹⁰

Aristotle's famous discussion in IX. 8 of the sense in which the virtuous agent is a 'self-lover' (*philautos*) suggests that he ascribes to him some self-regarding motivation of the kind described, though it is hard to give it a determinate place on the spectrum I have suggested. The virtuous agent will sacrifice everything for his friends and his country—wealth, honours, all external goods, life itself—but in so doing he will 'lay claim to the fine for himself' (1169ᵃ22–3). He will even resign to his friend the opportunity of doing fine things, instead of doing them himself, but even this sacrifice has the paradoxical feature that, in making it 'the good man appears to assign more of the fine to himself', since it is 'finer to cause one's friend to do them than to do them oneself' (1169ᵃ33–ᵇ1). It might be suggested that Aristotle is not here describing the agent's motivation, but rather the effect of his actions; his motivation is ultimately altruistic, in that his ultimate concern is the good of his friend or of his country, but in virtue of that very motivation his actions bring on himself a credit which was no part of his aim. But the description of him as 'laying claim to' the fine and 'assigning more of it to himself' surely pick out

---

⁹ Charles (1995: 166) cites the same example in much the same sense. To the best of my knowledge we hit on the example independently.

¹⁰ I take it as fundamental to understanding the concept of the *kalon* that to be *kalon* is to be attractive, to be such as to provide an incentive to choice and action via such emotional attitudes as love, admiration, and emulation. It is the failure to capture that aspect that is what is basically wrong with the suggestion of Owens (1981) that *kalon* should be translated 'right'. That rendering does indeed capture the fundamental normativity of the concept, but at the price of severing its links with the emotions and aesthetic responses. Owens is quite correct to point out that to someone with the appropriate moral sensibility an action's being right may itself be a ground of that sort of attractiveness (1981: 271, 273). But that is to say that for such a person a certain action may appear *kalon because* it is right; it is not a ground for translating *kalon* as 'right'.

the agent's intentions, as is confirmed by Aristotle's explanation of the sense in which the virtuous person lays claim to the fine: 'for he would rather choose to have intense pleasure for a short time than moderate pleasure for a long time, and to live finely for a year than in any old way for many years, and to do one fine and great action rather than many small ones. That is perhaps what happens to people who give their lives for others. So they choose for themselves something great and fine' (1169ª22–6). Here Aristotle is describing the virtuous agent's preferences, and explaining what he does in terms of them; he is not making the implausible claim that, independently of what actually motivates him, the outcome happens to coincide with those preferences. It remains, I think, indeterminate whether the self-sacrificer seeks the fine in the sense of the personally creditable or in that of the objectively noble. The difference is primarily one of emphasis, between 'something which it is *splendid-for-me* to do' and 'a splendid thing for someone to do, and it is I who do it'.

Our assumption so far has been that, whether or not consciously rehearsed, the concept of the fine is internal to the virtuous agent's reasons for acting; i.e. that it is ultimately because the agent sees his or her prospective actions as in one way or another fine that he or she is motivated to do them, and that the agent's (possibly retrospective) account of his or her reasons for acting contains 'because it is or was fine (*qua* courageous, etc.)' as an indispensable element. That assumption certainly conflicts with some of our ordinary beliefs about some types of virtuous action, notably instances of courage and benevolence. Some of the clearest (and most admirable) instances of these virtues appear to be motivated neither by the conception of the action as creditable to the agent nor as exemplifying an ideal type of behaviour, but rather to be focused on the particular circumstances, especially as they affect others. Consider the following example.

A wounded man lies out in no man's land crying for help, and a soldier crawls out from the front line trench under heavy fire and brings him in. Asked why, he says something like this:

'You could hear the poor devil out there on his own. It was pitiful. You can't just let someone die like that without trying to help. Someone had to have a go.'

'Why you?'

'Well, someone had to. Why not me? If it was me out there, I'd want someone to try to bring me in. You can't just walk away from something like that.'

'But plenty of people did.'

'Well, that's their look-out; I couldn't.'

Here we have courage and compassion in the highest degree, yet the concepts of a splendid kind of thing to do or an admirable type of action seem to play no part in the agent's account of his reasons. The nearest we come to an abstract description of the action is as something one just has to do. The action-type is seen, not as attractive, either for the agent or for people in general, but as compelling; and the compulsion which it imposes arises directly from the need of someone else.

Examples such as the above present a clear choice. Either Aristotle does not count such cases as satisfying the requirement that the virtuous agent does virtuous acts for the sake of the fine, on the ground that the concept of the fine does not figure among the agent's reasons for acting, or we must construe that requirement in such a way that that concept does not have to figure among the agent's reasons. The former alternative identifies a considerable flaw in Aristotle's theory, since he is unable to count as virtuous acts which we can recognize as being virtuous to the highest—indeed, sometimes to a saintly or heroic—degree. (How bizarre to suppose that we can count someone who throws himself on a grenade to save his comrades as courageous only on the assumption that he must somehow have been motivated by the thought that that was a fine thing to do!) The flaw is not merely that it requires us to reject paradigm cases; in addition to that, it presents as a requirement for virtuous action something which appears to us rather as a defect, or at least a disqualification from the highest degree of virtue. This defect is a degree of concern with the figure which the agent cuts which jars with the genuine selflessness of the true saint or hero.

The other alternative is to construe the requirement that the virtuous agent acts for the sake of the fine as *de re* rather than *de dicto*. On this construal it need not be the case that the agent is motivated by the action's presenting itself to him or her *as* fine or admirable. What is required is that the agent is motivated by the action's presenting itself in some way or other in which that action *is in fact* fine or admirable. Thus in our example the heroic soldier was motivated by the thought of 'saving that poor devil out there', and saving the poor devil out there was in fact an extremely fine and admirable thing to do.[11] This interpretation certainly brings Aristotle's theory closer to certain modern intuitions, and frees it from the suspicion of an unpleasing narcissism which the alternative threatens. On the other hand, the discussion of self-love in IX. 8 cited above (where it seems difficult to interpret 'laying claim to the fine' and 'assigning the fine to oneself' totally *de re*) leaves an uneasy feeling that perhaps Aristotle's theory *is* self-regarding to a degree bordering (to the modern eye) on narcissism, and that the total selflessness of the saint or hero is something foreign to his ethical outlook. It may be Aristotle's view that the virtuous person's primary concern must in the last resort be the shape of his or her own life (a shape that leaves room for altruism and self-sacrifice), and that total self-forgetfulness is, if not impossible, at least not altogether (perhaps not at all) admirable, perhaps because it amounts to losing sight of something which one ought never to lose sight of, one's responsibility for shaping oneself.[12]

---

[11] As suggested by Williams (1995), Hursthouse (1995), and Darwall (2002: ch. 4).

[12] Cooper (1996b/1999: 270–9, page refs. to (1999)) argues that to act for the sake of the fine is to be motivated by the order, symmetry, and determinateness of action-types, since those are said at *Met.* 1078ª31–ᵇ6 to be the highest kinds of fineness. (He here maintains a suggestion raised but not definitively adopted by Allan (1971).) I find it impossible to fit that characterization of *to kalon* to the kind of example discussed above.

Much more relevant is the characterization of *to kalon* at *Rhet.* 1366ª33–4 as 'what is praiseworthy as being choiceworthy for its own sake'. Irwin (1985) takes Aristotle to say in this passage (*Rhet.* 1366ª33–ᵇ8) that the ultimate ground on which something is praiseworthy is that it promotes the common good. He consequently argues that 'choosing an action because it is fine is choosing it because it is the kind of voluntary action it is, one that aims at the common good, not because it is or promotes success in achieving some result' (Irwin 1985: 136). (He makes essentially the same point in Irwin (1992: 295–7) and Irwin (1988: 439–44).) But while in that passage of the *Rhetoric* Aristotle says that virtue is a capacity for doing good (1366ª38) and that the greatest virtues are the most useful to others (ᵇ3–4), he does not say explicitly that in every case what makes a virtue praiseworthy, and therefore fine, is its contribution to the common good. It is certainly plausible to say that of e.g. courage and justice (though less so of other virtues, e.g. greatness of soul), but *Rhet.* 1359ª1–5 suggests a somewhat different attitude to courage. There Aristotle says that we often praise people for neglecting their own interest in order to do something fine, citing the example of Achilles who 'went to the aid of his comrade Patroclus in the knowledge that he would have to die, though he could have lived; for him such a death was finer, though to live was advantageous'. In fact, as Aristotle and his readers knew, what Achilles did was

(iii) The third condition is that virtuous actions must issue from a firmly established state of character (see below). The description of such states as not merely 'stable' but 'unchangeable' is problematic. Taken literally, it implies that virtues, once acquired, cannot be lost. That seems an excessively strict requirement (or alternatively an excessively optimistic generalization), but it may in fact be Aristotle's view. At III. 5, discussing responsibility for bad states of character, he says that someone may have been capable of not acquiring a bad state of character, but be incapable of remedying it once he or she has acquired it, comparing such a person to someone who had the choice of throwing a stone or not, but who can't get it back once he has thrown it (1114^{a}16–21). At least some states of character are unchangeable by the agent, and it may be Aristotle's view that this is true generally of virtues and vices. At 1100^{b}33–5 he says that no *makarios* (i.e. person living a perfect life) can ever become wretched (*athlios*), no matter what misfortunes befall him, 'for he will never do hateful and base things'. The thought is that however severely force of circumstances limits his or her capacity for the exercise of the virtues he or she will never acquire the contrary vices, which implies that once in place one's virtuous disposition is permanent.

On that interpretation of 'unchangeable' the statements at 1104^{a}25–9 and 1105^{a}15 to the effect that virtues are destroyed by bad acts must be taken as loose expressions of the thesis that such acts prevent virtues from developing. There is, however, the possibility that by 'unchangeable' Aristotle means no more than 'very hard to change'. Cf. *Cael.* 280^{b}34–281^{a}1 and Aspasius's comment on 1121^{b}12–13.

avenge the death of Patroclus; there is no suggestion in this passage that what made Achilles' action a fine one was that avenging one's fallen friend is a kind of act that promotes the common good. Rather, the emphasis is on the nobility of self-sacrifice. Is self-sacrifice, then, noble because it promotes the common good? Or is it simply that we admire people who care enough for their friends to give their lives to avenge them, and wish that we could have such friends? It does not seem to me that Aristotle gives a determinate answer to that question.

Even if it were granted that what makes all virtues, and hence all virtuous actions, fine is their being such as to promote the common good, it is of course a further question how far the belief that a given action is such as to promote the common good is part of the thought of the agent who chooses to do that action because it is fine. (See discussion above.)

Irwin's account is criticized by Rogers (1993).

1105ᵃ33–ᵇ1 Technical skills may be subordinated to external goals, whereas virtues cannot be. Thus one may exercise one's skill in pottery purely to earn one's living, whereas 'virtuous' action done for an external end (e.g. the 'honest' actions of Kant's grocer who treats his customers honestly purely because he wants to keep their custom) is not genuinely virtuous.

Presumably Aristotle believes that, unlike virtues of character, technical skills can be lost, e.g. through lack of practice. The difference is presumably that the motivation to practice the skill is external to the skill itself, whereas the motivation to act virtuously is internal to the virtue.

'the others, i.e. the technical skills': lit. 'the other technical skills'. A literal translation gives the wrong sense, since Aristotle is here distinguishing virtues of character from technical skills. Cf. 1103ᵃ32 and note. For the idiom cf. Plato, *Grg.* 473c, where *tōn politōn kai tōn allōn xenōn* (lit. 'of the citizens and the other foreigners') must be read as 'of the citizens and the others, i.e. foreigners'. Cf. *Grg.* 447c3, with Dodds's note. (I am indebted for this point and for the reference to Mr. J. O. Urmson.)

1105ᵇ2–3 'in the case of the virtues … no effect.' See above, p. 86.

1105ᵇ5–9 Aristotle here assigns definitional priority to the agent over the act: the virtuous agent is not defined as one who does acts which fall under specific virtue descriptions, such as 'courageous' or 'just'; rather, courageous acts are defined as the sort of thing that the courageous person does, etc. His theory is therefore an 'agent-centred', as opposed to an 'act-centred' one. (For the distinction see Annas (1981: 157–60).)

The distinction requires that it be possible to identify the virtuous agent independently of that agent's doing virtuous acts. Virtuous acts of type T being identified as those which are done by the T-type agent (e.g. 'courageous acts are those done by the courageous agent'), we must have a sufficiently informative specification of the agent to allow us to identify the acts in question. Conditions (i)–(iii) above are intended to satisfy this requirement; courageous acts are those done by the courageous agent, and the courageous agent is the one who does those acts with knowledge, from a reasoned choice of those acts for themselves, and from a stable state of character. But now conditions (i) and (ii) threaten the account with circularity, at least on the *de dicto* construal, since we have seen that on that construal the agent's knowledge is the knowledge that such and such an act is an instance of the virtue in question. And since an act's being an instance of e.g. courage is a necessary condition of the agent's knowing that it is an instance, the identification of the agent as courageous requires the prior identification of certain acts as instances of courage. But according to Aristotle no such priority is available; hence the theory is circular.

To resolve this difficulty, we need to distinguish different levels of generality in the content of (a) the definitions of kinds of acts and agents and (b) the virtuous agent's knowledge. Aristotle's claim is that the only totally general specification of a kind of act falling under a virtue-type T is 'the sort of act that the T agent does', but the specification of the T agent contains the ascription to him or her of various specific pieces of knowledge, e.g. that this act of handing over £10 is just in so far as it is paying a debt. But doesn't that require that paying one's debts is always just, and isn't that a description which holds independently of what just agents do? The answer to the first question is 'No'. The agent can know that this instance of handing over money is just *qua* paying a debt without its being true that either handing over money or paying debts is always just. Nor need the agent be in possession of any general rule for determining in precisely what circumstances paying one's debts is or is not just. The agent's knowledge may be of the case-by-case type which governs our mastery of many everyday concepts.

There is, then, no vicious circularity in Aristotle's claim that a necessary condition of an agent's being T is that he or she should know that this is an instance of a T-type action, even when the only general specification of 'T-type action' available to the agent is 'action such that a T agent would do'. A musician may know that exactly this is an instance of sensitive phrasing, even if the only general specification of sensitive phrasing that he or she can supply is 'the kind of phrasing that satisfies an expert musician'.

On the other hand, this does not resolve the difficulty about the definitional priority of just acts and the just agent raised above (Intro. n. 9). For Aristotle's account of the priority of just actions in V, 1129^{a}8–9, assumes that the just agent does possess a specification of just action independent of 'the kind of actions a just agent would do', viz. 'actions in conformity with law and principles of fairness'; and that is just the kind of independent specification which is denied here. There may indeed be some degree of indeterminacy in whether particular instances do conform to law, leaving room for individual judgement, but that judgement is guided by the prior conception, as it is not in the musical example. The case of justice is analogous to that of inexact sciences such as medicine; there is room for the individual doctor's judgement of what is the right dose to give this particular patient, but that judgement is guided by the independent specification 'the dose which will restore the patient to health', not merely by the specification 'whatever dose the expert doctor will prescribe'.

ᵇ8:   'in addition the one who acts'. I translate the manuscript text, including the definite article *ho*, which Bywater deletes from the OCT.

1105ᵇ11–12   While the rendering which best fits the word order of the Greek is 'No one would ever become good by failing to perform those actions', it is possible that Aristotle intends (perhaps in addition) 'No one would ever become good otherwise than by doing those actions'. His account of the acquisition of states of character entails both.

1105ᵇ12–18   Aristotle reiterates his insistence on the practical character of ethical enquiry (cf. 1103ᵇ26–9). The role of theory is to assist in the acquisition of good habits.

BOOK TWO

CHAPTER 5

Aristotle now proceeds to define virtue in the canonical way by genus and species, identifying its genus in this chapter and its species in the next. Since being good is a quality, the genus to which virtue belongs is that of a certain kind of quality. And since we are concerned with virtue of character—that is to say, the virtue of the desiderative soul (see ch. 1, 1103ᵃ14–15)—we have to find its genus among the qualities of that type of soul.

1105^{b}20–1   The above explains the content of the list of 'things that come to be' in the soul. The soul is specifically the desiderative soul, as Anon. notes, and the 'things that come to be in' it are ways in which that aspect of the personality is qualified. In general, things may be qualified in one way or another (a) in virtue of actually being affected, e.g. becoming hot (by being acted on); (b) in virtue of being able to do something or to be affected, e.g. being capable of moving, or of being heated; and (c) in virtue of being in one state or another, e.g. being hot. In Aristotelian terminology, to be affected is to undergo a *pathos*, to be able to do something or to be affected is to possess a *dunamis* (power or capacity), and to be in a state is to possess a *hexis*. Hence we find *pathē*, *dunameis*, and *hexeis* (the plurals of the Greek nouns listed in the preceding sentence) included among the kinds of quality listed in *Cat.* ch. 8. (The *Categories* list includes other kinds of qualities, e.g. various physical dimensions and secondary qualities such as sweetness, which are not applicable to the soul.)

The question about virtue of character, then, is the question whether we have a good character (a) in virtue of the ways our desiderative soul is affected, (b) in virtue of the capacities of our desiderative soul, or (c) in virtue of the states of our desiderative soul. We might wonder why, given that capacities are capacities for doing or being affected, acts of the desiderative soul are not included together with ways of being affected as possible candidates for the qualities which make our character good or bad. The answer to that question requires examination of what Aristotle counts as the ways in which the desiderative soul is affected.

1105^{b}20–3   The previous note elucidates *pathē* as 'ways of being affected', but *pathē* is rendered here and throughout as 'feelings'. The basic sense of the word (the internal accusative of the verb *paschein*, meaning to suffer, undergo, have done to one) is 'something one undergoes, something which happens to one'; hence being shipwrecked or falling ill would be paradigm *pathē*. Prominent among things that happen to one are occurrences of psychological states such as bodily sensations, emotions, and quasi-emotional states such as astonishment; they count as *pathē* in that they come upon one, by and large, unbidden. In general, the English 'feelings' is the word which answers best the Greek conception of episodic psychological *pathē*, capturing their spontaneous quality, and also registering the fact that typically they are objects of immediate awareness, 'things that one feels'.

But the relevant concept here is not simply that of episodic psychological occurrences; it is that of such occurrences in the desiderative soul, i.e. of conscious episodes of desire of one kind or another. Aristotle is seeking to define goodness of character, i.e. goodness in our role as agents, and his crucial insight is that goodness of character is defined as a certain state relating to our motivation. As all motivation springs from desire, the relative psychological episodes are motivational episodes, i.e. episodes of various kinds of desire.

Hence Aristotle elucidates the *pathē* of the desiderative soul via a list of types of motivational episode, beginning with *epithumia*, which is a general term for desire, most commonly applied to the bodily-based desires for food, drink, and sex, and continuing with a list of specific emotions. The latter are specific types of motivation, many of which will be discussed in later chapters as providing the motivations for the kinds of conduct which are the subject-matter of the specific virtues and vices (e.g. fear and boldness for courage and its opposed vices).

The only general characterization of feelings is provided by the concluding phrase (^b23) 'in general what is attended by pleasure and distress'. This is not a definition, since it does not state necessary and sufficient conditions (other things, e.g. activities, are attended by pleasure and distress), but an informative specification, picking up the desiderative character of feelings. Feelings are attended by pleasure and distress in so far as they characteristically involve envisaging actual and/or projected situations as desirable or undesirable, leading to pleasure in the actual or projected satisfaction of the relevant desires and distress in their frustration. (Thus an angry person typically regards him or herself as ill-treated, a situation which he or she finds unpleasant, wishes to retaliate, takes pleasure in the thought of future retaliation and the actual act of retaliation, is frustrated by inability to retaliate, etc.[13])

The above explains why Aristotle does not consider acts of the desiderative soul, as distinct from the *pathē* of the soul, as among its qualities. For the desiderative soul is active in desiring, and

---

[13] For fuller discussions see Leighton (1982), Cooper (1996a).

to desire is to undergo a *pathos*. So there are no acts specifically of the desiderative soul over and above its *pathē*. Of course
agents act, but their acts are not simply events in the desiderative
soul; their acts express their character, i.e. their states of soul (see
below).[14]

1105^{b}23-5 The translation 'those things in respect of which'
attempts to capture in idiomatic English the Greek construction,
whose word-for-word rendering is 'and capacities in respect of
which'. That construction is itself neutral between a realist construal of capacities, according to which they are forces in the soul
in virtue of which one is able to do this or that, and a reduction-
ist construal, according to which to have a capacity to F consists
precisely in its being true that one is able to F.

'[S]usceptible of' renders *pathētikoi*, an adjective formed from
pathos, lit. 'such as to undergo'.

1105^{b}25-6 On the construction see the preceding note.

At *Met.* 1022^{b}10-12, in the course of distinguishing various
senses of the term *hexis*, Aristotle gives one sense as 'a disposition
(*diathesis*) in respect of which the thing disposed is disposed well
or badly', giving the example of health. The present passage gives
a specific instance of that general characterization; states *of the
desiderative soul* are those in which the agent is well or badly
disposed *with respect to feelings*.[15] Aristotle does not immediately
conclude from this specification of 'state' that virtue is a state. He
has still to make explicit the conceptual connection between virtue
and goodness, which follows at ^{b}28–1106^{a}2.

1105^{b}27-8 '[V]iolently' and 'slackly' both have negative evaluative force, applying to inappropriate feelings, the former excessive, the latter inadequate. For elucidation of the notions of excess
and inadequacy, and of the related notion of a feeling which is 'in
between', see the next chapter.

---

[14] On the role of feelings in Aristotle's theory see Fortenbaugh (1975: esp. ch.
4); Kosman (1980); Cooper (1988); Sherman (1997: ch. 2) *Rhet.* II. 2–11 contains
illuminating discussions of the psychology of anger, fear, and other emotions and
emotion-related attitudes.
[15] For a detailed account of Aristotle's conception of *hexis* see Hutchinson (1986:
ch. 2).

1105^{b}28–1106^{a}2 See conclusion of the last note but one. The connection between virtue and goodness is established by consideration of our ordinary evaluative practice.

1106^{a}3–4 The definition of virtue of character as 'a state concerned with choice' (*hexis prohairetikē*) at 1106^{b}36 makes it clear that 'not without choice' correctly expresses Aristotle's considered view. 'Or' has the sense 'or rather, or, more precisely', as not infrequently in Aristotle (e.g. 1110^{a}2–3).

'[C]hoice' renders *prohairesis*, which is specifically choice or decision resulting from prior deliberation. For Aristotle's detailed discussion see III. 2.

1106^{a}4–6 'affected': lit. 'changed'. The contrast is between a temporary occurrence, such as feeling angry, and a lasting state, such as being ill-tempered. See *Cat.* 9^{b}19–32. Here again Aristotle appeals to what we ordinarily say (as also in ^{a}6–9).

1106^{a}9–10 See 1103^{a}18–26 and note.

BOOK TWO

CHAPTER 6

1106^{a}14–21 Having identified the genus of excellence of character as a state, Aristotle proceeds to establish its differentiating characteristics.

He begins by recapitulating the general connections which hold between the notions of the excellence of a certain kind of thing, being a good thing of that kind and the function or characteristic activity (*ergon*, lit. 'work') of that kind. In I. 7 he pointed out that, for kinds of things which have an *ergon*, an individual's being a good one of that kind and doing well as a thing of that kind is determined by that individual's performance of the *ergon* of the kind (1097^{b}25–7); thus a builder is a good builder, and does well as a builder, iff he or she builds well, and an eye is a good eye, and does well as an eye, iff it sees well. In that chapter he applies that general doctrine to the specific case of the human being (*anthrōpos*); having identified the *ergon* of the human being as rational activity of the soul (*psuchēs energeia kata logon*), he uses that specification to identify good performance of that *ergon* (which he controversially identifies with the good *for* human beings) as activity of the soul in accordance with excellence (*psuchēs energeia kat' aretēn*). There he relies on the thesis which he makes explicit here; that it is the excellence appropriate to the kind which makes the individual a good one of that kind and which makes the individual's performance of the function good.

1106ᵃ21–6 Aristotle follows the order of exposition of I. 7, in applying his general thesis to the case of humans and their *ergon*.

He does not identify excellence with the actual good performance of the function; e.g. he does not identify the excellence of the eye with its actually seeing well. For one does not cease to have excellent eyesight when one shuts one's eyes. In general excellence is a state, such that it is the possession of that state which accounts for one's reliably performing the function well. Nor is such a state described purely conditionally, as the state such that, if the conditions for performing the function are realized, one will perform the function well. Aristotle seeks to characterize states of excellence informatively, so as to exhibit how the good performance of the function flows from the possession of the state. As he states in ᵃ24–6 he will attempt such an informative account in the account of excellence of character which follows immediately.

Excellence (i.e. virtue) of character is, of course, merely one kind of human excellence (see 1103ᵃ14–18). The other kind, intellectual excellence ('excellence of thought') will be discussed in Books VI and X.

ᵃ24: 'we have already said'. The reference is probably to 1104ᵃ11–27.

1106ᵃ26–ᵇ16 The fundamental thesis is that virtue of character is a mean or middle state, i.e. a state in between two extremes. Aristotle employs the notion of a mean in two ways, one as the arithmetic mean of two numbers, and the other as an evaluatively defined notion, that of the right amount of some quantity, which is in between too much and too little of that quantity. The point of so doing is presumably to illustrate the less familiar notion of the evaluative mean by contrast with the more familiar arithmetical mean.

He starts by claiming at ª26–9 that every divisible continuum is divisible either arithmetically (into sections which are either equal to one another or unequal) or evaluatively (producing amounts which are too large, or too small, or neither). That claim is ambiguous between

  (i) Every continuum C is capable of being divided either arithmetically or evaluatively,

and

  (ii) For every continuum C, either C is capable of being divided arithmetically, or C is capable of being divided evaluatively.

(i) implies that every continuum is capable of being divided arithmetically, and is capable of being divided evaluatively (cf. 'Every leg of lamb can be roasted or boiled'); (ii) does not have that implication. (i) is, on an ordinary understanding, clearly false; e.g. it is just false that every line, including the line AB below,

A———————————————————B

is divisible into a section which is too long and one which is too short. Charity in interpretation, therefore, indicates that Aristotle should be understood as maintaining (ii) rather than (i) at ª26–9.

There is a residual problem in ª28–9, where the Greek terms rendered 'the larger and the smaller' in the translation are *huperbolē* and *elleipsis*, which are Aristotle's regular terms for 'too much' and 'too little', rendered generally in the translation as 'excess' and 'deficiency'. If that rendering is adopted here, then Aristotle is referring exclusively to the evaluative mean, and presumably providing the gloss on 'the equal' needed to allow it to be understood as 'what is in between too much and too little'. But that faces the difficulty that the sentence of which this clause is part makes a general claim about continua as such; I have accordingly preferred a non-evaluative rendering of *huperbolē* and *elleipsis* (found in Plato, *Prt.* 356a, 357a; Aristotle, *Met.* 1004ᵇ10–12), which continues the sense of the first part of the sentence.

ª29–36:   Elucidation of the arithmetic mean.

ª36–ᵇ5:   Elucidation of the evaluative mean. The Greek expressions rendered 'a lot' (*polu*) and 'a little' (*oligon*) have in context the evaluative nuances 'too much' and 'too little'. Milo was a champion wrestler, famous for his gargantuan appetite.

^{b}5–16:   Application of the notion of the evaluative mean to expertise in general. Aristotle claims that every expertise aims to achieve the evaluative mean in its product, appealing to the everyday judgement that the perfectly proportioned product of an art or craft would be spoiled by any addition or subtraction.

In some cases of expertise the notions of too much, too little, and the right amount apply not to the product but to the means of producing it. Thus an expert javelin-thrower aims to throw the javelin as far as possible, but in the run-up has to avoid both running too fast and running too slowly.

For the theses that the products of nature and of excellence are more perfect than those of the arts and crafts see e.g. *PA* 639^{b}19–21. For the contrast with excellence Aristotle seems to rely on the view that whereas the arts imitate nature, excellence (including virtue of character) perfects nature (see 1106^{a}15–24).

'[P]roduct' renders *ergon*, rendered 'function' at ^{a}16–23. Like the English 'work', the term applies both to the exercise of a skill and to the output of that exercise: the work of a sculptor is to create works of sculpture.

^{b}15–16:   'which aims at and hits the mean': the Greek is *tou mesou ... stochastikē*, lit. 'aiming at the mean'. Since the argument requires that the aim be successful, I have translated 'aims at and hits' here and at ^{b}28.[16]

---

[16] For a valuable discussion of the mean in relation to us see Brown (1997). I agree with her principal contention that 'in relation to us' means 'relative to the different situations in which we act', not 'relative to our individual characters'. But, as she acknowledges, 'there *are* [her italics] characteristics of the agent relevant to what the excellent response in a given situation will be' (p. 86). (That is made clear by Aristotle's discussions of the agent-relative character of generosity (1120^{b}7–11) and magnificence (1122^{b}23–6).) Hence her conclusion (which I think correct) is that 'the mean is not relative to agents over and above being relative to situations' (ibid.).

In general, Brown is right in maintaining (against e.g. Leighton (1995)) that it cannot be the case that the ethical mean relative to us is the mean relative to our individual character; that would produce the absurdity that whether one is excessively or insufficiently responsive to a given motivation is determined by one's prior degree of responsiveness to that very motivation; e.g. a naturally lecherous person would count as temperate if he or she went in for casual sex only occasionally, whereas the same degree of indulgence in a naturally temperate person would count as intemperance. But as indicated by the examples of generosity and magnificence, there are features of one's individual make-up, not strictly falling under the head of character but closely

1106ᵇ16-24 Application to virtue of character. The evaluative mean is applied first to feelings (ᵇ18-23), then more briefly to actions (ᵇ23-4), since the essential points are made with respect to feelings.

These points are:

   (i) Feelings vary in degree.

  (ii) In respect of feelings, one can go wrong either in the direction of insufficient feeling, or in the direction of excessive feeling.

 (iii) One has feelings in the right way when one avoids both ways of going wrong.

 (iv) What counts as going wrong is not a matter of a single dimension, e.g. of intensity of feeling. One can manifest either excessive or deficient feeling in a variety of ways.

(i)–(iii) are relatively unproblematic. It is a matter of common observation that we can feel more or less angry, envious, etc., and we commonly criticize people, including ourselves, for e.g. really going over the top on some occasion, or feeling less compassionate than we should. (The question as to whether every feeling is liable to be felt wrongly in both ways will be discussed below.) But we might well suppose from points (i)–(iii) alone that Aristotle's view about feelings is that any specific feeling is measured on a single scale of intensity, from e.g. the mildest perceptible irritation to raging, uncontrollable anger, and that the mean with respect to each is some point on that scale. Point (iv) (ᵇ21-3) corrects this misapprehension.

Here Aristotle points out that the appropriateness or inappropriateness of feelings is relative to the ground and to the circumstances of those feelings. (It is important to see that he is talking about feelings themselves here; actions come later. See below.) Thus there are some things which it is right to feel angry about (someone pushing past one in a queue, or being rude to one in a

connected with it, to which one's motivational dispositions are appropriately responsive. So someone with a strong head for drink may manifest temperance by drinking ten glasses in an evening, since he or she will be none the worse for it, whereas someone with lesser capacity might have to stop at two. Further, there is one special case in which one's character is among the circumstances to which one's behavioural dispositions should be responsive, viz. greatness of soul; since that virtue is the virtuous person's correct self-evaluation (see commentary on IV. 3), the great-souled person is appropriately responsive to the state of his or her character.

shop), but not very angry, while there are other things one ought to feel very angry about (social injustice, for instance), and other things one just shouldn't feel angry about at all (it's absurd to feel angry about losing a game of ludo). Again, you can feel angry about something which it's appropriate to feel angry about, and feel anger to the appropriate degree, but feel angry at the wrong people (you shouldn't feel angry at social outcasts, but at those who cast them out). Again, there are in Aristotle's view some times at which I shouldn't even feel anger (much less act on it); presumably even feeling anger at a tactless remark made in distraction by someone who has just lost a child shows a failure of sensibility.

The general point is clear: viz. that hitting the mean in respect of feeling is having one's feelings properly attuned to an indefinitely wide range of circumstances, which determine the appropriateness of each instance of emotional reaction. But there are problems. First, the last item on the list of circumstances is 'as one should'; is this intended to sum up the list as a whole, or is it itself an additional circumstance? If the latter, what circumstance? Is Aristotle suggesting that there is a way of going wrong in respect of a feeling independent of all the kinds of circumstances we have mentioned, which is just having that feeling in the wrong way? Is the idea that there is some kind of anger, or of fear, that one should never feel? Perhaps I could be angry at the right time, with the right people, for the right reason, with a view to the right goal, but yet with the wrong kind of anger. But does that make sense? How could my anger be the wrong kind of anger if it did not involve going wrong in one or other of those very ways? For these reasons I suggest that we do better to understand 'as one should' as summing up the list (with the force of 'and in general as one should' indicating that the list is not meant to be exhaustive), not as adding to it.

Having given this detailed specification of the application of the evaluative mean to feelings, Aristotle contents himself by stating that what has just been said applies to actions too. This raises the question of why the emphasis is on feelings rather than on actions, which we expect to be the focus of ethical evaluation.

Clearly, the central doctrine, that being in the mean is being appropriately sensitive to an indefinite range of circumstances, applies to actions as well as to feelings. Flying off the handle at a trivial slight is being excessively angry, just as feeling intense anger at such a slight is feeling excessively angry. Feelings are given the priority in Aristotle's account because they are what prompt us to action. Once we understand what it is to have our feelings in good or bad shape, we already understand what it is for our actions to be in good or bad shape. To act with or from excessive anger just is to act in the ways that excessive feeling prompts. But now why not say that excessive feeling is just what prompts to excessive action? Of course that is true as well. There is no definitional priority one way or the other. The crucial priority is the motivational priority of feeling. And that priority is crucial in Aristotle's theory of education in virtue.

Education in virtue does not consist in being trained to act in the right ways, but in being trained to want to act in those ways, and therefore to do those kinds of act. As Aristotle has said, following Plato, the crucial thing is being trained from youth to feel pleasure and distress in the right things, for 'that is correct education' (1104ᵇ11–13). To possess virtue of character is, as we have seen, to have one's desiderative soul in good order; and that order is the responsiveness of one's desires (in the form of one's feelings) to the multiple demands of appropriateness which it is the task of the practical intellect to identify. It is that responsiveness which is the source of the effortless appropriateness which is characteristic of the actions of the virtuous agent (who is also, necessarily, the agent possessing practical wisdom, i.e. the virtue of the practical intellect). Hence the order of Aristotle's exposition here.

1106ᵇ24–35 This section recapitulates the themes of the chapter so far.

ᵇ25–6:   'excess ... blame': reading *hē men huperbolē hamartanetai kai psegetai, kai hē elleipsis*. The manuscripts read *hē men huperbolē hamartanetai kai hē elleipsis psegetai*, 'excess is wrong and deficiency is blamed', which is unsatisfactory. The OCT deletes *psegetai*, giving 'excess and deficiency are wrong'. But the contrast with 'the mean is praised and right' suggests that Aristotle describes the extremes as both wrong and subject to blame.

^{b}29-30:   Aristotle supports his account of the multiplicity of ways in which one can diverge from the mean by reference to the metaphysical system of the Pythagorean school, whose origins date from the sixth century BC. They drew up a list of ten pairs of opposed fundamental principles (the Table of Opposites) from which they attempted to explain the nature of everything; the basic opposition was between Limit (or the Definite) and the Unlimited (or the Indefinite), of which the others were special cases, good being an instance of the former and bad of the latter. See *Met.* 985^{b}23-986^{a}26.

^{b}35:   A quotation from an unknown poet.

1106^{b}36-1107^{a}2   Formal definition of virtue of character.

'a state': established in ch. 5.

'concerned with choice': established at 1105^{a}31-2.

'in a mean in relation to us': established by the discussion of 1106^{a}26-^{b}28.

In that discussion Aristotle has explained what it is for feelings and actions to be excessive, deficient, and in a mean, but has not explicitly shown how those characterizations apply to states. Clearly their application to states derives from their application to feelings and actions. A state which is in a mean is one such that the agent's feelings and actions are reliably in a mean, and similarly for excessive and deficient states. Thus to be good-tempered (*praos*) is to be properly responsive to the occasions for feeling angry and for acting on those feelings (see above), avoiding the extremes both of bad temper and of its opposite 'unanger' (*aorgēsia*, apparently a word coined by Aristotle), i.e. being insufficiently responsive to occasions for anger. That is what Aristotle means by his statement (^{b}28) that virtue aims at the mean.

'a mean determined by reason, namely the reason by which the person of practical wisdom would determine it'.

Aristotle has so far said nothing whatever on how the ethical mean is determined. Hence, despite the 'then' which introduces the definition, the definition is not derived *as a whole* from the previous discussion. All that that discussion has established is that the mean in feelings and actions is feeling and acting to the right extent, neither too much nor too little. The questions 'What counts as too much and too little?' and 'How does one recognize what is too much and too little?' have not been raised.

He now asserts that the mean state is determined by reason: namely, the reason by which the person of practical wisdom would determine it. For elucidation we must turn to VI. 1, 1138^b18-34, where he returns to this question.

There he expands his reference to reason by saying that the mean is 'as correct reason says' (1138^b20) (or, alternatively, 'as the correct principle says'; cf. note on 1103^b32-4) illustrating this by the analogy of the right amount of medicine to give to a patient, which is determined 'as medical science and the person who possesses it (i.e. the doctor) prescribe' ($^b31-2$). Fixing on the right dose is a matter of medical expertise, and the doctor is the expert. So at least we know that fixing on the ethical mean is a matter of expertise (as opposed, for instance, to a matter of chance), and we have in the person of practical wisdom the expert whose role is analogous to that of the doctor.

But still, as Aristotle points out (1138^b25-32) we don't know very much; specifically, we don't yet know 'what is correct reason and what is its standard' ($^b34$). 'Standard' renders *horos*, a limit or boundary, which is what you apply when you determine, delimit, or define (*horizein*) something. So we don't yet know what the correct reason is by which the person of practical wisdom determines the ethical mean, and specifically what standard or definition that person applies. We are in the same position as someone who knows that the right dose is the one that the medical expert would prescribe, but does not know anything about the nature of medical expertise, and specifically does not know what criteria the medical expert would use to identify the right dose.

(Aristotle does not distinguish the two questions distinguished above, the answers to which are distinct, but connected. Applied to the medical case, the answer to the first question, 'What counts as the right dose?', is 'The dose which is most likely to restore the patient to health'. That is the standard which the doctor applies in deciding on the right dose, but that does not of itself answer the second question, 'How does the doctor recognize which dose is the right one?', which can now be rephrased as 'How does the doctor recognize which dose is the one most likely to restore the patient to health?' The answer to that question is likely to be 'By extrapolating from his or her experience of giving this and other medicines to a variety of patients'. The first question identifies the standard which the medicine has to satisfy, the second the method of identifying what satisfies it.)

The opening paragraph of VI. 1, cited above, is the introduction to Aristotle's discussion of intellectual excellence, and leads us to expect that that discussion will produce explicit answers to the questions 'What is correct reason?' and 'What is its standard?' That expectation is apparently disappointed, since *NE* appears to contain no explicit answer to either question. So must we accept that Aristotle does not go beyond the 'true but unclear' (1138ᵇ25–6) statement of that introductory paragraph in elucidating the nature of the correct reason by which the person of practical wisdom would determine the ethical mean?

That may be unduly pessimistic. The definition puts the person of practical wisdom in the role of expert in determining the mean, and Book VI contains an account of practical wisdom itself, in chapters 7–9 and 12–13. In the course of that account Aristotle says (1144ᵇ27–8) that practical wisdom itself is correct reason in these matters. But that gives no account of how the person of practical wisdom determines the mean, any more than 'Medical science is correct reason in medical matters' says how the doctor determines the correct dose. That is to say, we still need an answer to the second question, 'What is the standard (sc. which the person of practical wisdom applies)?' And the answer to the second question is more elusive.

This question raises fundamental problems about the nature of the practical intellect, which go far beyond the present study. The crucial problem, or rather set of problems, is that of whether the practical intellect is directed, when functioning properly, by a conception of the human good, and, if so, how determinate that conception is. If there is no such conception, or if that conception is as indeterminate as 'the good life' or 'the life of excellence', then it provides no standard or test for the person of practical wisdom to apply, leaving that person's judgement as the ultimate authority on where the mean lies in any particular case. If, on the other hand, there is a more determinate conception, e.g. 'the right response in terms of feeling and action is the response which promotes a life in which theoretical activity is the agent's supreme goal', that does provide a standard to apply, though its application may have to rely on the educated judgement of the person of practical wisdom. The question is especially problematic in that the relevant texts are indecisive, some pointing in one direction, others in the other.[17]

1107ᵃ2–8 Aristotle first states in brief the essence of virtue of character as an evaluative mean between two opposed vices, one of excess and the other of deficiency (ᵃ2–3), then (ᵃ3–6) spells out that account in more detail, recapitulating the connection of the states with feelings and action. In ᵃ6–8 he points out that while the nature of virtue of character is to be a mean, it is an extreme (i.e. the best of the three states) in point of value.

This central doctrine encounters a major difficulty, which emerges from consideration of particular cases. Good temper, for instance, is a mean between states of excess and of deficiency with respect to anger. Now is the state of excess with respect to anger that of being excessively prone to anger, or of being prone to excessive anger? The former is a matter of getting angry too often, indiscriminately, etc., the latter a matter of getting too angry on the occasions when one does get angry (which might not be too often, or indiscriminately). On the account given above, each of these defects counts as excess of feeling; so on that account either being excessively prone to anger or being prone to excessive anger constitutes being in an excessive state with regard to anger.

But now it is clear that some people might feel angry on an insufficient number or range of occasions, but feel excessively angry on those occasions when they do get angry. Cruelty and injustice, say, leave them cold; the only thing that rouses them is personal insult to themselves, but on those occasions they are ungovernable. Are such people in an excessive or a deficient state with respect to anger? Surely the answer is that in certain respects their state is deficient, and in others excessive. With respect to

---

[17] Of the enormous literature on this topic, the following are among the most significant items: Allan (1953); Bostock (2000); Broadie (1991); Cooper (1975); Dahl (1984); Engberg-Pedersen (1983); Irwin (1978, 1980a, 1988); Kenny (1978, 1979); McDowell (1979); Monan (1968); Reeve (1992); Sherman (1989); Sorabji (1973–4); Wiggins (1975–6); Woods (1986). I have set out my own view more fully in Taylor (1990), revised and expanded (in German) in Taylor (2003a).

anger they display a combination of the opposed vices; we may compare Aristotle's description of 'bold cowards' (*thrasudeiloi*), i.e. people who are swaggeringly bold in advance of danger but cowardly when the danger is imminent ($1115^{b}31-3$) and his statement at $1121^{a}30-2$ that most extravagant people are also ungenerous (since they take money from discreditable sources, something characteristic of the ungenerous person, to fund their extravagance).

We should not, then, think of excessive and deficient states as monolithic, such that a person who is badly disposed to a given motivation must be ascribed one or other exclusively. Rather, excess and deficiency in feeling and action should be thought of as opposite directions in which one's response to motivation may diverge from the ideal. No doubt the typical case diverges in the same direction across the board, so that the irascible person will tend both to be angry too often and to be too angry, but atypical cases can occur. The sense in which a virtue is a mean between two vices is not that it is one of a triad of exclusive and exhaustive states, but that it is free from either of the two opposed tendencies to inappropriate response.

But if the crucial notion is that of appropriate response, why should we suppose that there are just two directions of inappropriateness? We should rather take seriously Aristotle's own remarks on the multiplicity of ways of going wrong ($1106^{b}28-35$). Someone who is lacking in a sense of the appropriate occasion for a certain kind of response may be just as likely to fail to respond on an appropriate occasion as to respond on an inappropriate one. And if such a person does respond on an appropriate occasion, he or she may well respond in an inappropriate way. Even if we can find some description of the inappropriate response as 'too F' (too sentimental, say), there may well be an equally correct description as 'not G enough' (not perceptive enough), and in any case what is really wrong with the person and the response is the lack of the appropriate kind of sensitivity.

It thus appears that the explanatory power of the evaluative mean and its associated triadic model of virtues and their pairs of opposed vices is threatened by a rival model, that of appropriately trained sensitivity. While inappropriately trained sensitivity will issue in responses some of which may be characterized as variously excessive or deficient, those characterizations now appear rather as superficial than as basic.

1107ᵃ8–17 There are certain kinds of feeling and of action to which the notion of the evaluative mean does not apply, because it is always wrong to have and to do them, respectively; their being designated as those kinds implies their badness.

Aristotle's thought about these cases seems to be, not that they are exceptions to the general doctrine of the mean, but that, since they are themselves types of extreme feeling and action, there cannot be a mean amount of them. That is explicit in the case of his examples of feelings which are always bad, viz. *schadenfreude*, spite (i.e. being distressed by the good fortune of others, irrespective of their desert), and shamelessness. He counts the first two as the opposed extremes of a triad of which righteous indignation (*nemesis*) is the virtuous mean (1108ᵃ35–ᵇ6; to be discussed below) and the third as one extreme of a peculiar triad (peculiar because the mean is explicitly said not to be a virtue) of which the mean is shame and the opposed 'vice' (or defect) is a state in which one is ashamed of everything (1108ᵃ31–5; also to be discussed below). The examples of action-types which are always bad, *moicheia* (conventionally rendered 'adultery', but more strictly any kind of illicit sexual act with a free partner, see Dover (1974: 209)), theft, and murder are presumably thought of in a similar way, as actions prompted by excessive feelings, respectively excess of sexual desire, of acquisitiveness, and of anger. Consideration of such examples reinforces the difficulty for the general doctrine of the mean set out above. None of these types of action can be ascribed *as such* to the excess of any particular kind of motivation (e.g. Aristotle himself gives the example of someone motivated to illicit sex not by lust but for gain (1130ᵃ24–8)); nor must it be the case that any particular instance expresses one extreme to the exclusion of the other; a random murder committed by a psychopath may express a whole complex of attitudes, some excessive (excessive delight in power, e.g.) and some deficient (insufficient concern for others). Here again the key notion seems to be that of inappropriate, not excessive or deficient, response to the demands of the situation.[18]

---

[18] So Hursthouse (1980–1), criticized by Curzer (1996).

1107ª18–27 One would make a like mistake if one applied the distinction of mean and extremes to states which are already explicit instances of those classifications.

This appears to confirm the suggestion above. The actions and feelings which are always wrong are implicit instances of extremes, while intemperance and injustice are explicit instances; the mistake in applying the doctrine of the mean to them is the same in either case.

Aristotle has not, then, considered whether there might be exceptions to the doctrine of the mean, i.e. types of motivation which are *per se* good or bad, irrespective of considerations of the degree to which they are felt, and types of action which are good or bad, but which are not prompted by respectively mean and extreme motivational states. Benevolence and malevolence and actions springing from them are plausible instances.

In addition to the paper by Hursthouse cited in the note on 1107ª8–17, other significant discussions of the doctrine of the mean are those by Hardie (1964–5); Urmson (1973); and Bostock (2000: ch. 2, sects. 3–4). Bosley *et al.* (1995) is a collection of articles on the topic, of varying degrees of interest.

BOOK TWO

CHAPTER 7

1107ª28–32 The general account of virtue of character is now to be applied to the particular virtues, which are first listed along with their contrasted vices. '[T]he particulars', i.e. the particular virtues and vices, are themselves types; contrast 1104ª6 where 'the discussion of particular cases' refers to the discussion of individual instances of these types. Aristotle's use of the expression *ta kath' hekasta*, (lit. 'the things each by each', or in more standard English, 'the things taken one by one') normally rendered 'particulars', regularly contrasts what is said *of each* (*kath' hekasta*) of the things falling under a general type with what is said *kath' holou*, lit. 'of the whole', i.e. of the type universally. These things may be sub-types, e.g. species of a genus, or individuals; Aristotle systematically ignores that distinction.

Specific statements (*logoi epi merous*, lit. 'statements referring to a part') are statements about some sub-type, contrasted with universal statements about that type. For the claim that they are truer than universal statements, see on 1103ᵇ34–1104ª5 and 1104ª5–10 above. There it was pointed out that some ethical generalizations hold only for the most part, while others, though universally true, are unspecific, requiring to be fleshed out by the detail provided by particulars. It was further suggested that the definition of virtue of character was an example of the second class. If that is correct, then 'truer' appears to be an inapposite term, since what is intended is that the particular discussions are more detailed or informative. If, on the other hand, Aristotle had in mind the thesis that ethical generalizations hold only for the most part, the point might be that the more specific the proposition the fewer exceptions have to be allowed. But there is (to repeat) no ground to suppose that the universal definition of virtue of character holds only for the most part.

1107ª32   What has to agree with what? Perhaps 'What we say in general has to agree with what we say about the particular cases'.

1107ª32–3   The list of virtues and vices must have been displayed in the lecture room; the sentence reads like an instruction to note-takers.[19] The text of *EE* includes a list at 1220ᵇ38–1221ª12.

1107ª33–ᵇ4   'fear and boldness': the nouns are plural in the Greek. See note on 'pleasure and distress' at 1104ᵇ3–5 above.

Aristotle treats courage and its contrasted vices as concerned with a pair of opposed motivations, fear and *tharros*, translated 'boldness'. Fear is aversion to danger, *tharros* a range of positive attitudes to danger or harm. In ordinary Greek the term may apply to positive delight in danger, especially that of battle, to aggressive fury, typical of uncivilized peoples and of animals such as lions, to confidence inspired by the belief that one will surmount the danger and to calm or cheerful acceptance of danger or actual harm. (Hence the translation 'confidence', adopted by Ross rev. Ackrill/Urmson, Irwin, Crisp, and Rowe, seems to me too narrow. While *Rhet.* 1383ª17–19 does indeed define *tharros* as

---

[19] For other references in Aristotle to items in his lecture-room see Jackson (1920).

akin to confidence, specifically 'hope, accompanied by imaginative representation, that safety is near at hand and fearful things non-existent or far off', not all applications of the term and its cognates in *NE* fit that definition; see note on 1115^{a}17–24.) Aristotle's detailed discussion of courage (III. 6–9) explores these nuances among other topics.

The word translated 'overbold' is *thrasus*, the adjective cognate to *tharros*. Hence a literal rendering is simply 'bold'. But that would give the misleading impression that anyone characterized by *tharros* is *thrasus*, whereas Aristotle, departing from ordinary usage, restricts the application of the adjective to the person characterized by an excess of *tharros*.

(The rendering 'rash', preferred by Ross rev. Ackrill/Urmson, Irwin, Crisp, and Rowe, loses the etymological connection with the noun; Gauthier/Jolif, on the other hand, preserve it by their renderings: 'audace' for the noun and 'audacieux' for the adjective. Natali has 'ardimento' for the noun and 'temerario' for the adjective.)

The distinction of these two motivations allows Aristotle to distinguish deficiency of fear from excess of boldness. Being insufficiently averse to danger is not the same disposition as being too keen on it, as may be seen from the fact that one might have the former defect without having the latter; someone who is literally indifferent to danger (i.e. someone who has no fear of it whatever, nor any keenness for it whatever) satisfies that description. On the other hand, being too keen on danger surely implies being insufficiently averse to it. The fact that Aristotle applies the single term *deilos* ('cowardly') to the person who is excessively fearful and insufficiently bold indicates that he thinks that the two states are at least inseparable; it is unclear whether his view is, as Gauthier/Jolif maintain, that there is a single vice, cowardice, characterizable both as excess of fear and deficiency of boldness. But here too indifference shows that the two states are not even necessarily coextensive; the indifferent person has insufficient boldness without excessive fear. Aspasius, Anon., and Aquinas (on 1115^{b}29) all note the failure of coextensiveness in the former case, while excluding it in the latter. See also note on 1115^{b}28–32.

1107^{b}4 'pleasure and distress': plural in the Greek.

1107ᵇ5–6 'temperance' and 'intemperance' render respectively *sōphrosunē* and *akolasia*, which are not cognate as the English terms are. The root meanings of the Greek terms are respectively 'soundness of mind' and 'undisciplinedness', but Aristotle, in broad conformity with standard Greek usage, gives them the technical applications which he sets out.

1107ᵇ6–8 Aristotle's willingness to coin terms to designate states of character for which ordinary Greek usage has no name shows that his concern is not merely to codify ordinary usage. Cf. 1104ᵃ22–5, 1108ᵃ16–19. For a helpful discussion see Gottlieb (1994).

1107ᵇ8–10 '[G]enerosity' renders *eleutheriotēs*, the abstract noun formed from the adjective *eleutherios*. The adjective is cognate to *eleutheros*, 'free', and has the basic meaning 'characteristic of, or appropriate to, a free person' (as opposed to a slave). Since one of the qualities that a free person was expected to display was generosity, the term acquires, in Aristotle and other writers, the specific sense 'generous'. (The somewhat archaic terms 'liberality' and 'liberal', adopted by Ross rev. Ackrill/Urmson and by Gauthier/Jolif, preserve the semantic connection with freedom.) In other contexts in this translation the term is rendered 'reputable' (1118ᵇ4) or 'respectable' (1128ᵃ18); see notes on those passages.

The translation 'generosity' may be objected to on the ground that generosity is a form of altruism, whereas the Aristotelian virtue is simply the proper disposition towards the use of wealth.[20] (That objection would tell equally against the rendering 'liberality'.) While I agree that the virtue is described in that way, I nevertheless maintain that Aristotle sees generosity in the specific sense as the primary form of the virtue, and that that primacy justifies the translation. See the discussion of IV. 1 below.

The deficiency opposed to generosity would more naturally be called 'meanness' in English, but I have preferred 'ungenerosity' (a) to avoid excessive use of the word 'mean', (b) to capture the fact that Aristotle's term *aneleutheria* is cognate to his term for 'generosity'.

---

[20] See the discussions of Hare (1988) and Young (1994).

1107ᵇ14–16 The more precise discussions of the virtues and their contrasted vices follow in books III–IV, as follows: III. 6–9 (courage), III. 10–11 (temperance), IV. 1 (generosity), IV. 2 (magnificence), IV. 3 (greatness of soul), IV. 4 (its small-scale counterpart), IV. 5 (good temper), IV. 6–8 (the 'social' virtues of truthfulness, friendliness, and wit), IV. 9 (modesty). There is no discussion of indignation.[21]

Detailed discussion of these topics will be found in the commentary on the respective chapters. In the present chapter I confine myself for the most part to explanation of the translation of Aristotle's terminology.

1107ᵇ16–20 Since the characteristic expression of magnificence is conspicuous expenditure on projects of public benefit, such as the building of temples, 'munificence' is a possible alternative translation (adopted by Rowe). For reasons for preferring 'magnificence' see commentary on IV. 2.

1107ᵇ21–3 '[G]reatness of soul': 'magnanimity', which is simply the Latinization of the Greek *megalopsuchia*, has been standard in the literature from the medieval commentators onwards. But while the meaning of the English term is connected with that of the Latin, and thereby with that of Aristotle's Greek, it is narrower. The primary connotation of the English is a generous willingness to forgive injuries; that is certainly one aspect of *megalopsuchia*, but only a subsidiary one. Hence it has seemed better to adopt the more literal rendering. See commentary on IV. 3. (Ross rev. Ackrill/Urmson renders 'proper pride', Gauthier/Jolif 'magnanimité', Irwin 'magnanimity', Crisp and Rowe 'greatness of soul', Dirlmeier 'Hochsinnigkeit', Natali 'fierezza', glossed as 'a firm and clear consciousness of one's superiority in thought and action', Pakaluk 'greatness of heart' (2004: 247).)

'[S]mall-mindedness' is an exact rendering of the Greek *mikropsuchia*, the polar opposite of *megalopsuchia*. It is unfortunate that English does not offer 'great-mindedness' as the name for the virtue. ('High-mindedness', adopted by Ostwald, is too

---

[21] Piety (*hosiotēs* or *eusebeia*) is noticeably absent from the list of virtues. For an acute discussion of this issue, including the suggestion (which I think correct) that Aristotle supplies the missing discussion in his account of the theoretical life in Book X, see Broadie (2003).

closely bound up with connotations of Victorian earnestness to be acceptable.)

1107ᵇ30–1108ᵃ1   Aristotle points out that, since there is no fixed terminology for dispositions concerning honour, the application of terms is disputed. But this phenomenon is not restricted to cases where there is no established terminology, since even sets of established terms such as 'courageous', 'cowardly', and 'over-bold' are subject to disputes about their appropriate application (1108ᵇ19–26; cf. 1109ᵇ16–18).

'[A]mbitious' and 'unambitious' render respectively *philotimos* (lit. 'honour-loving') and *aphilotimos* (lit. 'not honour-loving'). Though the connotations of the English terms are somewhat wider than those of the Greek, since the ambitious person characteristically cares about other things, such as power and success, as well as honour, they seem more appropriate names for defective states of character than the literal renderings (which are adopted by Gauthier/Jolif, Irwin, Crisp, and Rowe). Ross rev. Ackrill/Urmson renders 'ambitious', Natali 'ambizioso'.

1108ᵃ4–9   Aristotle has to devise terminology for the dispositions to do with anger. The noun and adjective applying to good temper (*praotēs*, *praos*) and the adjective 'irascible' (*orgilos*) were in current use; 'irascibility','unanger', and 'unangry' (*orgilotēs*, *aorgēsia*, *aorgētos*), on the other hand, do not occur in extant texts before their use here, and at least the last two may well be coinages of Aristotle's own. Anon. says that *aorgēsia* is the only Aristotelian neologism, but he may intend to include the adjective as well as the noun.

1108ᵃ19–23   '[T]ruthful' and 'truthfulness' render *alēthēs* and *alētheia*, the ordinary Greek words for 'true' and 'truth' respectively. In IV. 7 the term for the truthful person is *alētheutikos*.

Aristotle's virtue of *alētheia* is more specific than truthfulness in the modern sense, i.e. a general attachment to telling the truth. The Aristotelian virtue is a disposition to a specific kind of truth-telling: namely, telling the truth about oneself, without exaggeration or insincere depreciation of one's merits. See commentary on IV. 7.

The terms rendered 'dissembling' and 'dissembler' (*eirōneia*, *eirōn*), whose original connotation is the general one of deception, have in Aristotle and other writers the more specific sense of insincere self-denigration. Since Socrates is often represented by Plato as adopting a pose of intellectual inferiority to his opponents in argument, *eirōneia* in the specific sense came to be regarded as one of his hallmarks (cf. 1127ᵇ22–6), giving rise to the expression 'Socratic irony'. For full discussion see Vlastos (1991: ch. 1).

1108ᵃ30–1 Since every virtue and vice is concerned with feelings (as well as with actions), Aristotle's thought must presumably be that shame and the other feelings mentioned in the following lines do not prompt to action; hence in these cases the mean is concerned with feelings exclusively. If that is his thought, it is not true; as well as exhibiting shame by such reactions as blushing, one may be motivated by shame e.g. to run away and hide. Similarly, indignation and its contrasted vices may motivate action.

Aristotle distinguishes between *pathēmata* (translated 'episodes (of feeling)') and *pathē* (rendered here 'kinds of feeling'), saying that the means in question are 'in' (*en*) the former and 'concerned with' (*peri*) the latter. Since the two terms are often used interchangeably, it is not easy to see what distinction is being drawn. The distinction suggested in the translation is certainly a possible rendering of the Greek, but must be regarded as conjectural.

Most translators (Ross rev. Ackrill/Urmson, Gauthier/Jolif, Irwin, and Crisp) treat the two terms as interchangeable, translating both as 'feelings' or 'passions'; Rowe distinguishes 'affective feelings' (*pathēmata*) from 'things that happen to people' (*pathē*).

1108ᵃ31–5 '[M]odest' renders *aidēmōn*, the adjective formed from the word for 'shame' (*aidōs*). The *aidēmōn* is the person who feels shame appropriately. Because of its strongly negative connotations 'shameful' is not a possible translation. (Ross rev. Ackrill/Urmson renders 'modest', Gauthier/Jolif 'pudique', Natali 'pudico', Irwin 'prone to shame', Crisp 'properly disposed to feel shame', Rowe 'having a sense of shame', Dirlmeier 'feinfühlig'.)

1108ᵃ35–ᵇ6 As mentioned above, Aristotle does not discuss indignation and its associated vices elsewhere in *NE*.

'Indignation' renders *nemesis*, which is also the Greek for 'retribution'—hence its sense as an English word. In Aristotle's taxonomy it is specifically righteous indignation, distress, or annoyance at undeserved good fortune on the part of others. '[S]pite' renders *phthonos*, and 'joy in misfortune' *epichairekakia*; other translators (Ross rev. Ackrill/Urmson, Irwin, and Crisp) render the former as 'envy' and the latter as 'spite'. Rowe has 'grudging ill will' for *phthonos* and 'malice' for *epichairekakia*, Gauthier/Jolif 'envie' for the former and 'joie maligne' for the latter, Natali 'invidia' for the former and 'malevolenza' for the latter. This diversity of renderings reflects the fact that there is no exact match between Aristotle's taxonomy of motivational attitudes and ours. 'Envy' is a more specific term than 'spite', since envy of another's good fortune springs from awareness that one oneself lacks that specific good, whereas spite may prompt one to grudge to others goods which one enjoys oneself (Aristotle distinguishes *phthonos* from *zēlos*, envy, on precisely this ground at *Rhet.* 1387ᵇ23–5, 1388ª30–6). Since Aristotle's remarks about *phthonos* in this context are unspecific, I have preferred to render it as 'spite'. On the other hand, the English term 'spite' applies as naturally to *epichairekakia* as to *phthonos*. Having chosen 'spite' to render *phthonos*, I have therefore chosen the exact, but clumsy rendering 'joy in misfortune'. 'Schadenfreude' (Dirlmeier's translation) gives an exact one-word equivalent, but is still too alien to be permissible in a translation into English.[22]

Aristotle attempts to fit indignation into the triadic structure required by his theory of the ethical mean. There are two feelings involved (cf. courage), pleasure and distress (specifically pleasure and distress at what happens to others), and indignation is a mean between spite, regarded as an excessive state (since the spiteful person is displeased at anyone's doing well, whether or not deservedly) and *schadenfreude*, which is regarded as the deficiency opposed to spite. But it is clear that there is no one feeling such that spite is too much of it and *schadenfreude* too little. The spiteful person is upset when other people do well, the *schadenfroh* is pleased when they do badly; both reactions express an

---

[22] The discussion of the pleasure of comedy in Plato, *Phlb.* 48–50, represents comic humour as consisting primarily in ridicule, which is essentially a sort of enjoyment of the misfortunes of others, i.e. what Aristotle calls *epichairekakia*. Plato's term for that is *phthonos* (48b1–11, 50a2–9).

underlying malevolence, which is why they are typically found in the same person, as Aspasius and Anon. note.

The failure of these dispositions to fit the triadic structure illustrates the inadequacy of that structure pointed out above. The appropriate reactions to the fortunes of others are to be pleased when people get their deserts, whether good or ill, and to be displeased when they do not get their deserts, again whether good or ill. Being pleased at undeserved ill fortune and upset at deserved good fortune are inappropriate reactions, but those reactions do not fall on any single continuum with each other or with the appropriate reactions.

(At *EE* 1221^{a}38–^{b}3 spite is opposed, not to *schadenfreude*, but to a nameless defect of complaisance, characterizing someone who is not upset even at undeserved good fortune. Unlike the contrast between spite and *schadenfreude*, that contrast does pick out extremes of a single motivational dimension; Aristotle does not identify the mean between those extremes. On the other hand, *EE* 1233^{b}18–26 gives the same triad as the present passage.)

Aristotle's discussion of *nemesis* in *Rhetoric* II. 9 is superior in that there he does not attempt to fit it into the triadic model. Instead he correctly points out that pleasure in people's getting their due and distress at their not getting their due, whether good or ill, are marks of good character (1386^{b}10–33), and contrasts that with a single opposite character marked by both spite and *schadenfreude*; the same person manifests both, since someone who is distressed by the existence of something (in this case the good fortune of others) is naturally pleased by its non-existence or destruction (^{b}33–1387^{a}3).[23]

On Aristotle's claim that *schadenfreude* and spite are always bad, see above on 1107^{a}8–17. If that is so, the reason is not, as he claims, that those reactions are themselves extremes (since there is no feeling of which either of them is either an excess or a deficiency), but because they are aspects of malevolence, which is an intrinsically bad motivation.

1108^{b}6–7 'There will be ... later': in Books III–IV (see above).

1108^{b}7–9 'after that ... a mean': in Book V. 1–4.

---

[23] For fuller discussion see Mills (1985). On *nemesis* see Burger (1991).

1108ᵇ9–10 Since Aristotle does not apply the doctrine of the mean to the intellectual excellences, '[a]nd similarly' must mean simply 'similarly we shall discuss the intellectual excellences', not 'similarly we show how each intellectual excellence is a mean'. The intellectual excellences are discussed in Book VI.

BOOK TWO

CHAPTER 8

1108ᵇ15–19 Once again, Aristotle illustrates the ethical mean by the arithmetical; cf. 1106ᵃ26–ᵇ16. If a given quantity is divided equally, the equal portions are smaller than the larger of the portions produced by an unequal division, and larger than the smaller. By analogy, the ethical mean exceeds the deficient state and falls short of the excessive in feelings and actions.

1108ᵇ19–26 The application to particular cases of the general principle just enunciated is that the courageous person *is* readier to face danger than the coward, but less ready than the overbold, etc. Aristotle, however, makes (ᵇ19–23) the different, though related, point that (because of that) the virtuous person *appears*, in comparison with one extreme, to be an instance of the other (which in fact he or she is not), and then (ᵇ23–6) cites that as the explanation of the fact that vicious people at one extreme typically *call* the virtuous person by the name of the other extreme. Presumably (though Aristotle does not say so) the mistaken appearance holds only in the eyes of the vicious; he surely cannot be supposing that courageous people seem to other courageous people, or to themselves, cowardly by comparison with the overbold.

1108ᵇ26–30 The same principle of illustration is used as in ᵇ15–19.

1108ᵇ33–4 Cf. the definition of 'opposites' (*enantia*) in *Cat.* 6ᵃ17–18: 'the things in the same genus which are furthest from one another are defined as opposites'.

1108ᵇ35–1109ᵃ19 Aristotle claims that, in the case of some triads, one extreme is further from the mean than the other both

(a) intrinsically and (b) in virtue of the fact that we are more prone to it than to the opposite extreme. It is hard to see in what the intrinsic asymmetry (a) consists. Perhaps Aristotle's point is that the virtuous person's behaviour overlaps to a greater extent with one extreme form of behaviour than the other; while the coward shuns all danger, the courageous and the overbold alike face some dangers (and the latter faces in addition some which the courageous person avoids). Similarly, the temperate and the 'insensible' agree in shunning some pleasures, while the intemperate person abstains from none. But with regard to avoiding danger, the courageous person's behaviour overlaps more with that of the coward, and with regard to enjoying pleasures the temperate person's behaviour overlaps more with that of the intemperate; hence the asymmetry disappears. It might be suggested that the asymmetry consists in the fact that, the impulses to avoid danger and to enjoy pleasures being biologically more basic, and therefore much more common, than their opposites, the virtues should be seen primarily as corrections of those basic impulses; but then we have moved from contrast (a) to contrast (b).

BOOK TWO

CHAPTER 9

1109^{a}24 'it is a hard task to be good': a traditional saying. See Hesiod *Works* 287–92; Plato, *Prt.* 339a–41e (discussing a poem of Simonides).

1109^{a}25 The same expression (*to meson*, lit. 'the middle') designates the mean and the centre of a circle.

1109^{a}30–^{b}8 The practical advice assumes the asymmetry (and its twofold grounds) identified in the preceding chapter.

^{a}32: From *Od.* 12. 219-20, where Odysseus, following the advice of Circe (not of Calypso, as Aristotle, doubtless quoting from memory, says), tells his helmsman to steer well away from the more dangerous Charybdis (and hence closer to Scylla).

1109^{b}3–4 'that will be clear … feel': cf. 1104^{b}3–5 and note on that passage.

1109ᵇ6–7 'as people ... planks'. Cf. Plato, *Prt.* 325d6–7.

1109ᵇ7–12 The hostility to pleasure expressed here is atypical of *NE* as a whole, for Aristotle insists that pleasure is an intrinsic element of the good life (1099ᵃ7–28), and is prepared at least to consider (and in the view of some to endorse) the claim that pleasure is identical with the highest good (1153ᵇ1–14). The explanation is presumably that in this context he is thinking primarily of bodily pleasures, especially considered as allurements towards intemperance.

ᵇ8: 'unbiased': lit. 'unbribed'. Aristotle compares us to members of a jury giving their verdict on pleasure.

ᵇ9–11: In *Il.* 3. 156–60 the elders of Troy say that Helen should be sent away lest her incredible attractiveness bring destruction on the city.

1109ᵇ14–16 'But that ... angry'. Cf. ᵇ20–3.

1109ᵇ16–18 'Sometimes ... manly'. Cf. 1107ᵇ31–1108ᵃ1, 1108ᵇ22–6.

1109ᵇ20–3 'But up to what point ... of them'. Cf. 1104ᵃ5–10 and note on that passage.

ᵃ21: 'determine by reason': alternatively, 'determine by one's principle'. Cf. note on 1103ᵇ32–4.

Since Aristotle's point is that, while some slight degree of deviation from the mean is permissible, it is not possible to specify the precise degree in a general formula, strict logic would require that 'is blameworthy' should be replaced by 'is not blameworthy'. But since the meaning is clear in the context, emendation of the text is unnecessary.

BOOK THREE

Having discussed virtue of character in general in Book II, Aristotle deals with the virtues individually from III. 6 to the end of Book IV. The intervening chapters are devoted to the discussion of concepts which are used in the characterization of agents in terms of the specific virtues and in the consequent evaluation of those agents and their states of character and actions. These are the voluntary and involuntary (chapters 1 and 5) and the cluster of concepts consisting of choice, deliberation, and wish (chapters 2–4).

The corresponding material in *EE* is found in Book II, as follows: voluntary and involuntary (corresponding to *NE* III. 1) in chapters 7–9, choice in chapter 10, and deliberation in chapter 11. *EE* has no discussion corresponding to *NE* III. 4. Some material in *NE* III. 5 corresponds to *EE* II. 6.

BOOK THREE

CHAPTER I

The subject of this chapter is the distinction between the voluntary and the involuntary. The use of that pair of terms is largely conventional. Aristotle makes use of two pairs of adjectives, one pair (*hekōn* and *akōn*) applied to agents, the other (*hekousion* and *akousion*) applied to the actions and *pathē* (see below) of agents. The pairs are connected thus; an agent acts (or suffers) *hekōn* iff what that agent does (or suffers) is *hekousion*, and acts or suffers *akōn* iff what he or she does (or suffers) is *akousion*. (While *hekōn* and *akōn* are grammatically adjectives, in that they are declined according to the number, gender, and case of the noun which they qualify, they function as adverbs, the standard construction in which they are used being 'X did such-and-such *hekōn* (*akōn*)', translated 'X did such-and-such voluntarily (involuntarily)'.) Since the application of the two pairs is thus extensionally equivalent, for theoretical purposes they can be treated as expressing a single contrast.

That contrast is not exactly matched by that between the use of any pair of terms in current philosophical English. English has at least the pairs 'voluntary/involuntary', 'intentional/unintentional', 'of one's own free will/against one's will'; each of those contrasts matches something in that between *hekousion* and *akousion*, but none maps that contrast precisely (see below). The terms 'voluntary' and 'involuntary' are used here largely because they are traditional; Aquinas has 'voluntarium' and 'involuntarium', Natali 'volontario' and 'involontario', and the pair is standard in English translations (though Rowe has 'voluntary' and 'countervoluntary'). Gauthier/Jolif has 'de son plein gré' and 'malgré soi', and Dirlmeier 'freiwillig' and 'unfreiwillig' (both corresponding to the English 'of one's own free will/against one's will').[1]

While it is tempting to assume that the distinction between the voluntary and the involuntary is a distinction between kinds of actions, it is clear that some of the things to which Aristotle applies that distinction are not actions, e.g. his first example of something involuntary is being blown off course in a storm, which is not an action of the steersman, but rather something which happens to him or her (see below). We need a broader notion of events in the history of an agent, including both what they do and what happens to them, of which the question arises whether the agent is to be held to account for them (see below), but of which not all are actions properly so called. This is not a local feature of Greek usage; e.g. crashing one's car through falling asleep at the wheel might be classified as something involuntary (for which the agent might in some cases be held responsible), but not as an action strictly speaking; again the convulsive movements of an epileptic's limbs appear to be a paradigm of the involuntary, and not to be actions.

The nature of Aristotle's enquiry into this area is as follows. In common with ordinary thought, he recognizes a broad distinction within the category of events in the history of an agent which is relevant to the moral and legal evaluation of those events and hence of the person in whose history they occur. Very roughly, some events occur because the person in whose history they occur wanted or chose that they should, others not because that person wanted or chose that they should. So those of the former kind

---

[1] On the problems of translation see Moline (1989).

belong to that person in the fullest sense, whereas those of the latter kind do not belong in that sense. Therefore, and again very roughly, in the former type of case the person is appropriately praised or blamed, or, in appropriate circumstances, rewarded or punished, whereas in the latter type of case those attitudes are withheld, being replaced where appropriate by exculpation or mitigation. Aristotle's enquiry takes the form of an attempt to lay down precise criteria demarcating those roughly sketched types of case, thus systematizing the initial rough distinction in line with standard practices of legal and moral evaluation.

1109^{b}30–2   It was established in II. 5–6 that virtue of character is concerned with actions and ways in which the appetitive soul is affected, i.e. feelings (see notes on 1105^{b}20–1, 1105^{b}20–3, and 1106^{b}16–24). The claim that praise and blame accrue to the voluntary, and excuse and sometimes pity to the involuntary, should be understood as applying both to actions and to things that happen to one (*pathē*), as demanded both by ordinary Greek usage and by Aristotle's inclusion of examples such as being blown off course (1110^{a}3, see above). In ordinary Greek an *akousion pathos* is something that happens to one against one's will, or at least not in accordance with one's will, whereas a *hekousion pathos* is something which happens to one in accordance with one's will (e.g. someone who consents to being killed suffers a *hekousion pathos*; cf. 1136^{a}13–14), and while one would not ordinarily be blamed for the former kind of *pathos*, one might well be blamed for the latter. It seems, then, that Aristotle here slides from the more specific application of *pathos*, i.e. to things which happen *in or to the appetitive soul* (i.e. feelings), to the wider application of the term, i.e. to things which happen *to the agent*.

^{b}31:   'praise and blame': plural in the Greek.

^{b}32:   '[E]xcuse' renders *suggnōmē*; the range of meaning of the term also includes sympathy, pardon, and mitigation. The term recurs in 1110^{a}24, and in default of particular evidence to the contrary it is to be assumed that the sense in the two passages is the same. For the specific sense of the word, and for the interpretation of the assertion that *suggnōmē* is accorded to the involuntary, see note on 1110^{a}23–6.

ᵇ34–5:   Aristotle once again adverts to the relevance of his enquiry to political practice.

1109ᵇ35–1110ᵃ4   Aristotle divides involuntary actions and *pathē* into two exclusive and exhaustive classes: (a) those which come about through force and (b) those which come about through error.

Events of type (a) are defined as those where (i) the originating cause of the event is external to the agent, and (ii) the agent contributes nothing to the event. Condition (ii) appears intended to exclude the cases of duress, etc. discussed immediately below, in which someone external to the agent causes that agent to act by inducing him or her to choose to act in one way rather than another. The passivity of the 'agent' in cases of force is emphasized by Aristotle's saying that in these cases 'the agent (or rather the person to whom the thing happens) contributes nothing' (ᵃ2–3; cf. note on 1106ᵃ3–4). Force is then direct physical force, whether exercised by inanimate things, such as the wind, or by agents, as when one is carried off by kidnappers (ᵃ3–4).

It appears from *EE* 1224ᵇ11–15 that Aristotle includes under this heading cases where one agent uses the body of another as an instrument to cause some effect (the example is that of one person's seizing the hand of another and using it to strike a third). Here Aristotle describes the person whose hand is used as the instrument as 'resisting in wish and desire'; so the sense in which the 'agent' contributes nothing to such cases is that he or she contributes nothing *by way of agency*, which is compatible with his or her body having a part to play in the causation of the effect. (Conversely, a physically helpless agent who has him or herself moved by people acting on his or her orders is not included under this heading, since the origin of his or her movements is not external, but internal to his or her will.) But it then follows immediately, as Aspasius points out, that there can be no *actions* which are involuntary in this way.

ᵇ35–1110ᵃ1:   'things that occur by force': a literal rendering of *ta biai ... ginomena*. In 1110ᵃ1 a representative instance of the property of being a thing of that kind is characterized by the adjective *biaion*, formed from the noun *bia* (force), and the adjective is applied in 1110ᵇ1 to the class of things possessing that property. In those passages the adjective thus has the sense 'enforced, occurring by force'. It can also mean 'forcible, enforcing', which is the sense required in 1110^{b}9, where Aristotle raises and rejects the suggestion that the pleasant and the fine are *biaia*, i.e. that they are external forces compelling us to act.

1110^{a}1 'error' renders *agnoia*, which may be either ignorance or false belief. As Aristotle applies the term in 1111^{a}3–21 to a wide range of cognitive failures of different types (see below), 'error' is intended to be equally non-specific.

1110^{a}4–8   Aristotle now turns to cases of action done under duress. A complication arises immediately from the phrase 'or for the sake of something fine', (^{a}4–5). If the latter phrase refers to actions done for some inducement, such as a monetary reward, they do not appear even plausible candidates for actions done under compulsion, and Aristotle appears to forget about them immediately. It is therefore more plausible to take the phrase as referring, not to a type of case separate from that of duress, but to another aspect of those very same cases. In Aristotle's example the duress takes the form of threats of death issued by a tyrant who has the parents and children of the prospective agent in his power. Saving the lives of one's family is plainly a fine thing to do, so submission to the tyrant's threat can be represented either as prompted by the fear of the greater evil of their death, or as directed towards the fine act of saving them. It is not clear whether Aristotle thinks that this dual aspect applies to every case of duress, or to some only. (Aspasius's suggestion 'such as are done for fear of a greater evil, rather than for the sake of something fine' (i.e. when one succumbs to the threat of a greater evil, such as the death of one's family, rather than resisting the threat for the sake of some fine end) would require *mallon ē* instead of the simple *ē*. His comment can be read as suggesting that the text should be emended accordingly.)

Stewart takes the reference to be to the alternatives open to the agent, viz. giving in to the threat for fear of the greater evil, or resisting it for the sake of the noble end. Whichever the agent does, the question arises as to whether he or she acted voluntarily.

Straight off, the result of the account of force above, that there can be no actions which are involuntary due to force, clashes with the common-sense description of instances of duress as cases in which people are forced or compelled to do something. But on the other side there is plausibility in Aristotle's 'rigorist' conclusion; cases of action under duress must be cases where the agent chose to act to escape the threat or other pressure, but in that event it was up to the agent whether to submit to the duress, and so the agent was not *strictly* compelled to act. These cases thus present a classic Aristotelian *aporia*, i.e. a clash of well-motivated views calling for resolution via philosophical examination (cf. the introduction to the discussion of *akrasia* in VII. 1, esp. 1145ᵇ2–7).

1110ᵃ8–19 A second kind of disputed case is that of action required by force of circumstances which do not arise from human agency; the example is that of jettisoning a ship's cargo to save the ship in a storm. The two types of disputed case mirror the two types of involuntary *pathos* distinguished above, in each case one type arising from human agency, the other from non-human forces (indeed, the same force, viz. the force of the wind, in both cases). The grounds for dispute are the same in both types of disputed case; on the one hand the agent is compelled to act to avoid the threatened evil (whether arising from human agency or from a non-human cause), on the other the agent chooses to avoid that evil rather than suffer it. Aristotle's solution is *stated* for force of circumstances only, but is clearly intended to apply to duress also.

The solution to the *aporia* is (characteristically) that there is some truth in each of the conflicting views. Actions of the disputed type are mixed, in that they have some characteristics of the voluntary and some of the involuntary. But the voluntary predominates: the individual instances of disputed action are voluntary, the involuntary element consisting in the fact that they are instances of action-types which, were it not for the necessitating circumstances, no one would perform voluntarily. While that appears to be the outline of the solution, there is some obscurity in detail.

ᵃ9–11: '[W]ithout qualification' renders *haplōs*, lit. 'simply'. A term applies *haplōs* when its application is not subject to any qualification, by contrast to qualified application expressed by e.g. 'for X' or 'compared to Y'; see *Top.* 115ᵇ29–35. In this instance the claim is that the term *hekōn* applies to an agent's jettisoning of cargo, not without qualification, but subject to the qualification 'to save oneself and the others'. (Equivalently, we can say that the expression 'jettisons *hekōn*' applies to the agent not without qualification, but subject to the qualification 'to save oneself and the others'.) But now the elucidation of that claim is problematic. It might be taken to mean that the unqualified sentence 'X jettisoned *hekōn*' is false, whereas the qualified claim 'X jettisoned *hekōn* to save himself and the others' is true. But there is no interpretation of *hekōn* which makes the first sentence false and the second true. If X jettisoned the cargo intentionally to save himself and the others, then X jettisoned the cargo intentionally; if X jettisoned the cargo willingly (i.e. without reluctance) to save himself and the others, then X jettisoned the cargo willingly; and if X chose to jettison the cargo to save himself and the others, then X chose to jettison the cargo. Of course, on all these interpretations we need the qualification to explain *why* X jettisoned the cargo *hekōn*; so the correct account of the contrast between the two sentences is not that the first is false and the second true, but that the second explains the action which it describes, whereas the first does not. If that is correct, the contrast is the same as that between 'John ran' and 'John ran to catch the bus'. We have then to consider how that contrast contributes to Aristotle's solution of the *aporia*.

That contribution becomes clearer if we paraphrase 'John ran to catch the bus' as 'John's intention in running was to catch the bus'. No corresponding paraphrase is available for 'John ran'; 'John's intention in running was to run' suggests (though it does not entail) that John ran just for the sake of running, which is *ex hypothesi* false. The point of Aristotle's contrast may, then, be that whereas 'X's intention in jettisoning was just to jettison' is always false (NB 'no one', ᵃ9), 'X's intention in jettisoning was to save himself and the others' will be true of any sensible person who jettisons.[2]

ᵃ11–14:   (i) The foregoing contrast is supposed to explain how the disputed actions are mixed in character. (ii) They are none the less more like the voluntary than the involuntary, since their being voluntary or involuntary is determined by their characteristics at the time of action, and at the time of action they result from the agent's choice.

---

[2]   At 1151ᵃ35–ᵇ3 Aristotle distinguishes something pursued for its own sake, which is said to be pursued *haplōs*, from something pursued for the sake of something else, which is said to be pursued incidentally (*kata sumbebēkos*).

ᵃ13–14:   I take Aristotle's point to be that what is assessed as voluntary or involuntary is a complete action, and actions are complete when and only when they are done. The Greek is *to de telos tēs praxeōs kata ton kairon estin*, lit. (on my construal of *telos*) 'the completion of the action is according to the occasion'. An alternative sense of *telos* is 'goal, end', and all the other translators render it in that sense: e.g. Irwin 'the goal of an action accords with the specific occasion', Rowe 'the end for which actions are done varies with the occasion'.

ᵃ15–18:   Aristotle elaborates the description of these actions as issuing from the agent, and therefore under the agent's control.

ᵃ18–19:   Statement of the conclusion of the *aporia*. While the disputed actions are voluntary (for the reasons given in ᵃ11–18), they are 'perhaps ... without qualification, involuntary', since no one would choose any such action for itself.

The reasons for counting the disputed kinds of actions as voluntary are clear, and we might expect them to decide the *aporia* in favour of the voluntary. But Aristotle still seeks to do justice to their 'mixed' character in the description of these kinds of actions as 'perhaps without qualification involuntary'. The explanation given at ᵃ19 confirms the suggestion given above; actions belonging to the type 'jettisoning' are without qualification (i.e. without such qualifications as 'to save oneself and the others') involuntary, in that no one would choose to perform acts of jettisoning just for their own sake; i.e. no one would jettison just for the sake of jettisoning.

A minor difficulty is that, strictly interpreted, that result would classify as mixed any act of a type performed only for the sake of some further end: e.g. no one would choose to brush their teeth for the sake of brushing their teeth. Aristotle's intended condition must be the stronger one that, without the circumstances necessitating the disputed action, everyone would seek to avoid performing acts of the necessitated type, since doing them would be not merely pointless, but a positive evil (e.g. something harmful, disgraceful, or unpleasant; cf. 1104ᵇ30–2).[3]

The crucial point is that acts of the disputed types involve a choice of evils. The agent indeed *chooses* between evils, and to

[3] So Hursthouse (1984: 259).

that extent his or her act is voluntary, but the necessity of making the choice of evils is itself *forced* on the agent by external circumstances, and is something which the agent would prefer to avoid, but is unable to. Hence the agent is compelled to act, intentionally indeed, but against his or her will. This explains why it is appropriate to see actions of those types as having something of the voluntary and something of the involuntary about them, i.e. as being mixed. While that appears to be the solution of the *aporia* which Aristotle is aiming at, his actual terminology does not express it particularly clearly.

1110ᵃ19–23 Aristotle here considers another type of situation in which the agent is faced with a choice of evils, viz. that between enduring torture or other ill-treatment for the sake of some noble end and giving in to it at the price of abandoning that end. In those circumstances endurance is praiseworthy, and therefore voluntary (though mixed, as in the previous cases). On the other hand, enduring such things for the sake of some trifling good is a mark of bad character. Aristotle does not value endurance for its own sake; it must be guided by a correct sense of values.

Aspasius and Anon. take Aristotle to be considering cases where an agent does something distressing or shameful with a view to achieving a good end; Aspasius's example is a case of action under duress, that of a man who obeys a tyrant's order to parade in public in women's clothing, in order to save his city from destruction and his family from death. Anon. gives the examples of lying in order to achieve a good end and of seducing a tyrant's wife in the course of a plot to overthrow him. This interpretation is accepted by Gauthier/Jolif (ii. 75) and by Stocker (1986), who finds in this passage evidence that Aristotle accepts the doctrine of 'dirty hands'. But Aristotle's use of the verb *hupomenein* ('endure') rather than *poiein* or *prattein* ('do') suggests strongly that he is discussing suffering distressing or degrading treatment, not doing distressing or degrading actions (contrast ᵃ23–5: 'praise is not accorded, but excuse, when one does something one should not' (*hotan ... praxēi tis ha mē dei*)).[4] This passage therefore does not express commitment to the 'dirty hands' doctrine, and

---

[4] So Kenny (1979: 33), following Aquinas. This is not to deny that enduring such treatment is something which the agent *does*; it is a *praxis* (ᵃ20), since the agent chooses to endure such treatment rather than abandon his or her noble end. The point

I am not aware of any other passage which does so explicitly. The discussion of duress at 1110ᵃ4–8 does indeed describe the situation of someone faced with the choice of *doing* something shameful or having his or her parents or children killed, but there Aristotle's focus is on the question of whether a shameful action done under duress is voluntary or involuntary, not on the question of whether one should do the shameful thing. He offers no explicit answer to the latter question. From elsewhere we learn on the one hand that there are some kinds of thing one should never do under any circumstances (1107ᵃ8–17), and on the other that obligations to one's parents should stand very high in one's priorities (IX. 2, 1164ᵇ33–1165ᵃ2, 1165ᵃ21–7). But even in the latter context Aristotle eschews general formulae, adhering instead to his usual line that it is not easy to determine such matters precisely, in view of the range of different factors involved (1164ᵇ27–30; cf. note on 1103ᵇ34–1104ᵃ5). It is likely, then, that his answer to the question of whether one should do the shameful thing to save one's family from the tyrant is 'It depends on the circumstances'. It is plausible that he supposes that if what is demanded is *very* shameful, e.g. murdering someone else, one should not do it even to save one's family, but that if it is only moderately shameful, as in Aspasius's example, one should do it. That seems to me as close as Aristotle comes to espousing the 'dirty hands' thesis.[5]

ᵃ20:   'praised': because in those circumstances making the right choice of evils is heroic. In the jettisoning case, by contrast, all that is called for is good sense (ᵃ10–11).

ᵃ22:   'the reverse': the opposition is that between noble goods and trifling goods, or no goods at all.

1110ᵃ23–6   Aristotle now turns to the case of the person who succumbs to torture, etc., and in consequence does what he or she should not do. Such a person deserves (or receives, the distinction is not drawn) excuse, provided that the pressure to which he or

is that the agent does not do anything shameful; what he or she does is voluntarily endure something shameful.

⁵ On 'dirty hands' see also Curzer (2005: 249–53).

she succumbs is such as to overstrain human nature, and which no one would endure.

ª24: '[E]xcuse' again renders *suggnōmē*; see above on 1109ᵇ32. Strictly, a successful plea of excuse establishes that the agent did no wrong, while pardon, mitigation, and sympathy are all attitudes which assume that, while the agent did wrong, blame and punishment should either be withheld altogether or moderated to some degree. Since the agent is here expressly said to have done what he or she should not, excuse in the strict sense might appear to be inapplicable. On the other hand, the distinction at 1109ᵇ33 between *suggnōmē* and pity would suggest that here the former term cannot mean 'sympathy' (i.e. feeling sorry for), since that term is virtually interchangeable with pity. We should therefore expect *suggnōmē* to mean either pardon or mitigation. But the grounds on which *suggnōmē* is said to be appropriate are that the agent was subject to pressure too great for human nature to stand up to (cf. the discussion of things too fearful for human nature, 1115ᵇ9–11), which implies that it was impossible for the agent to resist it. But in that case the sense in which the agent did what he or she should not have done is that the action was of a kind such that no one should do something of that kind, a description which allows that in the particular circumstances it was impossible for the agent to avoid doing it. But in that case the agent has, not merely grounds for pardon, but a sufficient excuse. While that sort of thing is the sort of thing one should not do, in these circumstances the agent cannot be held to be at fault for having done it. It seems, therefore, that 'excuse' is after all the rendering which best captures the sense of *suggnōmē* here.

This raises the question whether actions of this kind are voluntary.

(a) Since Aristotle has said at 1109ᵇ31–2 that *suggnōmē* applies to the involuntary, we might assume that actions of this kind are counted as involuntary. But that construes 1109ᵇ31–2 as saying that *suggnōmē* applies only to the involuntary (or perhaps that it applies to, and only to, the involuntary), whereas it might be taken as saying that it applies to the involuntary, allowing that it applies also to some voluntary events. But given that interpretation, 'praise and blame applies to the voluntary' (ᵇ31) must be interpreted as allowing some application of *suggnōmē* to the voluntary also. So either the applications of praise and blame on the one hand and *suggnōmē* on the other are asymmetrical (the former applying only to the voluntary, the latter to the involuntary and to some of the voluntary), or, assuming that the applications are symmetrical, actions excused because done under superhuman pressure are involuntary. The reading of ^{b}31–2 which takes the applications as symmetrical is certainly the most natural one. Our expectation must therefore be that Aristotle counts actions done under superhuman pressure as involuntary.[6]

(b) An obvious objection to that suggestion is that Aristotle regards these as simply another sort of mixed action, and therefore as belonging to a type of action which is as such voluntary (for the reasons given above). But the crucial point determining mixed actions as voluntary (though mixed) is that it is up to the agent whether or not to act (1110^a15–18). Is that condition satisfied in these cases, in which the agent is subject to pressure too strong for human nature to resist? If it is impossible for me (or indeed for any human being) to hold out against it, then in no sense is it up to me whether or not I do hold out. Such 'actions' seem not to be actions strictly speaking, but involuntary *pathē*, in which the agent is acted on by irresistible force, like the mariner swept away by a storm.

1110^{a}26–9   These lines qualify those immediately preceding. Things done under superhuman pressure merit excuse, but there are some things, e.g. matricide, which one cannot be forced to do. In such cases one should rather die, having suffered the worst.

^{a}26:   This clearly contrasts with the previous kind of case, implying that in those cases the agent *is* 'necessitated' to do the thing that one should not do. We should expect that to imply that the agent is compelled to do whatever it is, and that it is impossible for

---

[6] Most commentators take the opposite view. Sorabji (1980: 260–7) maintains that actions of this kind are counted as voluntary in this chapter (in contrast to V. 8 and *EE* II. 8 (see below)), but are none the less treated as pardonable by the application of equity (*epieikeia*), the virtue which mitigates the strict provisions of written law in the interests of fairness (discussed in V. 10). Kenny (1979: 34–5) and Meyer (1993: 98–100) agree that Aristotle holds such actions voluntary, the former suggesting that they are accorded *suggnōmē* in the sense of sympathy.

him or her not to do it. On whether Aristotle draws any distinction between necessity and compulsion see below.

^{a}27:   While the preceding line has apparently stated a psychological thesis, this line contains the moral thesis, that the things which one cannot be 'necessitated' to do one should never do under any circumstances (cf. 1107^{a}8–17, with note), but should rather die. The thought plainly is that it can never be right to choose such things (the example is matricide) as the lesser evil, since doing them is more evil than any alternative, however horrible, which one might have to undergo.

The juxtaposition of these two theses raises the question of what the connection between them is supposed to be. The simplest hypothesis is that the moral thesis is supported by the psychological one; since one cannot be made to do the evil act in such cases, it is up to oneself whether one does it, and that being so, one must never do it, no matter how terrible the cost. That analysis raises the further question of what is supposed to show that the psychological thesis is true. Aristotle has just acknowledged that there are pressures which are too much for human nature to cope with; but if so, what happens if one is put under such pressure with a view to causing one to commit matricide? If, as Aristotle maintains, the alternative of not committing matricide is always open to the agent, then it seems that his only recourse is to insist that in such cases superhuman pressure cannot be brought to bear. But that seems to be mere obstinate adherence to a moral thesis, independent of the facts.

The alternative is to suggest that superhuman pressure is itself relative to the scale of the evil which it is designed to cause. Human nature, on this view, contains a built-in value scale. Given the alternative of committing an evil of magnitude x, there is a degree of pressure y such that it is beyond the power of human nature to endure y rather than do x. But there is some magnitude of evil z such that, for any degree of pressure, it is never beyond the power of human nature to endure that pressure rather than do z. In that case the relation between the two theses expressed in ^{a}26 and ^{a}27 is reversed; rather than its being true that one should never do z because one cannot be made to do z, it is the case that one cannot be made to do z because one should never do z.

It should be noted that the thesis under consideration is not that one's psychological possibilities are determined by the values which one actually has. On that hypothesis someone who holds that matricide is the greatest evil cannot be forced to commit it, whereas someone who holds that it is not the greatest evil can be forced to commit it. That cannot be Aristotle's view, since he describes the plea of necessity put up by Alcmaeon in Euripides' play (see below) as absurd, though *ex hypothesi* Alcmaeon did not regard matricide as the greatest evil. Rather, the thesis would have to be that human psychological possibilities are determined by evaluative facts which hold independently of the actual evaluations of agents. While I doubt whether we are justified in attributing that thesis to Aristotle, I am unable to do more than express scepticism. It does seem, however, that he is faced with the choice of that thesis or the unsupported assertion that superhuman pressure is impossible in cases such as that of matricide.

ᵃ28–9:   In Euripides' lost play *Alcmaeon* Amphiarus, king of Argos, who was a seer, foresaw that his wife Eriphyle would cause his death and commanded their son Alcmaeon to avenge him, threatening him with his curse if he did not. Alcmaeon therefore killed his mother, pleading that he was compelled to do so in order to escape his father's curse.

1110ᵃ29–ᵇ1   Aristotle recapitulates the description of an agent faced with a choice of evils, specifically between undergoing something distressing, such as torture, and doing something shameful. The latter is described in ᵃ32–3 as 'the things one is necessitated to do', and in ᵃ33–ᵇ1 praise and censure are said to accrue to those people who are necessitated or not. Presumably what is intended is that people who endure what is distressing are praised (cf. ᵃ19–22) while those who are necessitated to do what is shameful are censured.

Clearly, Aristotle is no longer considering the case of those subject to superhuman pressure, who are excused for being necessitated to do what they should not (see above); the people now being considered are not excused, but censured. They are those who make the wrong choice of evils, choosing the greater evil (what is shameful) in preference to the lesser (what is distressing). But in what sense are they necessitated to make that choice?

Not, clearly, in the sense that it is impossible for them to do anything else (for if it were, how could they be censured?). The sense seems simply to be that they have to make that choice if they are to escape the other evil. (But of course they do not have to escape the other evil, and should not seek to do so.)

Here we have a notion of necessitation which is clearly distinct from compulsion. It is conditional on the attainment of a goal; i.e. it is what one has to do if one is to achieve one's goal, and actions necessitated in this way are thus clearly voluntary. If all actions done in the context of choice of evils are necessitated in this way, then all are voluntary, and their being voluntary is compatible with Aristotle's adhering to his rigorist account of things done under compulsion. Things done under compulsion are involuntary; actions done in the situation of choice of evils are necessitated, but not compelled, and are voluntary.

That may be Aristotle's intended final solution to the original *aporia*.[7] If so, it is inadequate. If it is sufficient for A's being necessitated to F that A has to F if A is to achieve his or her goal, then Alcmaeon was necessitated to kill his mother, since he had to do that if he was to escape his father's curse. But Aristotle treats the plea of necessity as absurd in that case. Again, we saw above that cases like Alcmaeon's, where people cannot be necessitated to act, are contrasted with cases of giving in to superhuman pressure, where they can be necessitated to act. It is incredible that all that Aristotle means is that people subject to superhuman pressure (like everyone else) have to act in the way they do if they are to achieve their goal, without being compelled to act in that way. In their case, necessity is compulsion, which is why (unlike other necessitated people) they are excused for doing what they should not.

Regrettably, I conclude that Aristotle is operating with two notions of necessity, which he has not distinguished from one another. One is the conditional notion of necessity, what one has to do if one is to achieve one's goal; that is distinct from compulsion, and actions which are necessary in that sense are voluntary. The other is the stronger notion of necessity exemplified by the cases of superhuman pressure; that form of necessity is a form of compulsion, and therefore constitutes an excuse.

---

[7] As Irwin holds (1980*b*: 121, 136).

1110ᵇ1–9   Restatement of the rigorist criterion for compulsion. Since Aristotle does not propose any modification of the criterion, he presumably thinks that cases of succumbing to superhuman pressure satisfy it. That commits him to treating those cases as not involving choice or any other aspect of agency (he repeats that in cases of compulsion the agent contributes nothing, ᵇ2–3). On one model of superhuman pressure the person subject to such pressure does act intentionally to escape from it; the effect of that degree of pressure is to make it impossible for the agent not to have that intention. Aristotle's rigorist criterion rules out that model. On his account the agent subject to superhuman pressure has to be impervious to reasons at all. That is not an altogether unrealistic view. Some situations, such as being caught in an earthquake, are presumably so terrifying that the agent ceases to be capable of any kind of choice or evaluation of reasons, and thereby becomes incapable of forming any intention at all, but merely responds in a biologically determined routine of behaviour directed towards escape. And one might think that some forms of torture are so extreme that their effect is the same. Aristotle's limitation of compulsion to such extreme cases may be criticized as unduly harsh, and he can also be criticized for failing to apply that account of compulsion to cases such as that of matricide;[8] it is not, however, inconsistent with his rigorist assumption.

1110ᵇ9–15   Aristotle's primary reason for rejecting the suggestion that the desires for pleasure and for the fine compel people to act is that, since these are the grounds of all action, if they are sources of compulsion, then all actions are done from compulsion, a conclusion he regards as absurd.

ᵇ9:   '[F]orcible' renders *biaion*; see note on 1109ᵇ35–1110ᵃ1.

ᵇ10:   The suggestion that pleasant and fine things compel agents to act rests on the conception of those things as external to the agent. Aristotle rejects that conception; see below.

---

[8] Urmson (1988: 44–5) suggests that Aristotle has, excusably, failed to envisage the possibility of such cases. His wording leaves it open whether he thinks that Aristotle has failed to envisage it altogether or, as I suggest, failed to envisage its application to matricide.

^{b}11:   Presumably Aristotle means that any action is motivated by considerations either of pleasure or of what is fine. At 1104^{b}30–1 he has identified three objects of choice, the pleasant, the advantageous, and the fine (see note on 1104^{b}30–1105^{a}1). The advantageous is what is instrumentally desirable, i.e. what promotes what is intrinsically desirable; the latter is here distinguished into the pleasant and the fine. The priority of the pleasant, asserted in the earlier passage (see note), is not mentioned here.

^{b}11–14:   People act (or more strictly, things happen to them (see above)) under compulsion when they are acted on by external force; hence they are not themselves the authors of their 'actions'. Since the pleasant and the fine are the ultimate objects of motivation, and therefore of the agent's internal springs of action, it is absurd to count them as forces external to the agent. It is a mark of this that while being acted on is something unpleasant, which people undergo against their will, acting for the sake of the pleasant or the fine is itself pleasant; taking pleasure in one's actions, then, marks them as one's own, in contrast to things that happen to one as the result of external force.

^{b}12:   '[U]nder forcible compulsion' renders *biai*, lit. 'by force'; a literal rendering is impossible since 'act by force' has the sense 'act by forcible means' instead of the desired sense 'act subject to force'. 'involuntarily': here the sense of 'against one's will' is strongly conveyed by *akontes*.

^{b}14–15:   The opponent is assumed to make the compromise proposal that while we are ourselves the source of our good actions, our bad actions are done under compulsion. This suggestion is summarily dismissed as arbitrary; it receives fuller consideration at 1114^{b}12–25.

     In this section Aristotle has not discussed the general thesis that all actions are causally determined, but the specific thesis that all actions are done under compulsion. Rejection of the specific thesis is compatible with acceptance of the general one; Aristotle discusses more general issues of determinism in chapter 5.

1110^{b}18–24   Aristotle turns now to the class of actions and *pathē* which occur through error (*di' agnoian*); all of these are non-voluntary (*ouch hekousia*), while those and only those which the agent regrets after they have occurred are involuntary (*akousia*). The involuntary through error is thus a subclass of the non-voluntary through error.[9]

It might appear that this distinction is that between what is contrary to the agent's intention (which is regretted) and that which is not in accordance with the agent's intention (some of which is not regretted). But subsequent regret does not demarcate what happens contrary to the agent's intention from what happens without the agent's having intended it. Suppose that I write two letters, one a letter of thanks to a tedious relative for an unwanted Christmas present, the other to a friend, in which I expand on the tediousness of the relative and the inappropriateness of the present; then, by mistake I put the letters in the wrong envelopes and post them. On discovering my error, I am not particularly sorry, since I don't particularly care whether the relative has been offended. It may still be true that my intention was to put the letters in the right envelopes, and that had I noticed my mistake before sealing the letters I would have corrected it, since I would not have gone so far as *intentionally* sending an insulting letter to my relative, though I do not particularly regret having done so *unintentionally*.[10]

The same point arises in the case of compulsion (though Aristotle does not discuss it in that context).[11] Suppose I am a ship's captain in the days of sail, taking a cargo of slaves from Africa to a slave port, say Savannah, where they are to be sold. I don't care

---

[9] Moline (1989) therefore departs from Aristotle in describing a case of unintentional but unregretted action as done not through ignorance but in ignorance, 'for even if she [i.e. the agent] had not been ignorant she might well have done the same thing'. Such a case would be the following: (a) one's enemy is hiding in the bushes, (b) one shoots him thinking that one is shooting a stag, (c) had one known that it was one's enemy, one would have shot him anyway. Aristotle has no discussion of such a case.

[10] So Bostock (2000: 111–12).

Irwin is therefore mistaken in commenting (1999a: 203) that the distinction between the involuntary and the non-voluntary is relevant not to the agent's responsibility but to his or her character, on the ground that being pleased at something one has done in ignorance shows what sort of actions one is willing and prepared to do. I may be pleased to have done unintentionally what I would be not willing or prepared to do intentionally. Irwin is, however, right that the distinction is relevant to the evaluation of character. Being pleased at something that has happened contrary to my intention reveals my wider wishes and valuations (see below) and thereby reveals something of my character. So Hursthouse (1984: 254–7).

[11] As Bostock points out (2000: 112 n. 17).

for this trade, but it's my job, and I carry it out conscientiously. On this particular voyage a storm drives me to take shelter in Boston, where the slaves are freed. While I am glad that things have thus been taken out of my hands, with this outcome, it is still the case that I intended to sail to Savannah and that had it not been for the storm I would have done so.[12] These examples bring out the distinction between the narrower notion of what happens contrary to one's specific intention and a wider notion of what happens contrary to one's wishes or valuations. We express that wider notion in the case of actions by saying that someone acted unwillingly or against his or her will, and in the case of things that happen to one that they happened against one's will. Regret is the mark of such actions and happenings; we regret what happens against our will, and in the case of action we regret having to do whatever it is, and do it regretfully. Typically this wider notion coincides with our intentions; hence typically we regret actions and happenings which are contrary to our intentions. But the examples above are cases where there is a split between our intentions and our wider wishes or evaluations; and when that occurs, actions and happenings contrary to intention need not be regretted.

Since the distinction between the non-voluntary and the involuntary thus proves to differentiate two kinds of things which happen by compulsion and two kinds of things which happen through error, Aristotle's original classification (1093ᵇ35–1110ᵃ4) of what comes about by force and what comes about through error as species of the involuntary requires modification. Those two species divide, not the involuntary, but the non-voluntary. Within each of those species the involuntary is a sub-species, consisting of those non-voluntary happenings which are regretted. (See diagram.)

[12] Kenny's example (1979: 29) of someone pleased at being carried by strong winds to the port of his choice describes a different case, that of something which happens according to the agent's intention, but not because the agent intended it. (Cf. being given a book which one intended to buy.) The cases are similar in that in each case (a) the factor determining the outcome is external force and (b) the agent is pleased by (or does not regret) the outcome, but dissimilar in that in the first case the outcome is contrary to the agent's intention, in the second in accordance with it. (Kenny's case is the analogue (substituting force for ignorance) of the one envisaged in n. 9 above.)

Hursthouse (1984: 256) produces an intermediate case in which, wanting to flee from a battle, but intending to stick to one's post (because one fears punishment), one is pleased to be forcibly removed from the field. Here, as in Kenny's case, one is forced to go where one antecedently wanted to go, but, as in my case, one's going there is contrary to one's intention.

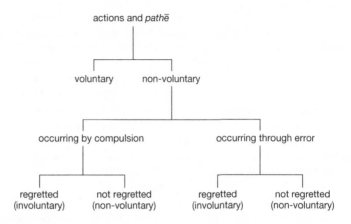

1110ᵇ24–7 Whereas the previous distinction falls within the class of things which happen through error, Aristotle now distinguishes acting through error from acting in error. Someone who acts in error while angry or drunk acts through or from anger or drunkenness, and hence not *through* error but *in* error. The ground of the distinction is causal; while error is a feature of what the agent does (the nature of the error is not specified at this point), the cause of the action is identified not as the error, but as the state of anger or drunkenness.

I assume that the error in question (a) is itself caused by anger or drunkenness and (b) is itself part of the explanation of the action. That is to say, Aristotle has in mind cases such as that of someone who commits some assault or damage while so drunk, or in such a furious rage, that he does not know what he is doing. On these assumptions there is an immediate problem of differentiating acting in error from acting through error. For presumably in every case of error the agent's state of error has some cause or other. If in cases where one's error stems from anger or drunkenness the action is attributable to those causes, *and not to the error itself,* will it not follow that one's action is *never* attributable to error, but always to the cause of the error? To avoid that conclusion, we must take it that Aristotle is assuming a distinction between cases where error can be attributed to some aspect of the agent's character, such as a failure to moderate one's temper or one's appetite for drink, and cases where such an attribution is not possible. That suggestion leaves the status of dispositions such as carelessness and negligence unclear (see below).

It is so far unclear what the point of the distinction is, and specifically how it relates to the voluntary/involuntary distinction, and thereby to liability for praise and blame. One possibility (to be explored below) is that Aristotle is moving to the position that voluntariness (and therefore liability to praise or blame) attaches to actions done in error, but not to those done through error.

1110^{b}28–1111^{a}2 'Now every ... acts involuntarily'. That certainly seems to be the point made in these lines, where Aristotle contrasts error about what it is right to do, which makes one a wicked person, from error about the particular circumstances of one's action, which can excuse one from blame. He is explicit that acts springing from the former type of error are not involuntary (^{b}31–2) and that they are blameworthy (^{b}33). It is unclear how these lines connect with those immediately preceding. One can see how anger or drunkenness might itself lead to this kind of error; drunkenness might make one think that it is a good idea to beat up someone whom one encounters in the street, or anger against the world might lead one to think that one is justified in doing so. But clearly moral error need not spring from anger or drunkenness, and equally clearly those states might cause other kinds of error, as instanced above. So it does not seem that the function of these lines is simply to elucidate the distinction between acting in error and acting through error which Aristotle has just drawn.

We should rather, I suggest, see Aristotle as moving towards the identification of the class of things which are involuntary through error by distinguishing that class from a number of others with which it might be confused. First (^{b}18–24), we have the class of things happening through error but not regretted, which are neither voluntary nor involuntary. Then (^{b}24–7), we have the class of things done not through error but in error. Their status with regard to the voluntary/involuntary distinction is left unclarified for the present. Finally (^{b}28–33), we have things done through error about what it is right to do, which are voluntary. Only when these have been distinguished is Aristotle able to identify the scope of the kind of error through which actions are involuntary, viz. error about the particular circumstances of the action (^{b}33–1111^{a}2).

ᵇ31–3: 'Error in one's choice'; one's choice (*prohairesis*) of action expresses one's reason for doing it, and therefore embodies a description of the action as being the right thing to do *qua* a certain type of thing (e.g. 'Massacring the children of one's enemy is the right thing for a warrior to do'). Where one's choice rests on a false evaluative belief, as in the example, one is guilty of error in one's choice.

'nor is universal error': not a further kind of error, but a further specification of error in one's choice, which is error about what *kind* of thing it is right to do, and therefore expressed in a universal proposition. That we have two specifications of one type of error rather than specifications of two distinct types is indicated by the singular 'this' in ᵇ33, which must refer both to error in one's choice and to universal error. So Aspasius, followed by Stewart.

ᵇ33–1111ᵃ1: 'in which and about which'. The precise distinction intended here is obscure, as it is in 1111ᵃ4, 'to do with what and in what circumstances'. Irwin renders 'which the action consists in and is concerned with', Rowe 'where action is located and what action is about', Crisp 'the circumstances of the action and what it is concerned with'. It is possible that no distinction is intended, the repetition being merely for stylistic effect; see note on 'is essentially related to and has to do with', 1104ᵇ18–21.

1111ᵃ3–6 Schematic specification of possible objects of error; agent, nature of action, surrounding circumstances, means, aim, and manner.

1111ᵃ6–15 Examples of the above types of error. Some come from literature, some from real life, and some from the kind of discussion of imaginary cases found in rhetorical training manuals, of which we have examples in the *Tetralogies* of the rhetorician Antiphon.

ᵃ6–7:   agent. None; Aristotle asserts that it is impossible (unless one is mad) to be in error about who one is. This is problematic; it seems that he has to count amnesia (including loss of memory of one's identity) as a sort of madness. Further, he overlooks cases such as Oedipus's ignorance that he was the son of Laius. Perhaps what he has in mind is the thesis that it is impossible to be aware that someone is doing something, but mistaken about whether the person doing it is oneself or someone else. While such mistakes do seem symptomatic of confused states of mind, they are not impossible; thus a semi-conscious accident victim may be dimly aware that someone is calling for help, but unaware that the person calling is him or herself.

^a8–13:   six examples, which apparently exemplify error about the nature of the action, surrounding circumstances and means. It is not entirely clear how the examples are distributed among the kinds of error (see below).

Six examples:

(i) Letting something slip out when one is talking (alternatively, as suggested by Stewart and Burnet, following Heliodorus, getting confused and hence saying something one didn't mean to say).

(ii) Not knowing that what one is saying is something not to be revealed.

(iii) Letting off a catapult while demonstrating it.

(iv) Mistaking one's son for an enemy (and killing him in consequence).

(v) Thinking that a sharpened spear has a button on the end (and hence killing someone in a fencing bout).

(vi) Thinking that a stone is a piece of pumice (and hence throwing it at someone and killing them).

These examples are of different types. (i) is a case of doing something (in this case blurting something out) without thinking; the error consists in not making use of relevant dispositional knowledge, e.g. that one shouldn't ask people how their ex-partner is getting on with his or her new lover. (Alternatively, it is a case of getting confused and saying one thing when you meant to say something else.) (ii) seems to depend on straightforward ignorance of fact; in the example the poet Aeschylus defended himself against the accusation of revealing the sacred mysteries of Eleusis by maintaining that, since he had not himself been initiated into the mysteries, he did not know that the things he was talking about were in fact secret. (iii) might cover one or other different errors; one might mistake the firing mechanism of the catapult for the safety catch, or one might intend just to point to the firing mechanism, but inadvertently touch it, thus letting the catapult off. In the first case one made a mistake, in the second one was insufficiently attentive to what one was doing. (iv)–(vi) are all cases in which false belief results in one's doing something unintentionally. It is indeterminate without further description how far the false beliefs themselves presuppose inattention. On the one hand, it is hard to see how someone who was paying the slightest attention to what they were doing could mistake a stone for a piece of pumice. On the other hand, in the circumstances it may have been only too easy (or even inevitable) to take one's son for an enemy.

Since Aristotle next goes on to a case of error about one's aim (see below), if he follows the order in which the types of error were listed above, the six examples above should include error 'about which' and error 'in which' (listed above without differentiation as 'surrounding circumstances'), and error about means, as well as error concerning the nature of the action. Examples (v) and (vi) are perhaps to be taken as concerned with means: respectively fencing *with* sharpened weapons and hitting someone *with* a stone. I am unable to suggest how the other four examples are supposed to be distributed among the other three kinds of error.

^a12:   Merope is a character in another lost play of Euripides. In the play she does not actually kill her son, whose identity is discovered at the last moment.

^a13–14:   (aim). Aiming to cure someone, one mistakenly gives them poison.

Note that the error is not error about what one's aim is, but about how that aim is to be achieved. This is another simple case of unintentional action stemming from false belief. Aristotle does not discuss whether it is possible to be in error about what one's aim is, as in cases of self-deception.

^a14–15:   (manner). Trying to touch someone lightly in sparring one hits them harder than one meant to.

Here the defect seems to consist in having insufficiently precise control over one's actions; cf. the second type of error involving the catapult mentioned above.

It is clear from the above that 'error' applies at least to not stopping to think, to ignorance of fact, to false belief, and to failure to exercise sufficient control over one's actions. Anyone who acts through error in any of these ways does so involuntarily (1111^a2, 15–16). Pity and excuse apply to them (1111^a1–2). It is yet to be determined whether this is to be understood as asserting that in every instance the agent is to be excused and/or pitied, or merely that instances of these kinds provide grounds for excuse and/or pity. If the former, then Aristotle seems to leave no room for culpable negligence; if the latter, then it may appear that blame applies after all to some instances of the involuntary. But see further on 1113ᵇ30–2 and on 1114ᵃ1–3.

1111ᵃ15–21   Summary of conclusions.

ᵃ18: 'the circumstances of the action': lit. 'in which the action [sc. is done]'. Aristotle appears to include in the application of this expression the nature of the action itself, since he does not mention it separately. This may signal his consciousness of the lack of any clear line of demarcation between the description of an action and the specification of the circumstances in which that action is performed.

ᵃ19–21:   on regret see above on 1110ᵇ18–24.

1111ᵃ22–4   Things that happen involuntarily having been defined as things that happen either by force or through error, the voluntary is defined as the negation of the involuntary. Hence voluntary actions are those which happen neither by force (i.e. their origin is not external, hence is internal to the agent) nor through error (i.e. the agent is not in error about the particular circumstances of the action). In fact, as pointed out in the note on 1110ᵇ 18–24 (end), the voluntary is the negation, not of the involuntary, but of the non-voluntary.

1111ᵃ24–ᵇ3   The suggestion that actions motivated either by spirit (see note on 1105ᵃ7–8) or by bodily desire (the primary sense of *epithumia*, but see below) are involuntary presupposes a tri-partite psychology similar to that of Plato's *Republic*, in which spirit and bodily appetite are the distinctive motivations of the non-rational parts of the soul, which are distinct from the intellect. (Aristotle does not himself accept this psychology; in I. 13 he distinguishes the intellect from a unitary aspect of the personality which he calls 'the appetitive and in general the desiderative', which includes both spirit and bodily appetite.) The suggestion (which is foreign to Plato himself) that in general actions done from appetite or from spirit are involuntary rests on the assumption that those motivations are forces external to the agent him or herself, who is implicitly identified with the intellect. Aristotle resists that picture, insisting that spirit and appetite belong no less to the agent than intellect does.

This section has some overlap with 1110^{b}9–15; see below.

^{a}25–6:   Aristotle assumes (a) that animals and children are motivated by either appetite or spirit and by nothing else and (b) that both animals and children act voluntarily. Both assumptions are questionable.

^{a}27–9:   Cf. 1110^{b}14–15.

^{a}29–31:   Though the primary application of *epithumia* is to bodily-based desires, especially those for food, drink, and sex, the noun and its cognates can be used, as here, in the general sense of 'want'. Since the opponent plainly uses the term in its restricted application in asserting the thesis, this particular response is an *ignoratio elenchi*.

^{a}32–3:   Cf. 1110^{b}11–13.

^{a}33–4:   Aristotle points out that the error which makes an action involuntary may arise from failure in calculation, as much as from spirit (or, he might have added, from appetite). This discussion does, indeed, imply recognition of the fact that cognitive failure may have motivational causes, as when desire of one kind or another leads one to overlook relevant circumstances (e.g. thirst might cause me not to notice that the water is contaminated). On the other hand, involuntary action may arise from error whose causation is squarely in the area of the intellect.

^{b}1–3:   This is Aristotle's principal argument against the suggestion.

BOOK THREE

CHAPTER 2

The topic of this chapter is choice, and that of the following chapter the connected concept of deliberation. Aristotle's conception of what choice is develops by stages over these two chapters.

His first step ($1111^{b}6-8$) is to identify it as a sub-type of the voluntary, which, given the account of the voluntary in the preceding chapter as a kind of actions and *pathē*, suggests that he is using the word as a collective noun designating a kind of actions (having the same extension as *to prohaireton*, 'that which is chosen'). He then proceeds in the rest of the chapter ($1111^{b}11-1112^{a}13$) to distinguish choice from a number of mental acts or states, before returning at the end ($1112^{a}13-17$) to his initial identification of it as a sub-type of the voluntary, specifically that which results from deliberation.

Deliberation is therefore the topic of the next chapter. Aristotle concludes that chapter by reverting to the topic of choice and its object, *to prohaireton* ($1113^{a}2-14$), culminating in the definition of choice as 'deliberative desire of the things which are up to us' ($^{a}10-11$; see below). Taking these two chapters together, then, his considered position is that the designation *to prohaireton* picks out a subclass of voluntary actions, viz. those which issue from choice resulting from deliberation, and that choice itself is the desire, resulting from deliberation, to act.

$1111^{b}5-6$ The reason that choice is a better discriminator of types of character than actions is that, as explained at $1105^{a}28-33$, one might act in a way characteristic of a particular virtue without thereby manifesting that virtue, if one's action did not issue from the appropriate choice. The same point holds for vice. See discussion of $1105^{a}30-3$ above.

$1111^{b}8-9$ Cf. $^{a}25-6$. The reason why children and non-human animals do not act from choice is that they do not act from deliberation; their actions are directed not towards the general (and relatively remote) goals assumed in deliberation, but towards the immediate goals presented by spirit and appetite. See further below.

$1111^{b}9-10$ On the thesis that actions done in unforeseen situations, in which there is no time for deliberation, are voluntary but not done from choice, see discussion of $1117^{a}9-22$.

$1111^{b}12-30$ Choice is distinguished in turn from each of the three kinds of *orexis* (see note on $1113^{a}9-12$): (a) *epithumia*, (b) spirit (treated together at $^{b}12-19$), (c) wish ($^{b}19-30$).

1111^b12–19:   Choice is distinguished from (a) *epithumia* (see on ^a29–31) and (b) spirit:

1. ^b12–13: Non-rational creatures are motivated by appetite and spirit, not by choice. This repeats ^a25–6.

2. ^b13–16: Cases where desire is in conflict with the agent's better judgement show choice to be distinct from desire.

The argument has two stages:

(i) In cases of conflict, the person who acts against his or her better judgement (i.e. the *akratēs*, rendered, in accordance with the basic meaning of the Greek term 'uncontrolled') acts in accordance with his or her desire, not in accordance with choice, while the person who abides by his or her better judgement (i.e. the *enkratēs*, or self-controlled person) acts in accordance with choice, not in accordance with desire.

(NB: The Greek literally construed reads: 'the *akratēs* acts desiring but not choosing, the *enkratēs* on the contrary choosing but not desiring'. This cannot of course mean that the former does not make a choice (since *akrasia* is action against one's choice (1148^a9), nor that the latter does not have any desire (since the *enkratēs* 'knowing that the desires are bad does not follow them because of his reason' (1145^b13–14). The sense of 'desiring but not choosing' is 'from desire, not from choice', and similarly for 'choosing but not desiring'.)

(ii) In cases of conflict, what opposes desire is not another desire, but choice. (This is presumably intended to rule out the suggestion that the *akratēs* and the *enkratēs* merely face a conflict between desires, not a conflict between desire and something distinct from desire, i.e. choice.)

It is clear that cases of conflict between long-term goals on the one hand and desires for immediate satisfaction on the other are not adequately characterized as conflicts between one desire and another. On the other hand, such conflicts clearly can occur, e.g. when the desire to remain comfortably in bed conflicts with the desire for a beer from the fridge. It is not clear whether Aristotle intends to deny the possibility of such conflict, or whether his point is merely that *akrasia* and *enkrateia* presuppose the other kind. The weaker point suffices for his overall argument.

3. ^b16–18: The internal object of desire is pleasure and the avoidance of what is unpleasant, but those are not the internal

object of choice. Aristotle is just going on to explain that the internal object of choice is the good (1112ᵃ7–8).

Heliodorus's paraphrase reads: 'desire is distressing and always has pleasure corresponding to it, but choice is neither distressing nor has pleasure corresponding to it'. This suggests that his text of Aristotle read '*hē men epithumia hēdeos kai lupēra, hē proairesis d' oute lupēra outh' hēdeos*' (*lupēra* replacing the OCT's *lupērou* in both places), i.e. 'desire is for what is pleasant and is distressing, but choice is neither distressing nor for the pleasant'. Since Aristotle says at 1119ᵃ4 that desire is accompanied by distress (*meta lupēs ... hē epithumia*), it is possible that that reading is correct. Both the main manuscripts of Aspasius read *epilupos*, supporting Heliodorus's reading: the reading *epilupou*, which Heylbut adopts in his text of Aspasius, is that of a corrector in one manuscript.

Aristotle has said at 1110ᵇ11 that whatever we do we do for the sake of the fine or the pleasant (see note on that passage). He is not, therefore, denying here that pleasure is an intrinsic good, but simply distinguishing the concept of pleasure from that of the good. *Epithumia* is the desire for food, drink, and sex because they are seen as pleasant; the question of how far these objects of desire are good requires the exercise in deliberation of further considerations than that they are pleasant, considerations which will involve the fine, in that the agent will have to consider the appropriate enjoyment of those objects.

4. ᵇ18–19: Choice is not spirit, since things done from spirit are least of all done from choice.

This claim is at odds with the discussion of *akrasia thumou* (i.e. acting against one's better judgement through giving in to spirit) in VII. 6. There the point is that since spirited reactions such as anger and indignation involve an element of evaluation, to the effect that one is being treated in inappropriate ways which one ought to resist, they are in accordance with reason in a way which bodily-based appetites are not (1149ᵃ32–ᵇ3). One would therefore expect Aristotle to say that things done from spirit contain more of an element of choice than things done from appetite, not less, as he implies here.

1111ᵇ19–30:   Choice is distinguished from wish. Choice is restricted to actions which the agent believes that he or she can do, whereas we can wish for things (known to be) outside our control, including the impossible.

ᵇ26–9: Aristotle contrasts our wish for ultimate ends such as health and happiness with our choice of what contributes to those ends. The latter include but are not restricted to instrumental means, since they also include things constitutive of ultimate ends: e.g. one might think that happiness (i.e. the achievement of a fully worthwhile life) consists in a life of philosophical contemplation, or in the conquest of the world, and hence choose to become a philosopher, or a conqueror. (Since choices are for objects at different levels of specificity, non-specific choices such as those just mentioned will require further more specific choices, such as the choice of a course of study, and so on down to decisions of what to do here and now.)

1111ᵇ30–1112ᵃ13 Choice is distinguished from belief.

1. ᵇ30–3: Choice is restricted to choice of things believed to be in our control, whereas belief is totally unrestricted in its subject-matter.
2. ᵇ33–4: Choice is evaluated as good or bad, belief as true or false.
3. 1112ᵃ1–3: Character is determined by good or bad choices, not by beliefs.
4. ᵃ3–5: We choose to do or avoid things, but have beliefs about what is the case (including what is to be chosen or avoided).
5. ᵃ5–7: Choice is praised for being of the right thing, belief for being true.
6. ᵃ7–8: Choice assumes knowledge that what is chosen is good, whereas we may believe what we do not know (to be true).
7. ᵃ8–11: People can choose to do things which they do not believe it best to do.

These arguments may be summed up as making the point that whereas belief is an assessment of how things are, choice has the practical function of determining how things are to be. Hence they have, in modern jargon, opposite directions of fit. The rational person seeks to accommodate his or her beliefs to how the world is, i.e. to maximize true and minimize false beliefs, but to change the world in conformity to his or her choices. Of course, choice must be guided by beliefs, since the range of possibilities open for choice is determined by how things are. But that in no way weakens the basic point.

1112^{a}13–17   Choice is identified as follows: action from choice is voluntary action issuing from deliberation.

^{a}15–16:   The argument is presumably: choice is accompanied by reasoning and thought (but reasoning and thought about how to act is deliberation), so choice is what has been deliberated. The supplied premiss presupposes the account of deliberation which follows in the next chapter.

^{a}16–17:   The word *prohairesis* is compounded from *hairesis*, 'choice', and the preposition *pro*, which, like the English 'before', may mean 'temporally prior to' or 'in preference to'. While the sense of the compounded noun is 'preferential choice', Aristotle plays on the ambiguity of the preposition to support his account of preferential choice as choice resulting from prior deliberation.

BOOK THREE

CHAPTER 3

On the connection of this chapter with the preceding one, see the introductory note to chapter 2.

1112^{a}18–34   The basic point is that deliberation, being thought undertaken with a view to the direction of action, is not undertaken in respect of subject-matters, where, for various reasons, no action is possible. Aristotle's classification of the types of subject-matter excluded from the scope of deliberation is for the most part self-explanatory.

^{a}21:   '[T]hings that are eternally so' include both timeless truths, such as mathematical truths, exemplified by the incommensurability of the diagonal and side of a square, and eternal truths, exemplified (in Aristotle's view) by the basic truths about the nature of the cosmos, which remain true for all time.

^{a}26–7:   The reason that there is no deliberating about droughts and rains is not that (like the movements of the heavenly bodies) they happen according to inevitable regularity, but that, though irregular, we cannot affect whether or not they happen. (Presumably Aristotle does not rule out deliberation about what to do in the event of drought or rain.)

^a28–9:   The Scythians, who lived in what is now southern Russia, including the Crimea, are an example of a people too remote to be affected by deliberation on the part of Greeks.

1112^b7 'more about the practical crafts than about the sciences': Aspasius mentions an alternative text (found in some manuscripts of Aristotle) which reads 'more about opinions than about the sciences'. See Barnes (1999: 42–3).

1112^b8–9 'for the most part': see note on 1103^b34–1104^a5. Deliberation presupposes some degree of uncertainty in the outcome combined with a sufficient degree of regularity in the subject-matter to allow of sensible planning.

1112^b11–16 Deliberation is directed towards the achievement of an aim which must be assumed in advance. The selection of the aim to be achieved cannot be part of the procedure of deliberation itself.

Aristotle's point is restricted to the conceptual point enunciated above. He says nothing about how one is to select the aim towards the achievement of which one's deliberation is directed. Consequently he does not exclude the possibility that the selection of the aim is, either wholly or in part, the work of the intellect. He does not even exclude the possibility that the aim assumed in deliberation at one level may be determined by deliberation at another level. Thus his claim that medical deliberation assumes the aim of healing the patient (on which see below) allows that the adoption of that aim may itself be the result of deliberation on whether to become a doctor (thereby adopting healing as the aim of one's practice) or whether to follow some other career. Higher-level deliberation (a) must be distinguished from lower-level, (b) must itself assume some given end, e.g. happiness (cf. 1111^b26–9, with note). Since deliberation cannot go on *ad infinitum* (1113^a2), every piece of deliberation, or every chain of such pieces, must begin from the assumption of some end which has not been selected by prior deliberation.

^b13: It might be objected that a doctor might well deliberate whether to cure the patient; he or she might, for instance, have been offered a bribe to poison the patient and deliberate whether it is best to do so, or to cure him or her. In that scenario we have a conflict between the aim assumed as internal to the practice of medicine and the external aim of enriching oneself. Aristotle's claim is that the practice of medicine assumes the healing of the patient as its internal aim, to the achievement of which medical deliberation (as distinct from other kinds of deliberation, such as the deliberation of the self-interested money-maker) is directed.

It may reasonably be objected that curing the patient is too narrow a conception of the internal aim of medical practice; modern medicine extends the notion of curing to that of improving the quality of life as far as possible, and counts consideration of whether to extend the life of the patient or to let nature take its course as legitimate objects of medical deliberation. While that requires a modification of Aristotle's specific conception of the internal aim of medical deliberation, it does not conflict with his central claim that what we may call technical or departmental deliberation presupposes some aim internal to the practice, an aim which is not selected by that departmental deliberation itself.

1112^b20–4 Aristotle compares the process of deliberation to that of geometrical analysis, in which the problem of how to construct a given figure is solved by working out that the desired figure can be constructed given the construction of a simpler figure, and that in turn given the construction of a simpler one, and so on until one reaches a figure which one knows how to construct.

1112^b28 'their origin is in us': cf. 1110^a15–17, 1111^a22–4.

1112^b30–1 'we seek a means . . . come about'. The Greek is *hote men di' hou ote de pōs ē dia tinos*, lit. 'sometimes by means of which (relative pronoun), sometimes how or by means of what/whom (interrogative pronoun)'. If, with all other translators, we render *dia tinos* as 'by means of what', it is obscure how 'by means of what' differs from 'by means of which'. Irwin and Crisp read the phrase as distinguishing the means (*di' hou*) from both the use of that means (*pōs*) and the means *to that use* (*dia tinos*); that reading requires a great deal to be supplied by the reader. I tentatively suggest reading *dia* *tinos* as 'through whose agency', assuming that Aristotle still has in mind the case of doing something through someone else's agency, mentioned at ^a27–8. (Aquinas's 'for the sake of what' (*propter quid*) is not a possible rendering of the Greek.)

1112^b33 'one's actions are for the sake of other things'. Aristotle has asserted at the opening of Book I that some activities (*energeiai*) have no end beyond their own exercise (1094^a3–5), and in VI. 5 he distinguishes action (*praxis*) from production (*poiēsis*) by claiming that the latter is directed towards the creation of an end distinct from itself, whereas the former has no end apart from its own excellent performance (1140^b6–7). In order to preserve the consistency of those passages with the present one, we must interpret Aristotle here as claiming that even actions done for their own sake are also done for the sake of something else, viz. happiness (cf. 1097^b2–5).

1112^b33–1113^a2 Neither one's ultimate aim nor the nature of the particular things with which one's action is concerned falls within the scope of deliberation. Hence the chain of deliberation has both a beginning and an end, and so does not go on for ever.

1113^a2–4 One deliberates about whether to Φ or not, and as a result of that deliberation one chooses to Φ (or not to Φ).

1113^a6 'the controlling element in himself': i.e. the practical intellect.

1113^a9–12 'Since the object ... with our deliberation'. Aristotle's picture of deliberation is that it is a process of thought by which our desire for an end is transmitted through a series of steps specifying the things conducive to that end to an instance of an action-type to be performed here and now. Thus I want a drink, conceive of a beer as a satisfying drink, want a beer, believe that to get a beer I must fetch one from the fridge, want to fetch a beer from the fridge, believe that to drink the beer I must open the can, and finally want (i.e. choose) to open the can.

   It is striking that Aristotle identifies choice with the final desire itself, not with some act (of the will, or of the mind) resulting from that desire. We might object that choice (or decision, which seems to be an equivalent concept) is an act performed at a particular moment in time, whereas desire is a state of mind which lasts for a time, but does not occur at any particular time. On the other hand, one may have chosen or decided to do something, without its being the case that there was some particular time at which one made that choice. That is to say, one may have passed from a state of not being decided whether or not to Φ into a state in which one is decided to Φ (or not to Φ), without that transition's having taken place at any particular moment. For Aristotle, having chosen is being in the state of having focused one's desire on an instance of an available action-type; if he were to speak of an act of choice, it would presumably be the act of focusing one's desire on such an instance, i.e. the act of *coming to desire* to Φ. But he does not speak of any such act, perhaps because he is aware that coming to be in such a state need not have occurred at any particular moment.

'[D]esire' renders *orexis*, which is Aristotle's generic term for wanting, its species being *boulēsis* (rational wish, *An.* 432^{b}5), *thumos* (cf. note on 1105^{a}7–8), and *epithumia* (cf. note on 1105^{b}20–3); cf. *MM* 1187^{b}37; *An.* 414^{b}2. See note on 1111^{b}12–30.

^{a}12 'in accordance with our deliberation': the Greek (which is that of the OCT) is *kata tēn bouleusin*. Gauthier/Jolif and Irwin adopt the alternative reading of some manuscripts, *kata tēn boulēsin*, 'in accordance with our wish', which is also possible, but loses the point that our final desire is shaped by our deliberation (see preceding note). The variant readings were known to Aspasius.
On deliberation see McDowell (1996).   ≤ Mele

BOOK THREE

CHAPTER 4

1113^{a}15 'We have said …': at 1111^{b}26. That assertion raises the problem of whether each person wishes for what is really good, or rather for what seems to him or her to be good.

1113^{a}17–22 Aristotle sets up an *aporia* (see note on 1110^{a}4–8) by raising an objection to both views. On the first, someone who

wishes for X in the mistaken belief that X is good, and is successful in getting X, does not get what he or she wished for, which
is paradoxical. On the second, there is nothing which is really,
or 'as such', what people wish for; one person wishes for one
thing, another for another. (It is not obvious why that counts as an
objection; at least it does not seem that the proponent of this view
should see it as such. By contrast, the proponent of the first view
must see the consequence as at least prima facie paradoxical.)

   The actual solution to the problem, such as it is, is provided by
the distinction between descriptions true of the things people wish
for, and the descriptions under which people wish for those things,
which may or may not be true of them. (Using Santas's terminology (1964), the description under which something is wished
for indentifies the intended object of the wish, while descriptions
true of that object specify the actual object of the wish. Thus I
may wish to marry an heiress, and hence wish to marry Jane in
the belief that she is an heiress, though she is in fact (unknown
to me) a pauper. In that case my being married to an heiress is
the intended object of my wish, my being married to Jane, and
being married to a pauper, the actual object.) The sense in which
the object of a wish is what is really good is that whatever we
wish for we wish for in the belief that it is really good, not in the
belief that it merely seems to be good. Hence if what we wish for
turns out, when we get it, not to be really good, there is a sense
in which we did get what we wished for (in that we wished for X,
and got X) and a sense in which we did not get what we wished
for (in that we wished for something really good, but did not get
something really good). The sense in which the object of a wish
is what seems good, rather than what is really good, is that the
only description true of all objects of wishing is 'seems good to
the person wishing it'. So the answer to the question 'Is the object
of a wish what is really good, or what seems good?' is 'In one
sense, that of the description under which the object is desired, the
object of wishing is what is really good. In another sense, that of
a description true of all objects of wish, the object of wish is what
seems good.' Both conflicting views are thus correct in a sense.

1113ª22–33 Aristotle's own solution also seeks (in accordance
with his usual practice) to show that each of the conflicting views is
correct in a sense. It relies on the distinction between a predicate's

applying without qualification (*haplōs*) and applying subject to a qualification (see note on 1110^a9-11). The predicate '... is the object of wish' applies without qualification to what is really good, but subject to the qualification 'for each person' to the apparent good. I.e. both the following propositions are true: 'What is really good is (without qualification) the object of wish' and 'What is the apparent good for each person is the object of wish for that person'.

$^a25-33$:   Aristotle's solution relies on the principle that, for many predicates, something is really or unqualifiedly F iff it appears F to an observer who occupies a position of special authority. The most obvious examples are secondary qualities such as tastes and colours, and in those cases the authoritative observer is the observer whose sensory receptive apparatus is (a) in correct working order and (b) employed in standard conditions. Thus we say that honey really is sweet, understanding by that that it tastes sweet to someone whose tastebuds are functioning properly and who uses them to taste honey in normal conditions (including the condition that the honey has not been adulterated so as to alter its taste). Again, the real colour of something is the colour it looks to have to a standard observer (excluding e.g. colour-blind people) in standard conditions (typically normal daylight). We should observe first that in these cases the standard observer is identified by the possession of properly functioning senses (raising problems of how such functioning is identified, which cannot be pursued here), and secondly that we normally regard the way things seem to the standard observer as constitutive of how they really are, rather than as a reliable guide to how they really are independent of the observer's judgement. E.g. we think that being really sweet just is tasting sweet to the normal person in normal conditions, not that sweetness is an intrinsic feature of certain things which normal people in normal conditions are good at detecting.

While Aristotle standardly (as here) uses secondary qualities as illustrative examples of the principle, he extends it (as here) to other predicates, including 'healthy', 'pleasant', and 'good' (cf. 1099^a21-4, 1166^a10-13, 1173^b22-5, 1176^a15-24). The importance of the principle lies in its application to this range of evaluative predicates, in that it offers a defence against Protagorean relativism. Thus the claim that the virtuous life is really the pleasantest life can meet the challenge of wicked or perverse pleasures by appeal to the principle that the good person (*spoudaios*) is authoritative, and that to that person virtue is pleasant and vice unpleasant. Hence virtue is really, i.e. unqualifiedly, pleasant, whereas vice is pleasant only to the vicious person.

In its extension to these cases it is unclear whether Aristotle regards the judgement of the *spoudaios* as constitutive of what is really the case (as in our normal construal of the secondary quality cases), or whether the *spoudaios* is rather a reliable guide to the way things are in themselves. On the most literal reading of ᵃ26–8 Aristotle says that things which are really healthy are healthy for those in good condition, but other things (i.e. things which are not really healthy) are healthy for those who are sick. Strictly that implies that things which are in themselves healthy preserve the health of those people who are already healthy, while things which are not in themselves healthy help to restore the health of the sick. But that leaves it obscure what it is for something to be in itself healthy. We have a much more plausible claim if we take Aristotle to be saying that what it is for something such as a diet to be healthy without qualification is for it to promote the health of those in good condition, whereas medication, etc. are not healthy as such, but healthy in so far as they restore sick people to health. But while that is certainly more plausible, it is not clear that it is what Aristotle is actually saying.

ᵃ29–33 is similarly inconclusive. The statements that 'in each thing the truth appears [to the good person]' (ᵃ30–1) and that the good person sees the truth in each (ᵃ31–2) strongly suggest that the good person is a reliable guide to what is there independently, but 'being as it were the standard and measure of them' (ᵃ33) points the other way. Literally, a standard (*kanōn*) and a measure (*metron*) is a measuring-stick, which we might take as another indication that the judgement of the *spoudaios* reports what is there independently, as a ruler measures the objective length of what it is laid against. But it is hard not to read this expression as a conscious response to the Protagorean claim that 'Man is the measure of all things', which certainly expresses the thesis that the way things are is constituted by the judgement of each individual.

If that is so, Aristotle is here saying that the reality of each kind of thing is constituted, not by the way it seems to each individual, but by the way it seems to the authoritative *spoudaios*. At least we have to acknowledge that the text is not decisive between the alternative construals.[13]

The identification of the authoritative judge as the *spoudaios* is also problematic. In general the word functions as a synonym for *agathos*, 'good', and is regularly used in *NE* to designate the person who is good through possessing the virtues of character and intellect. In the context of judgements about what is sweet, hot, etc., the *spoudaios* is the person in good condition with respect to the perception of those qualities, who is thereby properly equipped to be authoritative on whether things have those properties. But when it comes to judgements of what is really pleasant, or really good, the application of the term slides insensibly from 'the person best equipped to judge what is pleasant, or what is good' to 'the good person as characterized by Aristotle's evaluative theory'. The claim that it is the virtuous person by Aristotelian standards who is authoritative on what is good or pleasant is itself a substantive evaluative thesis, which requires more support than it receives from the analogy with the standard observer of secondary qualities.

In the present case, Aristotle applies his principle to yield the result that what is really good is what is wished for without qualification, in so far as it is what is wished for by the good person, whereas what seems good is what is wished for by anyone who wishes. This solution to the original *aporia* identifies what is really good as the actual object of a particular authoritative wish, whereas the solution which I suggested at the outset identifies it as the intended object of everyone's wish. The two solutions are compatible with one another.

1113ᵃ34-ᵇ1 The assertion that pleasure appears good but is not is clearly restricted to the pleasures of the non-virtuous person. The things that appear good to the virtuous person, including that person's pleasures, really are so (see above).

---

[13] Charles (1995: 156-8) argues for the view that the good person reliably perceives what is good in reality.

BOOK THREE

CHAPTER 5

1113^{b}3-4 'Since the end ... choose'. This repeats 1111^{b}26-7 and 1112^{b}11-12.

1113^{b}6-7 'So virtue ... as well'. See note on ^{b}11-14 below.

1113^{b}6-11 'where acting ... disgraceful by acting'. This elaborates the claim of 1110^{b}9-15 that we are equally responsible for good and bad actions.

^{b}8:   Saying Yes and No may be given as another example of opposites which are equally up to us, just as acting and not acting are. It is, however, possible that Aristotle is thinking of acting as itself a way of giving an affirmative answer to the question 'Should I Φ?' and not acting as a way of giving a negative answer to that question. Cf. VI. 2, 1139^{a}21-2, 'what assertion and denial are in thought, pursuit and avoidance are in desire', which seems to mean that pursuing some end is itself a way of asserting that the thing is to be pursued (or that it is good) and avoiding something a way of denying that it is to be pursued (or that it is good).

1113^{b}11-14 Since our actions, good and bad alike, are up to us, and since being good consists in doing good actions and being bad in doing bad actions, it follows that being good and being bad are up to us.

If, as the text prima facie suggests, this argument is intended to support the claim of ^{b}6-7 that virtue and vice are up to us, it fails, since Aristotle does not identify virtue and vice with the doing of good and bad actions. We *become* virtuous or vicious *as a result of* doing good or bad actions (1103^{b}12-21), but being virtuous is possessing a stable state of character disposing one to choose good actions for their own sake (1105^{a}30-3, with note), while vice is similarly a *hexis* (1103^{b}21-3). Hence either Aristotle's inference here is unsound, since its second premiss is false, or he is using the terms 'virtue' and 'vice' loosely, to stand for virtuous and vicious activity respectively.[14]

---

[14] Ackrill (1978a) favours the former alternative, Meyer (1993: 129-32) the latter. Ott (2000) maintains that this argument is not intended to support the thesis of

1113ᵇ14–15 'Saying ... blessed'. According to Anon., Aristotle is here adapting a line from the fifth-century comic poet Epicharmus (see Gauthier/Jolif's note). '[B]lessed' renders *makarios*, a term designating the highest degree of felicity, characteristic of the life of the gods. The thesis that no one attains blessedness involuntarily is a truism, especially in view of the connotation of 'against one's will' which attaches to *akōn*. The thesis that no one is voluntarily wicked (generally regarded, by contrast, as highly paradoxical; see 1145ᵇ25–8), is one of the central ethical theses maintained in various Platonic dialogues; see *Prt.* 345d–e; *Meno* 77–8; *Grg.* 475e, 509e; *Leg.* 860c–863e. In its Platonic version it depends on the premises that no one acts against his or her own interest except through error and that wickedness is against the agent's interest. Aristotle's rejection of the Platonic thesis depends on his account of error set out in chapter 1. The only sort of error in virtue of which actions are involuntary is error about the particular circumstances of the action; hence the kind of error manifested by someone who believes e.g. that it is in his or her interest to rob and murder makes the person's actions wicked, not involuntary (1110ᵇ30–1111ᵃ1).

1113ᵇ16–18 'what has been said': at 1112ᵇ31–2. The thesis that we are the origin (*archē*) of our actions is clearly synonymous with the thesis that the origin is in us (compare ᵇ18 with ᵇ20). The thought is clearly expressed in 1113ᵃ5–7; deliberation is completed when the agent brings the origin of the action back to himself, i.e. to the controlling element in himself (sc. the practical intellect).

Aristotle here supposes someone objecting to his account of our actions as originating from ourselves, with a view to maintaining that none of our actions is voluntary. The thought is clearly that our actions are voluntary iff they originate from us; hence they are involuntary iff their origins are external to us.

the voluntariness of both virtue and vice, but is directed *ad hominem* against Plato's claim (in *Laws* 860–7) that virtue is voluntary and vice involuntary. The crucial claim that being good and bad consist in doing good and bad actions respectively is a Platonic assumption which Aristotle 'exploits ... without endorsing it' (Ott 2000: 106). Against this, it seems that the passage up to ᵇ14 expresses Aristotle's own view; the argument against the asymmetry thesis (vice is involuntary, virtue voluntary) appears to begin at ᵇ14.

While actions done under compulsion are one kind of action whose origin is external to us, the objector is not reviving the thesis rejected at 1110ᵇ9–15 that all action are done under compulsion. Rather he or she should be understood as assuming some general thesis of causal determinism, according to which all events, including our actions, are parts of causal sequences whose origins lie indefinitely far back in time. On that view the origin of a person's action is not that person or anything 'in' that person, but whatever was the origin of the causal chain of which that action was part, whether the agent's genetic constitution, environmental factors in the agent's upbringing, or the original state of the universe and the causal laws governing its subsequent development.

1113ᵇ19–21 In his reply to the imagined objection Aristotle reaffirms the position that our actions have their origin in us, and are thereby voluntary.

It is disputed whether this reply involves denial of the causal determinist thesis assumed by the objector. The crucial question is the interpretation of 'we cannot take our actions back to any other origins than those in us'. Those who see Aristotle as an incompatibilist read these words as denying that our actions have any origins other than those in us.[15] Agents are then literally unmoved movers of actions, originating new chains of events. On the other hand, those who see Aristotle as a compatibilist[16] read the crucial phrase not as denying that our actions have origins other than their origins in us, but as denying that we can 'take our actions back' to those origins. The force of that denial amounts to this: whatever the causal antecedents of an agent's choices, provided that the actions in question do issue from those choices, they are thereby characterized as belonging to the agent and hence as falling with the scope of the agent's responsibility.[17]

1113ᵇ23–5 '[B]y force' has the sense established in ch. 1, i.e. 'under compulsion' (not 'forcibly').

---

[15] This position is maintained tentatively by Hardie (1980: 178) and more definitely by Furley (1977: 53).

[16] E.g. Stewart i. 225–9; Everson (1990); Meyer (1993: ch. 6 and 1998).

[17] Sorabji (1980) maintains the compromise position that the agent's origination of action is held by Aristotle to be incompatible, not with the prior causation of action, but with its prior necessitation. See esp. ch. 14.

'through error for which they are not themselves responsible': here Aristotle shows himself aware of a sort of error for which one is oneself responsible, which he discusses in more detail at ^{b}30–1114^{a}5.

1113^{b}26–30   Cf. Plato, *Prt.* 323c–d. The similarity is sufficiently marked to suggest a conscious reminiscence on Aristotle's part. See also 1114^{a}23–31.

1113^{b}30–2   Aristotle's first case of culpable error is that of error brought about through drunkenness. This description applies to a range of cases characterized at 1110^{b}24–7 as done 'in error' rather than 'through error' (see note on that passage). Aristotle points out that sometimes the penalty is doubled in such cases, explaining that people are punished for the error itself (in addition to the penalty for the action). Suppose that, while too drunk to notice where I am going, I knock over and smash a priceless vase. My being too drunk to notice where I was going is treated as an aggravating circumstance, and I am punished for being in that state in addition to the punishment for the act of damage. The reason I am punished for being in that state is that I got into it through getting drunk, and it was up to me whether or not I got drunk.

At ^{b}20–1 Aristotle has said that those things whose origins are in us are themselves up to us and voluntary. It is clear that he applies this doctrine not only to my getting drunk in the first place but also to my not noticing where I was going and to my smashing the vase; all of these had their origin in me, since it was up to me not to get drunk. Consistently with the discussion in chapter 1, this class of cases involving culpable error is not a class of involuntary acts. (So Alexander *Problem* 9, 129. 25–130. 6 Bruns (Sharples 36–7).)

Here we have a clear divergence between Aristotle's category of the voluntary and our own notion of the intentional. In the case as described I did not smash the vase intentionally (or intend to smash it). Nor need I have got drunk intentionally. I might even have got drunk without noticing that I was getting drunk. Aristotle will insist that I could, and should, have avoided getting drunk. While that is certainly true, and justifies blaming me both for having got drunk and for what I did when I was drunk, it brings out the width of the gap between Aristotle's wide conception of the origin of an action and the modern conception of intentional action.[18]

1113^b33–1114^a1   Error about the content of law is another kind of culpable error. Cf. 1110^b28–32. Here too actions done from this kind of error count as voluntary (1110^b32).

1114^a1–3   A third kind of culpable error is negligence. Cases of negligence raise the question of whether negligent actions are voluntary. On the one hand they seem voluntary by the criterion of 1113^b20–1; just as things done when drunk count as voluntary because their remote origin was in me, since I could have avoided getting drunk, so negligent actions count as voluntary for the same reason, since I could have avoided being negligent. On the other hand, it is clear that many of the cases of error about particulars cited in chapter 1 as causes of involuntariness could arise from negligence (e.g. letting off the catapult or not noticing that the spear was sharp). In order to bring those two discussions into consistency we have to assume that the treatment of particular error in chapter 1 is as a whole subject to the unstated qualification that that kind of error makes actions involuntary only when it is not itself culpable.

Taking the discussion of III. 1–5 as a whole, then, Aristotle is consistent in maintaining that all and only involuntary acts are excusable. Apparent counter-examples were acts done under superhuman pressure, which seemed prima facie to be voluntary but excusable, and the various kinds of acts of culpable negligence, which seemed prima facie to be involuntary but blameworthy. Of these the former turn out to be involuntary (on the assumption that the agent does not act intentionally) and the latter voluntary. That result, however, is squarely inconsistent with V. 8, 1136^a5–9,

---

[18] I therefore agree with Curren (1989: 266) that 'for Aristotle an agent may be responsible for something without having decided to bring it about, or having foreseen its coming about, provided its source and cause is the agent's character through the mediation of the agent's intellect'. I disagree, however, that Aristotle thereby holds people responsible for actions (including negligent actions) which are neither voluntary nor involuntary. The class of things which are neither voluntary nor involuntary is a subclass of thing which happen through error, whereas I have argued above that things done from culpable error, including things done through negligence, belong to the class of things which happen 'in error'. Curren does not discuss 1113^b20–1.

Roberts (1989: 24) seems to me correct in holding that Aristotle takes things done in culpable ignorance to be voluntary.

where Aristotle expressly identifies a kind of involuntary action as inexcusable: viz. actions done in error as a result of an unnatural *pathos*. Since the latter passage belongs to one of the books common to both *NE* and *EE*, generally supposed to have been written in the first instance for the latter, this may be an indication of some shift of view between the two versions of the lectures on ethics.

1114^{a}3–10　The account of negligent actions as voluntary assumes that one could have avoided being negligent in the first place. Aristotle now presents an objection which challenges that assumption. What if I am a naturally negligent person? The objection assumes that if it is just my nature to be negligent, then I can't help being negligent. Aristotle's reply simply rejects that assumption. He insists, in line with his general doctrine of the formation of character (see above), that we become negligent people by behaving negligently, and that behaving negligently or not is up to us.

Aristotle's thesis may be understood in either a stronger or a weaker version. Given the former, he claims that the acquisition of traits of character is determined wholly by the agent's actions; consequently, factors outside the agent's control, such as genetic constitution or environmental factors, play no role. Given the latter, his claim is that while such factors have some effect on the traits of character we acquire, they do not wholly determine it, leaving some scope for the agent to contribute to the formation of character traits. While the stronger claim is incredible, the weaker one fits our ordinary intuition that while people indeed have natural predispositions (whether genetically programmed, or environmentally influenced, or conditioned by both factors) to traits such as aggressiveness or laziness, they typically reinforce those predispositions by their behaviour. Aristotle's modest claim at 1114^{b}21–2 that we are in a way jointly responsible for our states of character suggests that the weaker version represents his view.

1114^{a}12–13　'If someone ... voluntarily': cf. 1113^{b}19–21.

1114^{a}13–21　In this passage Aristotle extends the application of the thesis that effects whose origins are in us are voluntary (1113^{b}19–21) from actions to states. So someone whose illness was brought about by causes internal to him or her is ill voluntarily

(^{a}15–16). Aristotle accepts the implication that in some such cases (not necessarily all) the effect may be irreversible, as it is impossible to get back a stone once one has thrown it (^{a}16–19). The fact that it is now out of my power to determine whether I am ill or well is compatible with its previously having been in my power to determine whether or not I became ill, and the latter is sufficient for its now being true that I am ill voluntarily.

Aristotle is not, then, merely asserting[19] the tautology that if I have done something I cannot make it the case that I have not done it. Nor does he restrict himself to pointing out that if I have voluntarily acquired some state of character, I cannot cease to have it merely by wishing to do so. While he does indeed make that point (^{a}12–14), he goes on (^{a}14–21) to make the stronger point that such voluntary acquisition of states may be irreversible.[20] See concluding paragraphs of note on 1105ᵃ30–3.

1114ᵃ21–31   The further extension of Aristotle's thesis to physical states with internal causes makes it clear that he is committed to the strong thesis that some voluntarily acquired states are irreversible. Blindness is the most obvious example.[21]

This passage too recalls *Prt.* 323d.

1114ᵃ31–ᵇ3   'Now suppose ... as well'. In this section Aristotle considers another version of the theory that our actions are not up to us. The supposition is that our actions are determined by our conception of the good, but we have no control over that conception, which varies from one individual to another as part of each individual's natural constitution. Aristotle uses the premiss that each person's conception of the good is part of that person's individual make-up to reject the claim that we have no control

---

[19] As Irwin maintains (1999*a*: 210).

[20] Bostock's attribution to Aristotle of the yet stronger thesis that voluntary acquisition of vices is always irreversible (2000: 116–17) is compatible with the text but not demanded by it.

[21] This seems to me decisive against the suggestion of Di Muzio (2000) that in this passage Aristotle is claiming no more than that someone who has voluntarily acquired a bad state of character (a) will not find it easy to reform, (b) will not be responsive to persuasion or punishment. Since Di Muzio acknowledges that Aristotle elsewhere says that some wicked people are incurable, his real target is Bostock's interpretation mentioned in the preceding note.

over that conception. His argument repeats that of ^{a}4–7. Just as our different natural predispositions leave scope for our actions to contribute to our states of character, so on this supposition our different natural conceptions of the good themselves leave room for us to modify those very conceptions in the course of our development. That is very much the situation assumed in Plato's Socratic dialogues. Socrates assumes that everyone acts in the light of their individual conception of the good, but treats that conception not as fixed, but as capable of modification, specifically by critical reflection prompted by argument.

1114ᵇ3–12 'If not ... natural goodness'. Aristotle now considers a variant of this theory, in which the conception of the good is assumed to be incapable of modification by voluntary action or by argument, but merely subject to natural development. The analogy with sight is crucial. While one's powers of sight develop as one grows to maturity, one cannot be taught or otherwise conditioned to see things in one way rather than another.

1114ᵇ12–16 'Now if that is true ... reference to that'. Aristotle's first response is that on that hypothesis good actions and virtue are no more voluntary than bad actions and vice, since *ex hypothesi* all actions are determined by the individual's conception of the good, which is itself immune from modification. While Aristotle presumably regards that conclusion as absurd, it is precisely the conclusion which the opponent is seeking to establish.

1114ᵇ16–21 Aristotle now considers two possible modifications of this hypothesis, either of which will allow actions to be voluntary:

(i) ^{b}16–17: the individual is after all able to make some contribution to his or her conception of the end (i.e. the moderate hypothesis of 1113ᵇ31–1114ᵇ1 is revived);

(ii) ^{b}17–19: though the conception of the good is fixed, the individual has the choice of actions via which that conception will be realized.

Either modification yields the result that vice will be no less voluntary than virtue (^{a}19–21).

1114ᵇ21–5 Aristotle concludes by restating his own commitment to the modest thesis that we are able to modify our own conception of the end, and thereby our states of character, which are therefore voluntary.

1114ᵇ26–30 Summary statement of the main headings of the general account of the virtues of character established in Books II and III. 1–5.

1114ᵇ30–1115ᵃ3 In a coda (in effect a footnote to the thesis that the virtues are voluntary) Aristotle reminds us of the discussion of 1114ᵃ12–31, which shows that states are voluntary in a different way from actions; while we are in control of our voluntary actions throughout, we may be in control of the initiation of states while not being able to control their persistence.

1115ᵃ4–6 Transition to the discussion of the individual virtues.

BOOK THREE

CHAPTER 6

1115ᵃ6–7 Cf. 1107ᵃ33–ᵇ4, with note on that passage; here too the nouns rendered 'fear and boldness' are plural in Greek.

1115ᵃ8–9 Qualifications are introduced at 1115ᵇ7–11.

1115ᵃ9 '[E]vils' renders *kaka*, things bad for the person who has them. The term applies both to the causes of harm and to the harm caused.

'[E]xpectation of evil' is accepted as the definition of fear in Plato, *Lach.* 198b and *Prt.* 358d–e (see also *Leg.* 646e). As a definition of the emotion it is defective, in that it ignores the element of distress at the prospect of harm and consequent desire to avoid harm which are partly constitutive of the emotion. The definition given at *Rhet.* 1382ᵃ22–3, 'distress or disturbance due to imagining some destructive or painful evil in the future', remedies the former defect.

On the other hand, 'expectation of evil' is closer to a correct account of the motive of fear, which prompts one to take some

precautionary step for fear of a possible danger, e.g. being vac-
cinated for fear of infection. In that case, unlike the case of the
emotion, unpleasant turbulence of mind is not essential, though the
element of desire to avoid harm is present. Aristotle's discussion
of the object of fear appears not to distinguish between fear as an
emotion and fear as a motive (see below).

1115ᵃ9–14 Aristotle begins his attempt to specify precisely the
feelings (*pathē*) with respect to which courage is the appropriate disposition. They have been identified generically as fear and
boldness, and fear has been conceptually connected to prospective
harm (see above), but Aristotle's view is that not every kind of
harm is such as to provide material for the exercise of courage. The
sentence 'the courageous person does not seem to be concerned
with all' is to be construed as contributing to the identification of
the specific subject-matter appropriate to the virtue: it is therefore
equivalent to 'courage is not as such concerned with all'. Since
Aristotle says that everyone fears poverty, etc., the courageous
person will of course be concerned with those things in so far as
he or she fears them; the point is that his or her courage does not
consist in being properly disposed with respect to them all. (The
idiom recurs at 1115ᵃ18–19, 22–4, 27–30.)

ᵃ12–14:   (a) What does Aristotle mean by his assertion that there
are some things which it is fine or noble to fear and disgraceful
not to?

(b) How does that claim support his thesis that not all the things
which we all fear provide the material for courage?

(a) The most natural interpretation of Aristotle's claim is that
there are some things which any right-thinking person will regard
as evils to be avoided, e.g. illness, poverty, and disgrace. Consequently, someone who doesn't care about his or her health or
reputation shows irresponsibility at best, depravity at worst. It is
less plausible to take him to mean that the thought of these things
should strike everyone with fear, so that there is something badly
wrong with someone who is not afraid of contracting cancer or of
losing his or her savings. That is to say, it is more natural to take
him to be talking here of the motive of fear than of the emotion.

(b) Given that interpretation, how does the claim that we all
ought to regard illness, etc. as evils to be avoided show that such

evils do not provide material for the exercise of courage? Should we attribute to him the following argument?

(i) We ought all to be courageous.

(ii) It is not the case that we ought all to be fearless with respect to illness, etc.

Therefore,

(iii) Being courageous does not consist in being fearless with respect to illness, etc.

That argument is perfectly sound, but the ambiguity between fear as a motive and fear as an emotion prevents it from supporting Aristotle's desired conclusion. For what premiss (ii) states is that it is not the case that we ought to lack the motive to avoid such evils as illness. And while it is true that courage does not consist in lacking the motive to avoid such evils, that has no tendency to show that courage may not be manifested in facing up to such evils. Someone who holds, against Aristotle, that courage may be manifested in such areas will point to e.g. a doctor remaining in a plague-stricken city as an example of courage as signal as that of a soldier who stands fast when his comrades all run away. Both individuals show a proper management of the emotion of fear, which enables them to hold fast to their conception of a noble goal despite their recognition of and aversion to the evil which threatens them (see below).

Another possible argument is

(i') Courage is a sort of fearlessness.

(ii') The right attitude to illness, etc. is not fearlessness.

Therefore,

(iii') Courage is not the right attitude to illness, etc.

This argument equivocates on 'fearlessness'; the sort of fearlessness which courage is, is not being overcome by the emotion of fear, whereas the sort of fearlessness which the right attitude to illness, etc. is not is the absence of the motive to avoid illness, etc. Here too the distinction between emotion and motive is crucial.

On modesty and shamelessness cf. 1108ª31-5, 1128ᵇ10-35.

1115ª17-24 'Perhaps ... is he courageous'. Following on from his conclusion that not every kind of harm provides the material for courage, Aristotle makes the positive suggestion that the specific area of courage is harm for which one is not at fault, but immediately rejects that too as insufficiently specific, producing counter-examples both of cases of fearlessness in that area which do not count as courage and of fearfulness which do not count as cowardice. In some of these cases (^{a}19–22) the term is applied by extension, on the basis of similarity to genuine cases of courage.

The alleged counter-examples are two cases of cheerfulness or calm when subject to harm (suffering a financial loss, and being about to be flogged), which are said not to be instance of courage, and two of fear of various harms (outrage against one's family and spite (i.e. someone else's malicious conduct)),[22] which are said not to be instances of cowardice. Each of the first two cases is described in vocabulary using words derived from *tharros*, indicating the wide range of applications of that term (see note on 1107^{a}33–^{b}4).

Aristotle's attempt to identify kinds of situation in which responses to actual or envisaged harm are not appropriately described in terms of fear and its opposed vices is at odds with his central thesis that the virtue is the disposition to respond appropriately to fear and boldness, and the vices dispositions to respond inappropriately. Situations such as those envisaged in the counter-examples can plainly call forth appropriate or inappropriate responses; one person meets financial disaster or goes to the flogging with composure, another suffers moral or emotional collapse; one man defies threats that his wife and children will be kidnapped and tortured, another succumbs and hands over state secrets. What is a case of courage or of cowardice must be settled case by case, not by consideration of the nature of the situation-type. It may indeed be the case that the ordinary Greek of Aristotle's day would not readily have recognized such

---

[22] I assume that both cases, outrage against one's family and spite, are cases of envisaged harm inflicted by others. *EE* 1229^{a}35–8 does indeed refer to the distress which the spiteful person expects to feel, saying that expectation of that distress is not a sort of fear; but here the point is different, viz. that fear of spite is not cowardice. The *EE* passage does not therefore support Irwin in his adoption of the alternative reading *gunaikas* for *gunaika* at ^{a}22 (also read by Aspasius), with the consequent translation 'is afraid of committing wanton aggression on women and children'. (On that reading the point would be that fear of one's own bad impulses is not a form of cowardice.) But fear of committing wanton aggression against women and children seems a most bizarre example to make Aristotle's point, whereas fear of outrage against one's family is a most natural one. (All other translators whom I have consulted translate as I do. Heliodorus and Anon. have the OCT reading.)

cases as instances of courage or its opposed defects; if that is so, Aristotle seems here to be guided by common beliefs which are opposed to the thrust of his own theory.

1115ᵃ24–6   Aristotle narrows down the field of courage to the greatest evils. The argument appears to be

(i) No one is more enduring than the person who endures the greatest evils.

(ii) No one is more enduring than the courageous person.
Therefore,

(iii) The courageous person is the person who endures the greatest evils.

That argument is formally invalid; all that follows from the premises is that the courageous person is just as enduring as the person who endures the greatest evils. (Just as, if no one is uglier than Tweedledum and no one is uglier than Tweedledee, it follows, not that Tweedledum is Tweedledee, but that Tweedledum and Tweedledee are equally ugly.) Further, even if we grant that the courageous person is the person who endures the greatest evils, it does not follow that courage consists exclusively in enduring the greatest evils.

1115ᵃ26–7   Contrast the Epicurean argument that death is *not* to be feared, precisely because nothing can affect the dead (for good or ill); *KD* 2; *Men.* 124–5; Lucr. III. 830–46.

1115ᵃ28–31   While death has been identified as the greatest evil, the field of courage is finally specified, not as any kind of death, but as the kind of death which calls for fine or noble action, i.e. death in battle. The crucial point is that virtuous actions are done for the sake of the fine (cf. note on 1105ᵃ30–3); Aristotle claims that the only circumstance in which one can act for the sake of the fine specifically *qua* the courageous (cf. that note) is in battle.

'[T]he finest circumstances' (ᵃ30) and 'the finest danger' (ᵃ31) are respectively circumstances and danger which allow for the performance of the finest actions.

'[B]attle' (ᵃ30 and 35) renders *polemos*, lit. 'war', but Aristotle is clearly thinking of death in combat. Dying e.g. of dysentery on campaign does not in his view provide an occasion for the exercise of courage.

In thus locating courage exclusively in the area of military combat, and particularly in his remark that his view is supported by the honours accorded to military heroes (^{a}31–2), Aristotle indicates that at least in the case of courage the fine for the sake of which the virtuous agent acts is conceived primarily as the splendid or glorious, rather than as the more abstractly noble or admirable (cf. note on 1105^{a}30–3). It is true that ordinarily, as he says at ^{b}5–6, there is no glory in drowning or dying of disease (for exceptions see below), but that does not prevent one from conducting oneself in such situations in a certain way because that is an admirable or noble thing to do. Suppose one thinks: 'Well, the ship's going down and we've no chance. So better to go down calmly and with dignity than screaming and struggling', or 'If I have to die of cancer I'm determined to make as little fuss and upset others as little as possible. That's the proper way to go.' Here, leaving aside questions of self-sacrifice (see below), one sets oneself to fulfil an ideal of appropriate behaviour which answers as closely to the notion of the *kalon* (fine) as does the more spectacular ideal of the splendid or the glorious.

1115^{a}35–^{b}3   Faced with imminent shipwreck, courageous people and experienced seamen are both fearless, but for different reasons. The latter are confident that their expertise will enable them to survive; on the distinction between genuine courage and confidence based on expertise see below on 1116^{b}3–23. The former have no hope of survival, but face death serenely (clearly because of their noble character (see above) though Aristotle does not recognize this as a case of acting for the sake of the fine). What is not clear is how their despising (*duscherainein*) that sort of death fits into the picture. Aristotle presumably means that they regard dying in a shipwreck as beneath their dignity, by contrast with meeting a glorious death on the battlefield. But why does that contribute to their fearlessness? Presumably the thought is that if you despise someone or something, you are not afraid of it. But normally that is because if you despise something, e.g. an enemy, you think that it is not able to harm you significantly. But drowning is going to deprive these people, not only of life, but also of the opportunity of a glorious death. So they ought to regard it as more harmful to them than death in battle, not less. Their despising that kind of death does not, therefore, help to explain their fearlessness, but makes it all the more remarkable.

1115ᵇ3–5 If imminent danger is to provide an occasion for the exercise of courage, at least one of the following conditions must be satisfied: (a) there is something you can do to resist the danger; (b) it is fine to die in such circumstances. Aristotle maintains that neither condition is satisfied in the cases presently under discussion.

On (b) see above. On (a), the requirement is that one is threatened by harm against which one can defend oneself (the Greek is '[circumstances] in which there is *alkē*, lit. 'defence' or 'resistance'), whereas in shipwreck or disease one is merely a passive victim. Courage requires resistance, not mere endurance or acceptance.

That courage requires action as opposed to mere passivity is surely correct, but Aristotle is wrong implicitly to equate passivity with endurance. Enduring a long and painful illness patiently and cheerfully is itself an activity calling for the highest degree of resolution. But in any case, the victim of shipwreck or illness is not necessarily restricted to endurance. Such situations may give rise to the possibility of actions of various kinds, some of them heroic in the highest degree. One can think of heroic efforts to save the ship or its company, or heroic cases of self-sacrifice, such as giving up the last place in the lifeboat, or the last dose of anti-plague serum, to someone else. (Such actions may even bring posthumous glory of the kind normally associated with death in battle; the self-sacrificial death of Captain Oates on Scott's Antarctic expedition is an obvious case.)

Aristotle thus conceives courage, strictly speaking (*kuriōs*, 1115ª32), extremely narrowly, as physical courage displayed on the battlefield. Courage in the face of other kinds of death, or more widely of other kinds of harm (Aristotle's example is financial loss) is explicitly said to be called courage by an extended use of the term, on the strength of its resemblance to courage in the strict sense (1115ª15, 19). That is as close as Aristotle comes to recognizing moral courage; he shows no interest in the detailed typology of that kind of courage, as exemplified e.g. in willingness to shoulder onerous responsibility, or in the resolution to do what one believes right at the cost, if necessary, of social obloquy and abandonment by one's friends. While Aristotle's insistence on courage in battle as courage in the strict sense may be influenced by considerations of the etymology of the Greek *andreia* (lit. 'manliness', from *anēr*, 'man'), it is over-simple to suggest that this narrow conception of courage is the Greek (by contrast with the wider modern) conception. For in Plato's *Laches* Socrates endorses a wider conception of courage as a sort of endurance (*karteria*) displayed not merely in battle but also in cases of shipwreck, disease, poverty, and political affairs generally, and even extending to resolution in resisting desires and the allure of pleasure (191d–192d). (The presence of the examples of shipwreck, disease, and financial loss in both authors makes it likely that Aristotle had that specific passage in mind in composing this chapter.) While that wide application of the term may have been to some extent revisionary of ordinary Greek conceptions, the fact that it is proposed by Socrates and accepted as unproblematic by his interlocutors indicates that it was not completely alien to the thought of the time.

BOOK THREE

CHAPTER 7

111$5^b$7-9　　The thesis that things which are fearful beyond human capacity (*huper anthrōpon*) are fearful to every sensible person is not a repetition of the point made above (^{a}10–14) that everyone ought to fear evils such as disgrace. There the point was that everyone should regard those as evils to be avoided if possible, but such evils are within ordinary capacity to cope with. One should not be struck with terror at the prospect of them, but face them appropriately. Here the point is that some evils are just too terrible for human beings to cope with; hence the inevitable response to them just is to be overwhelmed by terror. Presumably these are the same sort of thing as the sources of superhuman duress mentioned at 1110^{a}24–6 (see above) which 'overstrain human nature and which no one would endure'. Aristotle gives no examples here; 111$5^b$27 might suggest that being caught in an earthquake is one such case. The commentators cite earthquakes, lightning strikes (cf. *EE* 1229ᵇ27), and floods.

1115ᵇ9–10   In contrast to the above kind of case, things which are fearful, and things which inspire boldness 'for a human being' (*kat' anthrōpon*, i.e. within the capacity of humans to cope with) vary in magnitude and degree (i.e. degree of fearfulness and of boldness-inspiringness). The Greek adjectives *phoberon*, 'fearful', and *tharraleon*, 'inspiring boldness', apply alike to events and to aspects of events. Thus we might equally say that to a soldier who is naturally apprehensive but eager to do his duty combat is both *phoberon* and *tharraleon*, or that for him risking death is *phoberon* but doing his duty *tharraleon*. While Aristotle's doctrine is that courage is being correctly disposed to both feelings, fear and boldness, it is not clear whether he thinks that in every instance of courage the courageous person feels both. In some instances of courageous action, such as that of the martyr discussed below (see note on 1117ᵃ33–ᵇ16, with n. 28), it is plausible that the courageous person, while fully aware of the impending evil, feels no fear of it. Whether on every occasion the courageous agent feels *tharros* is uncertain because of the obscurity of what counts as feeling *tharros* (see note on 1107ᵃ33–ᵇ4). If meeting danger readily, in a calm frame of mind, itself counts as feeling *tharros* (as suggested by 1115ᵃ20–1 and 23–4), then in every case the courageous person will feel *tharros*. But if a more positive enthusiasm for the danger or some aspect of it is required, then that could surely be lacking to the courageous person. Aristotle's remarks about *tharros* are insufficiently detailed to settle this question.

1115ᵇ10–11   '[U]ndisturbed' renders *anekplēktos*, lit. 'not driven out of oneself', i.e. not overcome by fear. The courageous person is not overcome, to the extent that it is possible (or appropriate) for a human being not to be so. (By contrast to the situations just mentioned, where composure is impossible/inappropriate.)

1115ᵇ11–20   This passage summarizes the application to courage of the doctrine of the mean set out in III. 6.

ᵇ12:   'as reason prescribes': alternatively, 'as the principle prescribes'. Cf. 1103ᵇ32–4, 1107ᵃ1–2 (with notes). Repeated at 1115ᵇ19.

^b12–13:   On the claim that the virtuous agent acts for the sake of the fine see note on 1105^a30–3. The Greek rendered 'that is the goal proper to virtue' could also mean 'that is the goal proper to the virtue [sc. of courage]'. I have interpreted it as referring to virtue of character generally on the strength of 1120^a23–4.

^b12–15:   'for the sake of the fine': see note on 1105^a30–3.

^b15–19:   cf. 1106^b21–3, 1107^a15–16, 1109^a28–9, ^b14–16.

1115^b20–4 'The goal ... courageous actions'. The argument of this passage is obscure, and the text of ^b21 uncertain. I interpret conjecturally as follows.

1. ^b20–1 might be read (a) as a general claim about all activities, or (b) as a more specific claim about all virtuous acts. If (a), then the claim is presumably that every (intentional) activity has the aim of bringing about some state, e.g. the act of kicking a ball is directed to bringing about the state of the ball's being in motion. If (b), the claim would presumably be that every virtuous act has as its aim the expression or manifestation of that specific virtuous state of character; e.g. my aim in paying a debt is to act justly, and thereby to express or manifest the virtuous state of justice (cf. note on 1105^a30–3). Aristotle might intend (b) to be understood as a special case of (a), and indeed something like (b) has to be understood if (a) is to be relevant to the conclusion. It is therefore the simplest hypothesis to suppose him to have (b) in mind from the start.

2. ^b21: 'to the courageous person courage is something fine'; I follow Gauthier/Jolif and others in reading *kai tōi andreiōi dē* instead of the OCT's ungrammatical *kai tōi andreiōi de*. (*dē* is an emphatic particle, *de* the connective 'and', which merely duplicates *kai*.)

The argument is then: virtuous agents aim at expressing or manifesting their virtuous states of character, for the courageous agent courage is something fine, so courageous agents have the fine as their goal.

^b22:   'each thing is determined (or 'defined' (*horizetai*)) by its goal' appears to be a general point about the definition of actions; an action counts as e.g. building if its aim is a house's having been built, or as a just act if its aim is the manifestation or expression of the character-state of justice. If the reconstruction of the argument given above is correct, the argument does not require this step.

1115^{b}24–6   Cf. 1107^{b}1–2

1115^{b}26–8   The Greeks knew of Celtic peoples inhabiting a wide range of territories north of the Mediterranean, from Spain to Asia Minor. They were renowned for their insensate ferocity.

^{b}26:   '[I]nsensate' translates *analgētos*, lit. 'insensible to pain or suffering (*algos*)'. The parallel passage in *EE*, 1229^{b}28–30, describes the Celts as taking up their weapons and advancing against the waves, adding that they do this from spirit (*thumos* (see note on 1105^{a}7–8)) though they are aware how great the danger is. As martial or aggressive fury is sometimes counted as *tharros* (e.g. Plato, *Prt.* 351a–b (cf. note on 1107^{a}33–^{b}4)), we might expect Aristotle to ascribe this behaviour to an excess of *tharros*. Instead he ascribes it to an excess of fearlessness, which is logically equivalent to a deficiency of fear. It thus appears that his conception of *tharros* is narrower than that expressed in the *Protagoras* passage.

1115^{b}28–32   We might hope that the description of the person who has an excess of *tharros* would give us a clearer idea of what Aristotle's conception of the latter is. But what we get is apparently a description of someone who pretends to be courageous but is really cowardly, putting on a show of eagerness for combat in advance but shirking it when the time comes. Surely such a person is not really excessive in boldness, but merely pretends to be. Unless, therefore, Aristotle's description is quite irrelevant, we must take him to be describing, not (despite 'a boaster who puts on a pretence of courage', ^{b}29–30) someone who pretends to be eager for combat in advance though he is really cowardly all the time, but someone who is genuinely eager for combat in advance, but finds his eagerness ebbing away as battle approaches. But if boldness is just eagerness for battle, why are the Celts who are eager to fight the stormy sea not a paradigm of excess of that?

Perhaps the answer is that Aristotle's conception of boldness is that of *Rhet.* 1383^{a}17–19: 'hope, accompanied by imaginative representation, that safety is near at hand and fearful things nonexistent or far off'. The Celts are filled, not with hope that they will escape the waves, but with mad fury against them, while the 'bold coward' starts off by hoping to escape but loses hope as battle nears. But there are problems.

(a) In what sense is the hope of the 'bold coward' excess-ive? Is it unreasonable hope? But the courageous person normally hopes to escape, and in that case the hope is not unreasonable. Is the point that the bold coward starts off by making light of the dangers and exaggerating positive aspects of the coming combat, but tends towards reversing those assessments the closer battle looms? But in that case fear and boldness look less like inde-pendent feelings and more like necessarily interdependent aspects of the agent's attitude to danger. There are positive and negative aspects of envisaged danger, and the proper attitude to it consists in getting the balance between the two right. One can go wrong by tipping the balance either way; but either way the defect has to be described in the relation between the ways of representation. One can give too much weight to the fearful aspect (and thereby insufficient weight to the positive aspect, e.g. that we stand to win a glorious victory), or vice versa; but there is no room for the description of someone who, while giving some weight to one or other factor (or both), merely gives too much weight to the fearful without giving insufficient weight to the positive, or vice versa.[23] On the other hand, someone who gives no weight at all to either factor gives insufficient weight to both (see note on 1107^{a}33–^{b}4).

(b) We have seen that Aristotle applies terms implying bold-ness to people who are unruffled in situations where they have no hope of escape (suffering financial loss, 1115^{a}21–2, facing a flogging, 1115^{a}23–4). One way to deal with such cases would be to suggest that in these cases the term is applied purely to a style of behaviour, viz. remaining outwardly unmoved and unflinching, whereas when the term names a feeling, boldness is identical with hope or confidence of escape. But that is quite artificial; it is surely envisaged not simply that these people meet these disasters without weeping, trembling, etc., but that their calm demeanour expresses a calm and untroubled frame of mind. But is the effect of that not to identify boldness purely negatively, in effect identifying it with fearlessness? Not necessarily. Here too we may appeal to the idea of positive and negative assessments of the harm; the unruffled calm can be seen as the outward expression of such assessments as 'Well, one will just have to pick oneself up and start again' or

[23] Cf. Stocker (1990a: 140–2, 147).

'I mustn't give these bastards the satisfaction of seeing me break down. That'll show them.'

My suggestion, then, is that Aristotle's conception of boldness is primarily cognitive; it is positive assessment of envisaged danger or harm. Sheer animal fury, which in ordinary idiom counts as boldness (see above) lacks sufficient cognitive content to count, and it may be because he sees the Celts as driven on by an aggressive spirit close to that that he does not find it appropriate to describe them as overbold. But on the other hand hope or confidence of escape from danger (which Aristotle may identify with one another, though they are in fact distinct, the latter implying the former, but not vice versa) is not the only form of positive assessment; exciting, glorious, worthy of a Spartan, are all forms of that kind of assessment.[24]

1115ᵇ33–5   Cf. ᵇ15–19.

1116ᵃ1–2   As argued above, the connection between excess of fear and deficiency of boldness is not merely contingent. That is not inconsistent with Aristotle's assertion that the former is more obvious in the case of the coward.

1116ᵃ2–4   The sense in which the courageous person is the opposite of the coward, who lacks hope (i.e. is *duselpis*), is presumably that (normally) the former does not lack hope. In that case we should expect 'for confidence (Aristotle's term for the confident person is *euelpis*, lit. 'having good hope') is the mark of the bold person', rather than the converse.

1116ᵃ7–9   Aristotle's description of the overbold as impetuous people, who *are* eager before danger comes (as opposed to just seeming eager) confirms the suggestion made above on 1115ᵇ27–32.

1116ᵃ11–12   'because it is fine to do so or disgraceful not to': repeated at 1117ᵇ9. At 1117ᵃ17 'and' replaces 'or' in the formula.

---

[24] *tharros* is not, then, adequately characterized as an attitude to risk. Hence Urmson's suggestion (1973: 229–30; 1988: 64–5) that the Aristotelian triad of attitudes to fear (cowardice, bravery, insensitive fearlessness) requires to be supplemented by a triad of attitudes to risk (over-caution, caution, rashness), while sound in itself, is not a contribution to the discussion of Aristotle's account of courage.

It is clear that Aristotle treats the two formulations as interchange-able. The courageous person has the choice of acting courageously or failing to do so; the former is fine, the latter disgraceful.

1116ᵃ13–15 The negative evaluation of suicide as an act of cow-ardice occurs also at *EE* 1229ᵇ39–1230ᵃ4. In these passages the only motive considered is the desire to escape from suffering of one kind or another. At 1138ᵃ9–10 Aristotle refers incidentally to people who kill themselves from anger; he may be thinking of people who (like Ajax) kill themselves in indignation at some insult. If so, it is unclear whether he would count those cases too as acts of cowardice.[25]

BOOK THREE

CHAPTER 8

In this chapter Aristotle distinguishes from true courage five states which are ordinarily called types of courage, though strictly speak-ing they are not. They are ordinarily reckoned to be types of courage because they motivate (up to a point) the same kind of behaviour as true courage, but are different from the latter in respect of their motivational content.

1116ᵃ17–ᵇ3 1. Civic courage

ᵃ17: '[C]ivic' renders *politikē*, the kind of courage typically displayed by citizens (*politai*) in their role as soldiers, as distinct from that of professional (i.e. mercenary) soldiers, discussed under (2) below.

The quotations are from the *Iliad*: ᵃ23, 22. 100 (spoken by Hec-tor); ᵃ25–6, 8. 148–9 (spoken by Diomede); ᵃ34–5, 2. 391, 393 (spoken by Agamemnon, not by Hector (see note on 1109ᵃ32)). ᵃ35, 'will not be able to avoid the dogs'; i.e. he will be killed, and his corpse will lie unburied.

Civic courage is motivated by the sanctions imposed by the *polis*. Aristotle distinguishes two types of sanction:

(a) Those intended to imbue the citizens with a sense of the value of courage in battle. These include honours for distinguished

[25] See Dover (1974: 167–9).

conduct and public disgrace for cowardice, both of which may be enshrined in legal enactments (ᵃ18–29).

(b) Threats of physical punishment of shirkers, combined with methods of physical compulsion on the battlefield, such as beating any who turn back (ᵃ29–ᵇ3).

It is clear that the motivation provided by sanctions of type (b) differs from that of the courageous person; the latter acts 'for the sake of the fine', whereas those motivated by type (b) sanctions act out of the fear of physical punishment, or, in cases where flight is made physically impossible, under compulsion.

The case is less clear for type (a) sanctions; the person motivated by them acts from virtue (ᵃ27–8), and from desire for the fine and to avoid disgrace, which is seen as shameful (ᵃ28–9). The courageous person acts courageously 'because it is fine to do so and disgraceful not to' (1117ᵃ17). In general, virtuous states of character, including courage, result from correct training (see above, II. 3), and type (a) sanctions look as if they should be among the means of such training. Where, then, lies the difference between true courage and mere civic courage?

The difference, such as it is, must be this: the courageous person has fully internalized the values from which he or she acts, whereas the values motivating civic courage are external. The primary motivations of the civically courageous person are the desire for honour and the desire to avoid disgrace, i.e. to be favourably regarded, and to avoid being unfavourably regarded, by others. It is particularly significant that a central aspect of civic motivation is shame (ᵃ28), something which Aristotle regards as foreign to the motivation of the fully virtuous person (see on IV. 9 below). Shame is primarily the fear of being disgraced in the eyes of others;[26] it is thus the mirror image of the desire for honour, to stand well in the eyes of others, which in the case of civic courage is the form which desire for the fine takes (ᵃ28–9).

The person of civic courage is thus motivated primarily by considerations of social standing, by contrast with the person of true courage, who is motivated primarily by considerations of standing in his or her own eyes. The courageous person cares above all about doing what he or she sees as fine, not what others see as fine, and similarly for avoiding what he or she sees as disgraceful.

---

[26] See Williams (1993: esp. 78–82).

Of course the line is a tenuous one (Aristotle emphasizes that of the five types of apparent courage civic courage is the closest to genuine (^{a}17)). In both cases what the agent him or herself admires and shuns coincides with those same attitudes on the part of others. And, as we have seen (see note on 1115^{a}28–31), the thought that a certain kind of act is splendid or glorious, and thereby such as to attract the admiration of others, is central to the virtuous agent's thought of it as fine, above all in the case of courage. But if we are to preserve the distinction at all, we must insist on the opposition of the direction of priority; the person of civic courage thinks that facing the enemy toe to toe in the battle line is a fine thing to do because that is what wins one honour, and that flight is ignoble because it brings disgrace. The person of true courage thinks that those acts deserve respectively honour and disgrace because they are, respectively, intrinsically splendid and intrinsically disgraceful.

1116^{b}3–23   2. Courage based on experience

^{b}4–5:   Socrates defines courage at *Lach.* 199a–b as knowledge of what is frightening and confidence-inspiring (*tōn deinōn epistēmē ... kai tharraleōn*) and at *Prt.* 360d as wisdom concerning what is frightening and not (*sophia ... tōn deinōn kai mē deinōn*; the two formulae are interchangeable). These formulae express the Socratic thesis that courage is identical with knowledge of what is good and bad for the agent overall. That knowledge is explicitly in the *Laches* and implicitly in the *Protagoras* distinguished from technical expertise, which is relative, not to the overall good of the agent, but to the performance of a specific task. In the former dialogue (193a–d) people who undertake dangerous activities without technical knowledge are said to more courageous than the corresponding experts. Aristotle's citing the Socratic thesis as supporting the identity of expert courage with true courage is therefore careless.

^{b}15–19:   The reference is to a battle near the city of Coronea in Boeotia in 353, at which the citizen militia of Coronea held their ground and were killed when their mercenary allies fled.

1116^{b}23–1117^{a}9   3. Spirit

On spirit see notes on 1105ᵃ7–8 and 1115ᵇ26–8. Aristotle here distinguishes the role of spirit as the primary motivation in savage beasts and ferocious humans such as the Celts from its role in the courageous agent, where it is subsidiary to the primary motivation to realize fine action. The thought is clearly that in seeking that goal the courageous agent is energized by the aggressive and retaliatory force of spirit.

ᵇ31–3:   The point seems to be that animals attack only from fear, as is shown by the fact that if they can hide instead (as they can in a wood) they do not attack.

1117ᵃ4–5:   Aggressiveness prompted by spirit counts as an expression of courage when and only when it is directed to the goal of achieving the fine, so that the appropriate actions are chosen under that description.

1117ᵃ9–22   4. Confidence

A reprise of (2), since the confidence is that of experts. Cf. the confidence of sailors mentioned at 1115ᵇ1–4. The only new material is the brief mention of Dutch courage at ᵃ14–15.

ᵃ12–13:   'for the reasons stated': see 1115ᵇ11–24.

ᵃ17–22:   The translation is equivalent to 'It takes a braver person to be unafraid in sudden danger than in one you can prepare for'. Another possible rendering is: 'Being unafraid in sudden danger is more strongly indicative of courage than being unafraid in situations you can prepare for'. Aristotle may intend both, perhaps not differentiating between the two.

In any case this passage is in tension with the claim at 1105ᵇ31–2 that a virtuous act is done from choice, since choice presupposes deliberation (1112ᵃ14–16, 1113ᵃ9–11), whereas here it is the undeliberated character of action in sudden danger which makes it the action of a more courageous agent. Could it be Aristotle's position that while the act in the situation of sudden danger is not a courageous *act*, since it is not the result of deliberate choice, it is yet the output of a more courageous *character*, i.e. a character more in tune with the requirements of courage than one where the agent can act courageously only as the result of deliberation? That seems required by Aristotle's assertion at 1111^{b}9–10 that 'sudden' actions are voluntary, but not done from choice.

On the other hand, that attributes to Aristotle the highly counterintuitive position that the best kind of courage issues in acts which are not themselves courageous acts. That position is avoided if we interpret Aristotle as holding that, while the acts of the courageous agent in a situation of unforeseen danger do not indeed result from deliberation there and then, they nevertheless express the agent's rational, i.e. deliberate, choice. The crucial point is that, while in that situation the agent acts without working out the right thing to do, his or her act is not purely instinctive, but rational. The agent acts for reasons, and can say afterwards what those reasons were, thus recapitulating a pattern of practical reasoning which was not gone through in advance or at the time of action. Though not *deliberated*, the action was *deliberate*, in the sense of 'deliberate' which is equivalent to 'intentional'. (Another equivalent expression is 'on purpose'; in sudden danger the courageous agent certainly acts on purpose, and is in no doubt what that purpose is.) As a result of his or her correct training, the courageous agent has internalized a pattern of response to situations of danger which enables him or her to respond correctly immediately, without having to stop to think. But that is not to say that the action is done without thought. Rather, we can say that all the crucial thinking has been done in advance, leaving only a gap for the recognition of the situation as calling for this response or that; once that gap is filled by perception, action follows immediately (cf. 1109^{b}22–3, 1147^{a}26–31).[27]

The recognition of a kind of action which, though not issuing from actual deliberation nevertheless expresses a pattern of practical reason which can be recapitulated *ex post facto* in deliberative form has the further advantage of solving a difficulty in Aristotle's account of *akrasia*: namely, his recognition of impetuous *akrasia* (*propeteia*), in which the agent is led astray by passion before completing his or her deliberation (1150^{b}19–28). The difficulty is that, *akrasia* being action contrary to one's rational choice (*prohairesis*, 1147^{b}9–11), the impetuous person, who does not complete his or her deliberation, cannot make a rational choice, and therefore cannot act against it, and so cannot be akratic. Here too, as in the case

---

[27] See Irwin *ad loc.*; also Stewart i. 245 (on 1111^{b}9); Mele (1981).

of sudden danger, we have to see the impetuous person as having internalized a pattern of practical reasoning such that, were that pattern to be realized in actual thought, it would result in the correct choice; the impetuous person, then, acts contrary to the choice that he or she would have made had he or she deliberated. The crucial difference between that person and the courageous person in sudden danger is that in the latter case the internalized pattern of practical reasoning is effective, whereas in the former it is ineffective. It then becomes a problem to specify what it is to have internalized a pattern of reasoning which is ineffective; but that problem belongs to Aristotle's account of *akrasia*, not to the present discussion.

While preferring the account of actions in situations of unforeseen danger as in accordance with the agent's reasoned choice in the way described above, I have to acknowledge that that conflicts with the letter of 1111ᵇ9–10. I do not see how to make all Aristotle's statements on this topic consistent with one another.

1117ᵃ23–7   5. Ignorance

ᵃ23–4:   The difference between the confident and the ignorant is that the 'courage' of the former depends on their estimate (which may be correct) of their ability to cope with the danger, whereas that of the latter depends on their ignorance of the true nature of the danger.

ᵃ26–7:   The event described took place during a battle at Corinth in 392.

BOOK THREE
CHAPTER 9

1117ᵃ29   'boldness and fear': plural in the Greek.

1117ᵃ29–32   Aristotle here appears to contrast being unafraid in the face of danger with keeping one's head in the face of situations which inspire boldness, e.g. not getting over-excited at the prospect of victory and glory. Both are required of the courageous person, but courage consists rather in the former than in the latter. This presumably picks up the point made at 1108ᵇ35–1109ᵃ19, that of the two opposed extremes, cowardice is more opposed to courage than overboldness is. On that thesis see note on that passage.

1117ᵃ33 'as we have said': this has not in fact been said in so many words, though it was implied by the argument of ch. 6 that people are called courageous for facing the most fearful things.

1117ᵃ33–ᵇ16 In this passage Aristotle emphasizes that courage consists in facing what the agent recognizes as the greatest evils: death and the consequent loss of all those features which make the virtuous life supremely worth living. Since the virtuous agent has more to lose than anyone else, death is more of an evil to him or her than to anyone else (ᵇ10–13). Hence facing these evils is distressing, and something which even the courageous person does reluctantly (ᵃ33–4, ᵇ6–7).

There is an obvious tension between this passage and the assertion of 1104ᵇ7–8 that 'the person who endures frightening things with pleasure, or at least without distress, is courageous, while the person who feels distress at doing so is cowardly' (see note on 1104ᵇ5–8). Aristotle appears to be conscious of the difficulty, and to attempt to meet it by his example of boxers, who put up with all the unpleasantness of arduous training and being knocked about in the ring for the sake of the rewards of victory, which will indeed be very pleasant when they come, but which, when one actually is in the ring, are overshadowed by the pain one is enduring. It is not clear that this provides an adequate answer. First, it presents the value of courage as purely instrumental, like that of a painful medical procedure. In itself, courage is something irksome, which is worth while only for the sake of subsequent rewards. Secondly, those rewards are represented as bestowed by others, which tends at the least to assimilate true courage to civic virtue, from which Aristotle has just distinguished it (see above). 1104ᵇ7–8 demands of the courageous person some kind of positive response to the actual situation of courageous action, which appears to be excluded by the present passage.

A better solution of the difficulty is provided by Aristotle's own account of courage as the appropriate response, not merely to fear, but also to *tharros* (see note on 1115ᵇ27–32). The courageous agent does indeed regard imminent death as involving a loss which he or she shrinks from and would prefer not to have to undergo. But at the same time he or she regards the very act of undergoing that loss as something admirable, and as such faces it either gladly or at the least without hesitation. Every sane person, in Aristotle's view, faces death reluctantly. The difference between the courageous person and the coward is that reluctance is the latter's overall attitude (since the value of the courageous act is either outweighed or not present to his or her mind at all), whereas for the courageous person reluctance is the response to the situation *qua* loss of goods, which is outweighed by the value of the situation *qua* courageous act. Hence the courageous person's overall attitude is pleasure, or at least ready acceptance.[28]

---

[28] Duff (1987) 10–11 gives an excellent account of *tharros* (and hence of courage) along these lines. He describes a martyr who 'goes willingly (even gladly) to her death, because she sees that this is required of her: she is of good hope and good cheer; she exhibits, I suggest, an appropriate kind of *tharsos* [an alternative spelling of *tharros*]. Her *tharsos* does not consist in any expectation of survival—she has none—nor in a love of danger for its own sake—she finds neither value nor pleasure in mere danger. It consists rather in her *hopeful confidence* [author's italics] in the worth of her action and her sacrifice: she is happy and willing to give up her life in this cause. ... Her *tharsos* provides an appropriate *pathos* which partly constitutes her courage: she takes pleasure in facing the right dangers for the right reasons; her passion speaks with the same voice as reason, since it is informed by her understanding of what is good and noble'.

Duff further suggests (p. 11) that the martyr's natural fear of death is not simply outweighed by *tharros* thus described, but transformed, so that the painful expectation of death, though still present, no longer disturbs her or prompts her to flight. Stocker (1990a) makes a similar suggestion. He describes the eagerness of the courageous warrior as follows: 'Rather than a light and easy eagerness it will be a more solemn, studied or regretting eagerness ... attaining victory is pleasurable, but acting courageously need not be pleasurable and may indeed be painful ... Such solemnity, regret and lack of pleasure need not involve indecision, vacillation, ambivalence or other lack of whole-heartedness. The fear had by courageous warriors does not involve conflict. Rather, there is the regret or sadness that the goal involves such a risk ... the fear and the confidence have interpenetrated each other, losing their separate identities' (pp. 144–5).

While these studies provide much valuable insight into certain special types of courage, it is perhaps an exaggeration to insist that Aristotle's courageous person must be *completely* free of the inclination to avoid pain or death, and hence *totally* unconflicted (Duff 1987: 13). Such might perhaps be the state of someone of superhuman courage (see VII. 1, 1145ª19–25), but it is not clear that Aristotle requires it of the ordinarily courageous person. One might well query whether someone in the exalted state of Duff's martyr feels any fear at all. If her negative assessment of the situation is no more than sadness at the prospect of the loss of what she has valued in life, that seems insufficient to amount to fear; and in any case she need not even feel that, if her sorrow at parting from life is turned into the joy of witnessing for her faith. Even a person with no motivational conflict, like Stocker's warrior, might feel regret at having to be in a situation demanding self-sacrifice, and be glad if, in the event, that sacrifice was not required. But the martyr might count self-sacrifice as a

So Aspasius 98. 24–5: 'the exercise of courage is accompanied by a certain reluctance and distress, but nevertheless the distress is overcome by the pleasure of aiming at what is fine.' Heliodorus misses the point, emphasizing the courageous person's sufferings to the extent that any pleasure threatens to disappear.

1117ᵇ17–20 Really courageous people will give their lives only when it is noble to do so, whereas inferior people may be prepared to give their lives for trifling gains. Hence a military commander (especially one whose cause is ignoble) might be better advised to enlist the latter than the former. (Once again, Aristotle seems to be thinking primarily of mercenaries, who might be induced to fight e.g. by a promise of loot which would have no attraction to truly courageous soldiers.)

1117ᵇ21–2 Note that even a discussion containing as much detail as the foregoing is still described as an outline. Cf. 1103ᵇ34–1104ᵃ2, with note on 1103ᵇ34–1104ᵃ5.

For *EE*'s discussion of courage see III. 1. Mills (1980) compares the two treatments in detail, arguing that *EE*'s discussion is the earlier.

BOOK THREE

CHAPTER 10

1117ᵇ23–4 '[F]or these ... parts' explains why courage and temperance are grouped together. The explanation assumes a

privilege rather than a burden, and be disappointed, rather than relieved, to be given a last-minute reprieve.

   It may be thought that only totally unconflicted courage can be distinguished from self-control (*enkrateia*). That seems to me a mistake; the self-controlled person has bad desires which he or she controls through reason (1145ᵇ12–13), but the desire to avoid pain and death, even in circumstances when undergoing them is fine, is not a bad desire, but an aspect of properly functioning human nature (see above). In the case of fear, the *enkratēs* would be someone who was by instinct cowardly, i.e. someone who instinctively sought to shun any and every distress, but mastered that bad impulse through reason. A normally courageous person, on the other hand, is not someone cowardly by nature, but someone who, faced with imminent and serious harm, feels the appropriate amounts of fear and *tharros*. Such a person can still feel some degree of genuine motivational conflict, provided that his or her overall attitude is as described above. So Gauthier/Jolif ii. 226–7.

   Charles (1995: 143–8) gives a similar account of courage to that given in the text above. Other perceptive discussions of Aristotelian courage are those by Pears (1980); Young (1980); Leighton (1988); and Heil (1996).

psychology resembling that of Plato's *Republic*, in which spirit and bodily appetite belong to different non-rational parts of the soul, courage being the virtue of the spirited part and temperance that of the appetitive part. Cf. note on 1111ᵃ24–ᵇ3. Since, as pointed out in that note, Aristotle does not himself accept the tri-partite psychology, the claim that courage and temperance seem to belong to the non-rational parts must be a reference to what he takes to be ordinary opinion. So Anon.

While Socrates does himself assign courage to the spirited part in the *Republic*, defining it as 'the retention by the spirited part, amid pleasures and pains, of the commands of reason about what is to be feared and not' (442c), his account of temperance does not assign it to the appetitive element, or to any element in particular. Temperance is an agreement between the three parts of the soul that reason is to rule (442c–d).

1117ᵇ24–6   The reference is to 1107ᵇ4–6. The point that temperance is less concerned with distress than with pleasure is explained at 1118ᵇ28–33.

1117ᵇ27–8   As the sphere of courage was confined to a specific kind of fearful thing, death in battle, so Aristotle proceeds to limit the sphere of temperance to a specific set of bodily pleasures, those of touch. His method of eliminating first non-bodily pleasures and then the other bodily pleasures appeals to our practice of applying the terms 'temperate' and 'intemperate'; these, he claims, are applied only to states of character involving pleasures of touch.

1117ᵇ31   'the intellect': lit. 'thought'.
Aspasius objects to the wording of Aristotle's statement that in intellectual pleasures the intellect is affected, on the ground that pleasure belongs not to thought but to the passive part of the soul.[29] He takes this to be a loose statement of Aristotle's actual view: viz. that people who are having some intellectual pleasure are affected in the passive part of the soul in consequence of having the thought that they have achieved their desired object. In effect this is to analyse intellectual enjoyment as (a) the state of being pleased that one has achieved one's goal, (b) some passive state caused

---

[29] See Urmson (1967: 325).

by state (a). Analyses of that kind lose the connection between activity or actuality (*energeia*) and pleasure which is central to Aristotle's account.[30]

1118^{a}1 Aristotle must presumably be referring to further instances of non-bodily pleasures, viz. pleasure in money-making and in friendship, and making the point that people who are excessively fond of those things are not called intemperate, any more than gossips are. Though, in these cases as in any other, distress is caused by the loss of what one takes pleasure in (see 1119^{a}3–5), it is unclear why Aristotle identifies these classes of people in terms of distress rather than directly in terms of pleasure.

1118^{a}1–16 Bodily pleasures are classified according to the senses: sight, hearing, smell, taste, and touch. In these lines the first three kinds are excluded from the sphere of temperance and intemperance by the same criterion as the non-bodily pleasures.

Prima facie, Aristotle's conception of bodily pleasures is much more restrictive than our ordinary conception of physical pleasures, i.e. pleasures in primarily physical activities. The enjoyment of e.g. dancing, swimming, or sailing does not appear to be reducible to the enjoyment of the exercise of any bodily sense or combination of such enjoyments. A possible answer to this objection[31] is that it is in fact Aristotle's view that in every case what is enjoyed is the perception of these activities, which consists in the exercise of one or other of the bodily senses.[32]

In any case Aristotle would presumably argue, as above, that people are not called temperate or intemperate in respect of that kind of physical pleasures.

^{a}11–12: Perfumes are associated with sex, and dainty dishes (*opsa*, strictly dishes such as cheese or fish intended to give a relish to the staple bread) with immoderate enjoyment of food.

^{a}13–16: The argument is presumably that, though people other than the intemperate enjoy the smell of food when they are hungry, it is characteristic of the intemperate to enjoy the specific kinds of smell mentioned at ^{a}11–12.

---

[30] See Urmson (1967); Bostock (2000); Taylor (2003*b*).
[31] Proposed by Bostock (1988).
[32] For further discussion see Taylor (2003*b*).

An alternative interpretation, adopted by Gauthier/Jolif, Dirlmeier, Irwin, and Natali, is that it is characteristic of the intemperate, and of them alone, to enjoy the smell of food without being hungry.

1118ᵃ16–23 Aristotle asserts that, whereas humans appreciate scents such as those of flowers and sounds such as music intrinsically, animals are attracted to scents and sounds only instrumentally, as signs leading them to food. He presumably regards aesthetic appreciation as such as peculiar to humans. To the extent that aesthetic activity involves appreciation of certain types of experience for their own sake, abstracted from the biologically determined goals of survival and reproduction, we can see why that kind of activity would have little or no place in the lives of most non-human animals.

ᵃ21–2: The quotation is from *Il.* 3. 24.

1118ᵃ23–ᵇ1 Aristotle next excludes the pleasures of taste from the sphere of temperance and intemperance, leaving only the pleasure of touch as its specific sphere. The pleasures proper to the intemperate person are those of food, drink, and sex, all of which are kinds of tactile pleasure.

ᵃ25: 'slavish and bestial': i.e. appropriate to slaves and beasts.

ᵃ26–9: Aristotle restricts the role of taste to the judgement or discrimination of flavours, which he treats as a special type of expertise, employed by wine-tasters, pastry-cooks, and the like. He relies on this specialized conception for his thesis that taste is not among the objects characteristically enjoyed by intemperate people. But while it may be useful to define taste as the sense by which we discriminate flavours (cf. *An.* 418ᵃ11–13), that by no means supports the identification of the enjoyment of taste with the enjoyment of the process of making refined discriminations of taste, or of the discriminations thus produced. One does not have to be a whisky connoisseur to enjoy the taste of whisky, and the more intemperate one's enjoyment of whisky is, the less likely one is to be interested in fine discriminations of taste. But one may enjoy it for the taste (no doubt among other features, see below), for all that.[33]

---

[33] Cf. Young (1988: 536–8).

^a29:   'they do not at all enjoy those': 'they' may be the experts themselves (so Ross rev. Ackrill/Urmson), or perhaps people in general (so Irwin, Crisp, and Rowe). Which Aristotle intends is immaterial to his central point, that intemperate people do not enjoy tastes.

^a30–2:   The pleasures of food, drink, and sex, which are the pleasures characteristic of the intemperate, are all forms of tactile pleasure.

Having eliminated taste, Aristotle is left with tactile sensations as the specific objects of the intemperate enjoyment of food and drink. The example in ^a32–^b1 indicates that he is thinking of the sensation of the stuff sliding down the gullet, but he may have other sensations in mind as well, such as the feeling of a full stomach. While the latter may indeed be part of the attraction of over-indulgence in food and drink, it is hard to take seriously the suggestion that even for the greediest person the actual sensation of swallowing is significant, still less that it is central. Besides the exclusion of the pleasure of taste, one of the most curious features of Aristotle's discussion of intemperance as regards drink is his neglect of the importance of alcoholic effect. In most cases, immoderate drinking is the immoderate drinking of alcohol, and Aristotle must have been thinking primarily of wine-drinkers, yet he says nothing about intoxication as an object of intemperate pleasure.[34]

^a31–2:   'what are called "the pleasures of Aphrodite".' The ordinary Greek word for sex is *taphrodisia*, lit. 'the things of Aphrodite' (the goddess of love). Aristotle makes slightly heavy weather of pointing out its literal meaning.

Aristotle's claim that sexual pleasure arises wholly from touch makes no distinction between the pleasure of touching, including stroking, fondling, etc., and the pleasure of being touched, including being stroked, etc. In either case physical contact causes pleasant bodily sensations, and it may be that Aristotle assumes that all sexual pleasure consists in enjoying such sensations. It is unclear how that view applies to cases such as the enjoyment of pornography. Aristotle may take it for granted that all such cases involve masturbation, in which the enjoyment is obviously tactile.

---

[34]   Cf. Young (1988: 538–9).

Alternatively, he may count sensations of sexual arousal, including those of orgasm, as themselves tactile, even if they are not caused by touching. In that case the notion of touch has been extended to include proprioception. See further on $1118^{b}6-8$ below.

$1118^{b}1-2$ 'the most common'. Aristotle appears to say here that touch alone of the senses is universal to all creatures which have any kind of perception. Cf. *An.* $413^{b}5-8$, 'just as the nutritive faculty can exist apart from touch and all perception, so can touch exist apart from the other senses', and $414^{a}2-3$. Aristotle regards taste as a species of touch, viz. the tactile discrimination by the tongue of flavour, which he regards as an effect produced in the wet by the dry; e.g. salt, which is a dry substance, is tasted when it acts on some moisture which is then perceived when it comes into contact with the tongue. See *Sens.* $441^{b}19-20$, and for full discussion Johansen (1997: ch. 4). Hence his most precise doctrine is that touch, including taste, is common to all animals, whereas the other senses are not (*Sens.* $436^{b}13-18$). He cannot, then, be attempting here to distinguish touch *from taste* on the ground that the former alone is common to all animals.

Sisko (2003) suggests that by 'most common' Aristotle means not 'having the widest application' but 'functionally most basic', citing *HA* $511^{b}1-3$, $520^{b}10-11$, where blood is said to be the most common of the homoiomerous constituents of sanguineous animals (despite the fact that other stuffs such as skin and sinew are equally found in all such animals), in the sense that blood is the basic nutrient of sanguineous animals (cf. *PA* $651^{a}14$, $652^{a}7$). Aristotle is here distinguishing touch from taste, he suggests, on the ground that it is the pleasure of touch (i.e. of the tactile sensation of swallowing) which explains why animals consume their food (*PA* $690^{b}35-691^{a}2$), while the pleasure of taste merely explains why they taste it. Hence touch has the most functionally basic role in the activity of feeding, and the enjoyment of touch in swallowing is therefore the most animal-like of the pleasures of the senses.

$1118^{b}4$ '[M]ost reputable' renders *eleutheriōtatai*, lit. 'most appropriate to a free person'. Gauthier/Jolif and Rowe translate literally; Ross rev. Ackrill/Urmson has 'most refined', Irwin 'most civilized', Crisp 'most genteel', Dirlmeier 'ungezwungensten' (i.e.

'most unconstrained', a translation which he describes as make-shift), Natali 'i piu liberali'.

1118ᵇ6–8 The certain parts are plainly the gullet (and perhaps also the stomach, see above) for food and drink and the sexual organs. With regard to the latter Aristotle's thesis appears to be that the specific object of sexual pleasure is tactile sensation in, or involving, the sexual organs. Again, there is no clear distinction drawn between the enjoyment of touching someone else's sexual organs and the enjoyment of touching one's own, or of having them touched by someone else. How does this account deal with the sexual enjoyment of kissing (as distinct from oral sex), or of touching other parts of the body, such as the small of one's lover's back, or their ear-lobes, or of having those parts of one's own body touched? Perhaps Aristotle counts such activity as sexual only in so far as it causes either genital contact or genital sensation.[35]

BOOK THREE

CHAPTER 11

1118ᵇ8–15 The contrast is between the generic desires for food, drink, and sex, which are biologically based, and hence common to all animals, and the varieties of them, which are dependent on individual taste (or perhaps on tastes peculiar to particular cultures), and thus acquired in the process of upbringing. Aristotle points out that even the latter have a certain natural element in them; while different individuals (or different kinds of people) prefer different kinds of food, still (e.g.) all humans agree in preferring one kind of cereal or another to grass or leaves.[36]

b11: 'as Homer says': loosely based on *Il.* 24. 129–31.

1118ᵇ18–19 'natural desire ... deficiency'; presumably a loose expression of the thesis that natural desire is *for* the filling up of a deficiency.

That thesis forms part of what appears to be Plato's favoured account of pleasure: namely, that pleasure is the perceived filling

---

[35] For fuller discussion see Urmson (1967) and Taylor (1988).
[36] On the importance of the contrast see Young (1988: 528–32).

up of a natural deficiency; see *Grg.* 494–7; *Resp.* 585d–e; *Phlb.* 31–2. Criticism of that theory is central to Aristotle's own accounts of pleasure in *NE* VII and X.[37]

1118ᵇ19–20   'belly-mad': the literal translation of *gastrimargoi*, one of several Greek terms for 'gluttons'.

'it': the belly (*gastēr*).

1118ᵇ21–7   Here again we have the usual formula specifying the various ways of going wrong. Cf. 1115ᵇ15–19 and the other passages cited in the note on that passage.

A non-standard feature of the occurrence of the formula here is the appearance of 'more than most people do' as a way in which one might enjoy something excessively (ᵇ23–4, 27). If it is interpreted purely statistically, it is plainly not a sufficient condition for excess; by definition, anyone who is unusually keen on something enjoys it more than most people do, but it does not follow that such a person enjoys whatever it is too much. 'Most people' must therefore be understood as itself a normative expression, having the force of 'people of sound judgement'.

ᵇ26:   'any such things': obviously not any of the hateful things which one should not enjoy at all, but any of the objects of individual desires.

1118ᵇ28–33   Aristotle clarifies the relation of temperance to distress by comparison with courage. In the case of the latter, the relation to distress is central, since the courageous person is defined as one who endures fearful things (which are necessarily distressing; see above on 1117ᵃ33–ᵇ16) and the coward as one who does not endure them. The temperate person, by contrast, is not defined by reference to the endurance of distress, nor the intemperate by lack of endurance. Temperance and intemperance are defined by their attitude to pleasure, to which distress is peripheral, in that the intemperate person is distressed when he or she fails to get the pleasure he or she wants, while the temperate person finds neither the lack of pleasure nor abstention from pleasure distressing.

[37] See Taylor (2003*b*).

1119^a1–3 The reference of 'the rest' is ambiguous, depending on whether the intemperate person is characterized as desiring all pleasant things (in which case 'the rest' refers to things other than pleasant things) or the most pleasant things (in which case 'the rest' refers to the remaining pleasant things). Perhaps the ambiguity is deliberate. Another possibility is that 'or' has the sense 'or rather' (see note on 1106^a3–4).

1119^a5–11 Cf. 1107^b6–8.

1119^a11–15 Cf. note on 1118^b21–7.

^a13–14: 'anything like that': see note on 1118^b26.

1119^a20 'as correct reason prescribes' (alternatively, 'as the correct principle prescribes'): cf. 1115^b12 and the other passages referred to in the note on that passage.

BOOK THREE

CHAPTER 12

1119^a21–3 Though the acquisition of states of character is voluntary (III. 5), Aristotle nevertheless holds that cowardice is closer to being involuntary than intemperance is, since we become intemperate by seeking out inappropriate pleasures, whereas we become cowardly by developing habits of shunning distress in situations in which it is thrust upon us against our will.

1119^a23–4 A further alleged reason for regarding cowardice as closer to the involuntary. Aristotle is perhaps thinking of people who are driven out of their minds by extremes of suffering. It is not clear why indulgence in extreme forms of pleasure should not be seen as having a similar effect.

1119^a27–31 Cowardice as such appears less involuntary than cowardly actions (such as throwing away one's shield in order to run away unencumbered, the paradigm instance of cowardly action for the Greeks). The latter seem (wrongly, in Aristotle's view; see above) to be done under compulsion, since one has to do them to avoid suffering, whereas there is no suffering, and hence no element of compulsion, involved in cowardice as such.

1119ᵃ31–3   The reverse is the case with intemperance and intemperate actions. There is no element of compulsion in the latter, since they are pleasant, not distressing (but cf. the suggestion of 1111ᵃ24–5 that things done from desire are involuntary), whereas becoming intemperate may seem to be involuntary, since no one desires to become intemperate. Presumably what Aristotle means by the latter claim is that no one acts with the explicit aim of becoming intemperate; rather, one aims to secure this pleasure or that, and even if one is aware that the effect of those particular actions is that one will become intemperate, still that is not the reason for which one does them.

1119ᵃ33–ᵇ15   The term *akolasia* and its cognates (whose literal sense is 'being unpunished, undisciplined' from the verb *kolazein*, to punish) apply both to the intemperance of adults and to the naughtiness of children. Aristotle here explains the resemblance which accounts for this dual application.

ᵇ2–3:   'the posterior is called after the prior'. In cases where a term has a primary and a secondary use, the secondary is always derived from the primary. In this case the priority could be temporal, in which case the adult state is called after that of the child (as Gauthier/Jolif, Ross rev. Ackrill/Urmson, and Rowe make explicit in their translations). On the other hand, Aristotle appears to suggest here that the direction of priority is the reverse; it is because children live according to desire and have a strong appetite for pleasure that they are instances of the general principle that bad appetites need disciplining. It seems to me, therefore, more likely that Aristotle's view is that the application of the term to adults is primary. Aspasius, followed by Natali in his note (p. 477), explicitly leaves the question of priority unresolved; Heliodorus takes the priority to be temporal.

ᵇ13–15:   'Just as ... accordance with reason'. Cf. the description of the 'appetitive and in general desiderative' part of the soul in I. 13 as derivatively rational, in that it is subject and obedient to reason (1102ᵇ30–1), and as 'something which listens to reason as to a father' (1103ᵃ3).

Stewart takes this sentence as decisive in favour of the thesis of temporal priority discussed above. But the use of the child/tutor relationship as an illustration of the relationship between appetite and reason is compatible with both the competing accounts of priority.

1119^{b}15–18   The agreement of reason and desire is echoed in the description of the conditions for correct choice in VI. 2. The conception (of the goal to be achieved and of the means to it) must be true and the desire right, and the one must say the same things as the other pursues (1139^{a}24–6); the good to be achieved by practical thought is truth in agreement with right desire (^{a}29–31).

'[R]eason' (rather than 'principle') is the appropriate translation of *logos* in this context, where Aristotle is discussing in the abstract the relation between the rational and appetitive elements of the soul.

Cf. 1115^{b}12, 19, 1119^{a}20.

For *EE*'s discussion of temperance see III. 2.

BOOK FOUR

CHAPTER I

1119ᵇ22–8 Cf. 1107ᵇ8–14.

The word translated 'wealth' (*chrēmata*, lit. 'things, things for use') frequently has the sense 'money', but Aristotle gives it the wider application of possessions whose value is measured in money. Since his topic is the virtue specific to the use of wealth and its opposed vices, that application is appropriate. Generosity is not confined to the appropriate use of money itself, but extends to the proper use of the things money can buy; a typical act of generosity would be making someone a handsome gift, not necessarily a gift of money.

ᵇ28: 'excesses and deficiencies': the plurals are explained at 1121ᵃ10–12.

1119ᵇ28–1120ᵃ3 The vices opposed to generosity are ungenerosity (*aneleutheria*) and extravagance (*asōtia*). The former, defined at 1107ᵇ13–14 as excess in acquiring wealth and deficiency in giving it away, is here more loosely characterized as caring about wealth more than one ought. The more precise characterization is repeated at 1121ᵃ14–16, and discussed more fully at 1121ᵇ12–1122ᵃ16.

With regard to extravagance, Aristotle distinguishes the strict application of the term from an extended one. The strict application derives from the root meaning of the term *asōtos*, which is 'unsparing' (from the verb *sōzō*, 'save' or 'spare'). The *asōtos* strictly speaking is the person who is unsparing of his or her resources, to the extent that he or she uses them up altogether. Aristotle's term for resources is *ousia*, which is also the word for being, essence, or substance. (I have used 'substance' in the translation, in the somewhat archaic sense of 'wealth, property' (as in 'a person of some substance') to capture this usage.) Perhaps influenced by this range of meanings of *ousia*, Aristotle maintains that being unsparing of one's resources is itself an application derivative from the most fundamental way of being unsparing, viz. being unsparing of one's life, being self-destructive. Using up one's resources is a way of being self-destructive, since one's resources are what one has to live on, and hence it counts as being *asōtos*. (It is likely that Aristotle is influenced in this fanciful etymologizing by another sense of *asōtos*, namely 'beyond help, incapable of being saved'. Since the self-destroyer is *asōtos* in that sense, he or she can the more readily be seen as *asōtos* in the sense of 'unsparing' (of him or herself).)

In contrast with this alleged strict application, Aristotle points to the derived application to those who spend excessive amounts on intemperate enjoyments. This is a looser application, in that it is not necessarily the case that those who are extravagant in this sense use up their resources entirely. In applying the term in this way, Aristotle says, we combine the notion of wasting one's resources with that of expenditure on unworthy objects. But his claim that the term *asōtos* applies strictly only to those who destroy their resources, and loosely or derivatively to those who waste them on inappropriate objects, seems quite gratuitous.

1120^{a}4–8   Aristotle derives the conclusion that generosity is the appropriate use of wealth from the general principle that things which have a use are put to the best use by the person best qualified to use them; e.g. a flute is put to its best use by an expert flautist.[1] As this is a general principle, applying alike to excellence of character and other kinds of excellence, such as technical skill, I translate *aretē* as 'excellence', rather than as 'virtue' at ^{a}6 and ^{a}7, though the specific type of excellence referred to in the latter passage is the virtue of character concerned with wealth. I revert to the translation 'virtue' at ^{a}11–12, where Aristotle is once again speaking specifically about excellence of character. (This is one passage where the translation policy stated in the Preliminary Note to the translation has the cost of requiring a shift between terms which does not correspond to the Greek.)

---

[1] I see no force whatever in Young's argument (1994: 323) that because *chrēmata* has the basic meaning 'useful things' (see note on 1119^{b}22–8 above), counting wealth as something useful 'verges on a category mistake'. Young himself correctly sees that Aristotle's account of the virtue depends on 'the correct conception of the nature of wealth: an abundance of property, properly put to use' (p. 330). On that account wealth is useful by definition: so how can it be close to a category mistake to count it as something useful?

See Blankenship's comment (Young 1994: 338–9).

1120ᵃ8–15 Since a virtue of character is a standing motivational state, prompting the agent to act well in a certain respect, generosity prompts the agent to act well as regards his or her wealth. Acting well consists in using one's wealth appropriately, i.e. in expending it in the right way. Acquiring and keeping wealth is a pre-condition of its use, not the use itself. It is the use of wealth, not its acquisition, which provides the opportunity for the fine actions which are characteristic of the virtuous agent, and which the agent chooses because they are fine (cf. the discussion of 'acting for the sake of the fine' at 1105ᵃ30–3). Aristotle's thought is that while the generous person both acquires and disposes of wealth appropriately, it is the appropriate expenditure which is noble and praiseworthy; the appropriate acquisition is merely not discreditable. That seems right; generosity strikes us as demanding gratitude and admiration, whereas appropriate acquisition, e.g. not screwing the last penny out of one's tenants or not charging exorbitant interest on a loan, is merely common honesty, and hence to be taken for granted.

ᵃ14:   'are associated with', renders *hepetai*, lit. 'follows' or 'follows from'. A literal rendering would mislead in suggesting either temporal succession or logical consequence, whereas Aristotle seems rather to have in mind the constitutive relation, that it is in virtue of giving in the right way that one acts well.

1120ᵃ23–4 'Virtuous actions are fine and are done because they are fine': lit. 'are fine and for the sake of the fine'. See discussion referred to in the previous note.

1120ᵃ24–7 'because it is fine': see above.
    'to whom …': the standard abbreviated list of conditions for correct action: cf. 1106ᵇ21–3, 1107ᵃ15–16, 1109ᵃ28–9, ᵇ14–16, 1115ᵇ15–19, 1118ᵇ21–7, 1119ᵇ15–18.

1120ᵃ26–7 'he will do so … in any way'. Cf. 1104ᵇ5–8 (with note); contrast 1117ᵃ33–ᵇ16 (with note).

1120ᵇ1 The generous person will give because it is fine to do so (see above), but the sum that he or she takes from his or her resources, and the act of taking it, will be seen, not as fine in themselves, but as necessary for the fine act of generosity.

1120^{b}4–6 'It is highly characteristic ... excessive in giving'. 'Excessive' cannot imply improper excess, which is the vice of extravagance; it must mean 'more than normal' or 'more than expected'.

1120^{b}7–11 '[M]eans' renders *ousia* at ^{b}7 and ^{b}9 (see note on 1119^{b}28–1120^{a}3). (The term is translated 'fortune' at ^{b}12, and 'means' at ^{b}24.)

1120^{b}11–14 'The more generous ... their works'. A reminiscence of Plato, *Resp.* 330b–c.

1120^{b}14–24 Contrast the prudence ascribed to the generous person at ^{b}2–3.[2]

1120^{b}20–1 'But all the same . . . and so on'. Cf. note on 1120^{a}24–7.

1120^{b}27–32 Summary of Aristotle's account of the virtue of generosity.

1120^{b}33–1121^{a}1 '[I]s associated with' again renders *hepetai*, which here, however, applies not to the constitutive relation, as in

---

[2] In a sensitive discussion Hare (1988) points out that *eleutheriotēs* combines 'good stewardship' (i.e. financial prudence) with the love of giving (generosity properly so called, which is an aspect of benevolence), and that the two can be in tension with one another. This is an instance of that tension.

Good stewardship will include the appropriate use of wealth for one's own benefit (e.g. in providing for one's retirement), whereas generosity is a form of altruism. Hence Young (1994: 333–4) distinguishes Aristotelian liberality from generosity. But while the *eleutherios* is characterized without specific reference to generosity at 1120^{b}23–4 as 'the one who spends according to his means and on what he should', it is none the less clear that Aristotle regards generosity in the specific sense as the primary form of the virtue. He says that it is more characteristic of the *eleutherios* to give to whom one should than to take from whom one should, and that giving is a form of conferring benefits (*eu poiein*) which attracts gratitude and love (1120^{a}8–23). It is true that he explicitly counts expenditure (*dapanē*) under the head of giving at 1121^{a}12, in the context of a discussion of the vices opposed to *eleutheriotēs*. But the natural way to take 1120^{a}8–9, which introduces the discussion of the virtuous person, is as saying that expenditure and giving are different uses of wealth, just as acquisition and conservation are different aspects of getting it. And that statement leads on to the section just cited, where giving is clearly giving to others. Again, the description at 1121^{b}3–7 of what is wrong with the *doseis* of the extravagant person is chiefly concerned with giving to the wrong sort of people, such as flatterers.

Contrary, then, to Young's suggestion (following Aspasius) that Aristotle uses *dosis* and *lēpsis* as generic terms covering the various ways of dispensing and acquiring wealth (1994: 318 n. 12), it seems to me that the predominant sense of *dosis* in IV. 1 is 'giving'.

1120^{a}12–13 (see above) but to things (specifically correct giving and correct taking) that naturally and typically go together.

1121^{a}1–4 Aristotle is presumably not envisaging a case where the generous person has, untypically, been guilty of extravagance, but rather one in which a proper exercise of generosity has, for reasons beyond the giver's control, gone wrong: e.g. if one gives money to a friend to enable him to set up in business, but instead the friend loses the money on the horses. Given such an event, the generous person will be upset, to the extent that it is appropriate to someone of good character to be so. Aspasius and Anon. take the case to be one where the generous person acts under duress, e.g. when a tyrant exacts money for some evil purpose.

^{a}3–4:　'for it is a mark ... things one should': cf. 1104^{b}11–13.

1121^{a}7 'does not agree with Simonides': a possible alternative reading is 'does not agree with the saying of Simonides'. Either reading suggests that in one of his poems Simonides said something to the effect that one should be more upset at spending what one should not than at not spending what one should. His extant verses do not contain any such sentiment. He is said to have had a reputation for meanness; see Anon. and Gauthier/Jolif ii. 258.

1121^{a}15 'but on a small scale': the qualification is explained by 1122^{a}3–7. (Aquinas and Ross in his original translation render 'except on a small scale'.)

1121^{a}19–30 Extravagant people are of better character then ungenerous people, since they have generous instincts, which will make them generous if shaped by the right experience and training; ungenerous people, by contrast, are selfish.

^{a}23–4:　'or changed in some other way': it is not entirely clear what other kind of influence Aristotle is contrasting with habituation. Perhaps he is thinking of experience, e.g. of having lost money through ill-advised giving, which might be sufficient of itself to motivate better judgement in giving, even without any further moral education. But the line between experience and education is not a clear one.

ᵃ30: 'not even himself'. Presumably Aristotle's thought is that acquiring wealth is of no benefit to the person of bad character (as the ungenerous person is *ex hypothesi*), since all goods have to be directed by practical wisdom, which in turn requires goodness of character (1144ᵇ30–2).

1121ᵃ30–2 Cf. note on 1107ᵃ2–8 (p.111).

1121ᵇ1 'because they do not care about what is fine': cf. note on 1120ᵃ8–15. (Also ᵇ4–5, 9–10.)

1121ᵇ6 'people of good character': lit. 'people moderate (or "measured" (*metriois*)) in character'. Aristotle is exploiting the connection, of both sound and meaning, between *metrios* and *mesos*. Someone whose character is properly proportioned or measured is in a mean state as defined by the doctrine of the ethical mean (i.e. a state between excess and deficiency of motivation).

1121ᵇ9–10 '[I]ndulgences' renders *akolasias*, lit. 'intemperances', i.e. the pleasures characteristic of the intemperate person; cf. III. 10.
'those pleasures': the Greek is simply 'the pleasures', but the context determines that it is specifically intemperate pleasures which are referred to.

1121ᵇ12–13 'ungenerosity is irremediable'. Aspasius takes 'irremediable' to be an overstatement of Aristotle's view, viz. that ungenerosity is very difficult to remedy. See note on 1105ᵃ30–3, (iii).

1121ᵇ17–31 Aristotle points out that the two aspects of ungenerosity, excess in taking and deficiency in giving, do not necessarily go together. His examples are exclusively of tight-fisted people who are scrupulous about not taking from improper sources, whether from genuine honesty (ᵃ24–8) or from fear of retaliation if they treat others dishonestly (ᵃ28–30).

ᵃ30–1: 'they are content neither to take nor to give'. Cf. Plato, *Resp.* 359a1–2, where Glaucon describes the origin of social justice as 'an agreement not to do or suffer wrong'. Anon. notes this parallel.

Aristotle could equally well have pointed to examples of people who take indiscriminately but are not tight-fisted, e.g. a generous brothel-keeper. In fact his treatment of people who take excessively (1121ᵇ31–1122ª12) does not mention this possibility.

1122ª7–13 '[G]ambler' renders *kubeutēs*, lit. 'dice-player'. It is unclear whether Aristotle is thinking of people who cheat at dice, or whether he thinks that making a profit from gambling is disgraceful whether or not one cheats.

'[F]ootpad' renders *lōpodutēs*, lit. 'someone who steals other people's clothes' (from public baths or gymnasia, or by stripping travellers). It is the term for a petty thief, while *lēistēs*, here rendered 'robber', implies theft on a larger scale (it is also the word for 'pirate'). Aristotle groups the last two together on the ground that their dishonesty, unlike that of the gambler, involves taking risks.

ª7:   Burnet, following Aspasius, deletes 'and robber'.

ª13:   '[D]iscreditable' translates *aneleutheroi* (qualifying *lēpseis*, instances of acquiring). See note on 1123ª9–18.

1122ª13–16 Of the two vices opposed to generosity, ungenerosity is worse than extravagance. Cf. note on 1121ª19–30. For the general principle that one extreme can be further from the mean than the other, see note on 1108ᵇ50–1109ª19.

For *EE*'s discussion see III. 4.

BOOK FOUR

CHAPTER 2

1122ª18–23 The topic of this chapter, *megaloprepeia*, is a character-state more specific to the conditions of the Greek city-state than most of the virtues of character with which Aristotle deals. It is the disposition to expend substantial amounts of one's private wealth on projects which both benefit the city and, by the element of display which such projects involve, bring credit on the individual who provides them. The exercise of this state thus consists in public munificence, but since Aristotle clearly takes the element of display to be essential, 'magnificence' (which is in any case the ordinary meaning of the word; see below) is a more appropriate translation than 'munificence' (the latter adopted by Rowe). In principle, one might be munificent without display, in that one might (a) expend large sums on projects which attract no public attention or admiration (e.g. funding a secret programme of cancer research) or (b) exercise munificence anonymously. But, as Aristotle's discussion makes clear, display and the admiration it attracts are part of the *raison d'être* of *megaloprepeia*.

The noun and its cognate adjective are formed from the adjective *megas*, 'great', and the verb *prepō*, whose root meanings are 'to be conspicuous' and 'to be fitting'. Its standard meaning is 'splendour, magnificence', which combines both root meanings of the verb; what is splendid is what is appropriately conspicuous. Aristotle's own etymology (which is on this occasion accurate) combines the notions of fittingness and grandeur (^{a}23).

Many Greek cities, notably Athens, required individual wealthy citizens to finance public projects from their private resources. Some of these, such as fitting out warships, equipping and training choruses for dramatic festivals, and funding various religious ceremonials, are mentioned in this chapter. Another type of magnificence was the provision by private individuals of public buildings, such as temples, libraries, or public gymnasia (or, in the Roman world, baths).

^{a}20–1:   'it does not extend to all activities involving wealth as generosity does, but only to those involving expenditure': but at 1120^{a}8–15 Aristotle has said that generosity is primarily concerned with the use of wealth, i.e. giving, which is distinguished from its acquisition (see note).[3]

The basic distinction between the two virtues is that magnificence is a specific form of generosity, distinguished from the generic virtue both by its scale and by its objects: it is large-scale public generosity, i.e. the generous provision of public goods.

Typically, large-scale public generosity (i.e. magnificence) costs more than private generosity, but all the same some particular act

---

[3] This is another symptom of the tension between prudence and love of giving pointed out by Hare (1988). See previous note.

Young (1994: 319) raises the question why Aristotle counts *eleutheriotēs* as a single virtue, rather than identifying two, one concerned with giving, the other with acquisition. The answer is that the proper use of wealth requires that it be appropriately acquired and conserved.

of private generosity might involve greater expenditure than some magnificent act.[4] Here again Aristotle speaks *hōs epi to polu*.[5]

1122ᵃ24–6 Since different types of public provision require different levels of expenditure, what counts as grandeur is relative to the level of expenditure involved. Spending on a public dinner the amount it would take to fit out a warship would be, not grandeur (as the same amount spent on the warship would be), but 'vulgarity'. Equally, spending on a warship the amount that would pay for a grand dinner would be, not grandeur, but 'shabbiness'. Aristotle here applies the theory of the mean relative to us; cf. note on 1106ᵃ26–ᵇ16.

ᵃ25:   'a sacred embassy'. The types of public provision mentioned above included providing for the equipment and expenses of state delegations attending religious festivals in other cities (including the Olympic and other Panhellenic Games).

1122ᵃ27 The quotation is from *Od.* 17. 420.

1122ᵃ28–9 Because generosity is the generic virtue, magnificence a specific form of it (see note on ᵃ20–1 above).

1122ᵃ30–1 '[S]habbiness' renders *mikroprepeia*, the polar opposite of *megaloprepeia*. '[V]ulgarity' renders *banausia*, the state of being a *banausos*, lit. 'manual worker', hence 'uneducated, vulgar person'. '[B]ad taste' renders *apeirokalia*, lit. 'lack of experience of what is fine'.

1122ᵃ33–4 'We shall discuss these points later': at 1123ᵃ19–33.

1122ᵃ35–ᵇ2 'As we said ... objects'. Cf. II. 1–3, with commentary.

1122ᵇ2–6 The exercise of magnificence consists in large expenditure on grand objects. The objects must be grand enough to justify the size of the expenditure, and the expenditure must be

---

[4] NB: generosity was described at 1120ᵇ19–20 as exercised 'alike on a large and on a small scale'.

[5] Young's hesitation (1994: 314–18) in accepting that Aristotle distinguishes magnificence from generosity (at least partly) in respect of scale seems to me unjustified.

adequate for the grandeur of the object, or even greater. In thus allowing that magnificent expenditure might exceed the grandeur of the object, Aristotle must implicitly distinguish appropriate from inappropriate excess. The latter is vulgarity (as in the example given above). But what is appropriate excess? Aristotle's thought would appear to be that what counts as appropriate expenditure allows for a certain degree of extra elaboration and refinement over and above what is strictly adequate (while not tipping over into vulgarity). So it would be adequate to produce a beautiful temple if the details of the frieze were picked out with gold paint, but an appropriately rich person might appropriately spend out on gold leaf instead, thus making the temple even more beautiful. As in the case of the trainer prescribing a diet for athletes at different stages of training, what is appropriate depends on the circumstances of the individual case (cf. notes on 1104^{a}5-10, 1106^{a}26-^{b}16, and 1109^{b}20-3).

1122^{b}6-7 'because it is fine': cf. note on 1105^{a}30-3.

1122^{b}7 'gladly': cf. note on 1104^{b}5-8.

1122^{b}10-14 The difference between magnificence and simple generosity is not merely that the magnificent person typically spends more than the generous (that distinction was made at ^{a}26-9). Here the point is that the acts of the magnificent person exceed those of the generous in scale (*megethos*), so that the former will produce a grander result than the latter, even from the same expenditure. The magnificent person must, then, have a sense of style and grandeur superior to that of the generous person, which makes him or her a better judge of what is really grand (cf. ^{a}34-5). That may be because the magnificent person is typically concerned with the public domain, and therefore with things on a grand scale, whereas generosity is typically private beneficence.

1122^{b}14-18 'Possessions ... excellence': lit 'the excellence (*aretē*) of a possession (*ktēmatos*) is not the same as that of a work (or "product" (*ergou*))'.

Aristotle's point is that the value of the things on which the magnificent person expends his or her wealth is not identical with their monetary value (which measures their value as possessions), but is determined by their grandeur and fineness (including beauty). So a more expensive statue or tragic chorus is not necessarily more valuable than a less expensive one, if the latter has higher aesthetic value. Aristotle assumes that objects of greater aesthetic value arouse greater admiration in those who encounter them, but he is not thereby committed to the view that the higher value consists in the higher degree of admiration.

1122ᵇ20 '[R]itual objects' renders *kataskeuai*, which has a range of meanings, including 'preparations, provisions, devices' and 'furniture and fittings'. Most translators take it that Aristotle is here referring to religious buildings: Crisp and Irwin have 'temples', Ross rev. Ackrill/Urmson 'buildings', Gauthier/Jolif 'constructions', Dirlmeier 'Bauten', Natali 'erezione di templi'. The word does not, however, seem clearly attested as designating permanent buildings. Rowe's 'ritual paraphernalia' seems closer to the attested senses.

1122ᵇ26–9 'That is why … properly'. Aristotle's thought is that a poor person who undertakes something magnificent will spend more than he or she can afford and still not do the thing properly.

1122ᵇ29–32 The suggestion is that the admiration of the spectator is not exclusively determined by the splendour of the object or undertaking itself, but is at least enhanced by the spectator's beliefs about the status of the person providing it.

1123ᵃ2–4 The context makes it clear that the guests in question are not private guests, but official guests whom the magnificent person is entertaining on behalf of the city; the giving and returning of gifts occurs in the same context. So the things '[i]n the private sphere' (1122ᵇ35) appear to be restricted to weddings and similar events (1123ᵃ1).

1123ᵃ4–5 The gifts which the magnificent person confers on the city (statues, buildings, etc.) are like votive offerings, in that they are prestigious objects of public admiration. (Sometimes, indeed, such things would themselves be votive offerings in the sense of being dedicated to a deity.)

1123ᵃ6–7 The parenthesis explains why the magnificent person's provision of a fine house for him or herself does not contradict the claim of the previous sentence; the fine house is itself an ornament to the city.

1123ᵃ10–18 Aristotle reverts to the relativity of magnificence (see note on 1122ᵃ24–6), distinguishing between magnificence without qualification (*haplōs* (Bywater's editorial addition); cf. note on 1110ᵃ9–11), which is large expenditure on grand objects, from magnificence in a particular area, which is spending a lot for a thing of a certain kind on an outstanding example of that kind. In the latter kind of magnificence the sum expended, though large for a thing of that kind, such as a toy, need not be a large sum. Aristotle expects the magnificent person to be magnificent in everything, large and small alike.

Given that, it is odd that Aristotle describes the value of a magnificent gift for a child as not merely small but mean (or 'petty'). The Greek is *aneleutheron*, lit. 'unworthy of a free person', and it normally carries strong overtones of disapproval and contempt, implying meanness or small-mindedness. (It is also the adjective for 'ungenerous' (1107ᵇ13, 1122ᵃ5).) Aristotle presumably does not wish to describe the *act* of buying the fine ball or oil-flask for the child as *aneleutheron*, because that would imply that the magnificent person should not do it, whereas at ᵃ16–17 he says that the magnificent person should do magnificently whatever kind of thing he or she does, and giving a gift of this kind is acting magnificently when it comes to giving presents to children. The sense in which the *price* of the gift is *aneleutheron* is presumably that it is not big enough for a free person to bother about.

1123ᵃ22 'members of his dining club': the reference is to a type of club (*eranos*) whose members typically brought their own food to the communal meal. Hence the expense for the host on each occasion would be modest in comparison with the lavish outlay appropriate for a wedding feast.

1123ᵃ23–4 The solemnity of costly purple robes would be out of keeping with the buffoonery appropriate to the chorus of a comedy.

The text leaves it indeterminate whether the reference is to a general practice of comedy production at Megara, or to some particular occasion. Translators generally assume the former, as does Anon. Anon. and Heliodorus take the reference to be to stage-hangings rather than to costumes.

1123ᵃ24–7 It is striking that Aristotle characterizes the vulgar person not only as overspending when economy is appropriate but as underspending when lavishness is called for. That fits the vulgar person's lack of the perception of what is appropriate which is characteristic of the virtuous person in general (1109ᵇ22–3) and of the magnificent person in particular (1122ᵃ34–5), but is at odds with what Aristotle has just identified as the motivation characteristic of the vulgar person: namely, to display his or her wealth and thereby attract the admiration of others. Perhaps Aristotle assumes that someone with that motivation will typically overspend, while occasionally underspending.

Aristotle's description makes it clear that the magnificent person too will expect the admiration of others, and there is nothing in his description which precludes the magnificent person from wanting that admiration. But for all that, the magnificent person's motivation differs from that of the vulgar person; the latter wants to show off his or her wealth and to be admired for it, whereas the former wants to do what is fine (1122ᵇ6–7, 1123ᵃ24–5), specifically what is fine in contributing to the common good (1123ᵃ4–5). In so far as the magnificent person wants to be admired, it is to be admired for doing what is fine in that way; the vulgar person just wants to be admired, and does not care whether the things for which he or she is admired are fine.

1123ᵃ27–31 The shabby person, by contrast, always underspends, even on those occasions on which he or she spends a lot.

1123ᵃ31–3 In the light of Aristotle's remark on the comparatively unobjectionable character of the states opposed to magnificence, it seems appropriate here, exceptionally, to render *kakiai* as 'defects' rather than 'vices'.

For *EE*'s discussion see III. 6.

BOOK FOUR

CHAPTER 3

Greatness of soul, the virtue discussed in this chapter, is unique among Aristotle's virtues of character in its self-referential and second-order nature. It is self-referential in that it consists in the virtuous agent's correct self-evaluation, and second-order in that it is the virtue of correct self-evaluation on the ground of possession of the other virtues. The great-souled person is someone who thinks him or herself worthy of great things and is actually worthy of them (1123^b1-2), and the respect in which the great-souled person is worthy of great things is that that person possesses complete virtue (1123^b26-30, $^b35-1124^a4$). That certainly includes complete virtue of character, and, while Aristotle is not explicit on the point, it is likely that it extends to intellectual excellence, and therefore total human excellence.[6]

Aristotle's application of the term in the context of his catalogue of virtues of character is somewhat more specific than that warranted by ordinary usage, which applies it to various aspects of the grandeur of spirit typical of those who are (or think themselves) superior to others: these aspects include courage, pride (extending to arrogance), and clemency. In *An. Post.* II, 97^b15-25, Aristotle distinguishes two kinds of *megalopsuchia*, and treats the term as ambiguous on the grounds of that distinction: the two kinds are pride, characteristic of Achilles, Ajax, and Alcibiades, and resolution in misfortune, characteristic of Lysander and Socrates. The latter application is also found in the description in *NE* I, 1100^b30-3, of the virtuous person in misfortune: 'Yet even in such circumstances nobility shines through, when one endures many great misfortunes equably, not through insensitivity, but because one is noble and great-souled.' In the context of the list of virtues it is the other aspect which predominates; the self-destructive pride of Achilles, Ajax, and Alcibiades springs from their sense of self-worth, and it is that sense, properly employed by the virtuous agent, which Aristotle identifies as the virtue. But the two

---

[6] On the other hand, the text gives little support for Gauthier's contention (Gauthier/Jolif ii. 272–7, 290–2, following Stewart i. 335–7 and Gauthier (1951: 104–14)) that the great-souled person must be a philosopher in the sense of someone living the theoretical life described in Book X.

aspects distinguished in the *Posterior Analytics* are connected, in that endurance of misfortune is itself an expression of the virtuous agent's sense of values, which counts good and ill fortune as unimportant in comparison with goodness of character (1124ᵃ13–16).

The discussion is complicated by Aristotle's characterization of the virtuous agent's self-evaluation. While we might expect the idea of self-worth to be captured by such a formula as 'thinking oneself to be good, and actually being so', Aristotle expresses it in terms of thinking oneself worthy of great things, while actually being so. This raises the question of what are the great things of which the virtuous agent is and believes him or herself to be worthy. For Aristotle, human goods are divided into the excellences, intellectual excellence and excellence of character, on the one hand, and 'external' goods, such as health, good looks, wealth, and honour, on the other, with the former having priority in value, in that while the external goods may enhance the value of a good life, and their absence detract from it, no life can be good which is not centred on the cultivation of the excellences. Since the great-souled person is worthy of great things because of his or her excellence, the things of which he or she is worthy cannot be the excellences themselves, but must therefore be the external goods. But this raises the difficulty that the external goods are themselves of inferior value to the excellences. In this chapter Aristotle identifies the greatest of the external goods as honour (1123ᵇ17–21), but the great-souled person regards even honour as of little worth in comparison with the excellence which merits it (1124ᵃ16–20). This chapter therefore exhibits a certain tension in Aristotle's description of the self-assessment characteristic of the great-souled person.[7] See further below.

1123ᵇ5 '[S]ound-minded' renders *sōphrōn*, translated 'temperate' in the context of Aristotle's treatment of the virtue of temperance (*sōphrosunē*). 'Soundness of mind' is the root meaning of the noun and its cognates, and the terms are frequently applied in that wider sense as well as in the specific sense of having the proper disposition to the bodily appetites. To be *sōphrōn* in the wide sense is to have a proper sense of one's own limitations and

---

[7] Cf. Cooper (1989: 196), who points out that the tension is more explicitly stated at *EE* 1232ᵇ9–16.

the proper relationships to others which those limitations imply; in consequence of that proper sense, the *sōphrōn* will respect the norms governing interpersonal relations and hence abstain from encroachment on what properly belongs to others. Since bodily desires such as those for food, drink, and sex are a particularly potent stimulus to overstepping the limits of one's proper conduct to others, the mastery of those desires is seen as central to *sōphrosunē*, to such an extent that it becomes, as in Aristotle's ethical theory, the primary application of the term. The wider sense is prominent in some Platonic dialogues, usually considered early, notably *Protagoras* (especially in Protagoras's myth) and *Charmides*.

The application of the term here is justified by the thought that the person in question is someone of modest deserts who has a realistic sense of his or her own worth, and is not therefore inclined to claim more than is appropriate. That realistic sense of self-worth, while necessary for greatness of soul, is not sufficient, since the necessary condition of greatness may not be satisfied.

1123^{b}8–9 Vain people are specifically those who unrealistically think themselves worthy of *great* things; those who overvalue themselves without thinking themselves worthy of great things are not counted as vain. (Heliodorus takes Aristotle's point to be that those who are worthy of great things, but think themselves worthy of even greater, are not counted as vain. The Greek is certainly capable of that construal.)

1123^{b}11–13 'The most small-minded ... so much?'. *Ex hypothesi*, people who are in fact worthy of great things but believe themselves not to be undervalue themselves by a wide margin; so if they were not in fact worthy of great things, undervaluation by such a wide margin would produce an extremely low self-evaluation.

1123^{b}13–15 'Now the great-souled ... his worth'. Cf. 1107^{a}6–8.[8]

---

[8] Curzer (1990) sees this claim as the expression of a conceptual tension between the theory of the mean and the Homeric ideal of great or heroic virtue, a tension which he thinks Aristotle is only partially successful in resolving. I think that he exaggerates the problem. He is right in pointing out that greatness of soul is unique among the virtues in involving the two components identified in the introductory note to this chapter, viz. complete virtue and correct self-assessment. But both components fit the

1123ᵇ15–24 The thesis that honour is the greatest of external goods is derived from ordinary beliefs. In Book IX (1169ᵇ9–10) Aristotle refers to the common belief that friends are the greatest of external goods. He sees friendship and honour as closely connected, in that (a) virtuous people wish their friends to be honoured (1169ª20, 29–30) and (b) being liked is similar to being honoured (1159ª16–17).[9]

ᵇ21: 'honour and dishonour': plural in the Greek, referring to particular instances of the bestowing of honour and dishonour, or to kinds of honour and dishonour, or both. Cf. note on 1104ᵇ3–5.

1123ᵇ24–6 Small-minded people rate themselves lower than their actual worth, and *a fortiori* lower than the worth of the great-souled person. Vain people rate themselves equal to the worth of the great-souled person (in that they think themselves worthy of great things (1123ᵇ8–9)), and hence above their own actual worth.

1123ᵇ29–32 The great-souled person, who is most deserving of honour, must be completely good. Hence he or she cannot manifest any particular vice, e.g. cowardice or injustice.

Running away headlong is what a coward does; the Greek translated 'headlong' is *paraseisanti*, lit. 'swinging one's arms' (to run away faster).

1123ᵇ32 'holds nothing of importance': i.e. holds none of the inducements to vicious conduct, such as safety or riches, of any importance. The virtuous person of course holds virtue itself, and the fine, for the sake of which he or she acts, of importance.

1124ª1–4 Cf. introductory note to the commentary on this chapter.

doctrine of the mean: (a) even heroic virtue is a mean between opposed defects, as Curzer himself describes (1990: 534–7); (b) the great-souled person's correct self-assessment is, as Aristotle says, a mean between over-evaluation and under-evaluation of one's own merits, which itself involves an appropriate desire for honour, i.e. a desire which is neither excessive nor deficient. Because greatness of soul is conceptually more complex than the other virtues of character, it fits the doctrine of the mean in a more complex way; but it does fit it, none the less.

⁹ See Gauthier (1951: 104).

ª1–2:   '[O]rnament' renders *kosmos*. As the Greek term also has the meaning 'order, system' (whence the English 'cosmos'), White (1992: 254) (following a suggestion of Hardie (1978: 63)) translates 'like an ordered system of the virtues', thus identifying greatness of soul with total virtue (see his discussion, pp. 255–71). But Aristotle's placing of it in his list of virtues of character makes it clear that he regards it, not as identical with the whole of virtue, but as one virtue among others. *kosmos*, in the sense of 'ornament' captures its supervenient character.[10] As pointed out in the introductory note, complete virtue is a component of greatness of soul, and is therefore not identical with it.[11]

How does greatness of soul make the virtues greater (ª2)? Presumably because the great-souled person's sense of self-worth acts as a stimulus to yet greater virtue. For details see Pakaluk (2004: 252–4, 265–7).

ª4:   '[C]omplete virtue' translates *kalokagathia*, the nominalization of the expression *kalos kai agathos* (lit. 'fine and good'), which standardly connotes overall excellence. In *EE* Aristotle identifies it with complete excellence (1248ᵇ8–13, 1249ª16–17).

---

[10] Schütrumpf (1989: 12) translates *kosmos* as 'endowment'. He does not explain this somewhat unusual use of the latter term, but appears to gloss it a few lines later as 'fulfilment'. It is unclear whether these terms are intended as equivalent to the sense 'ornament, enhancement' assumed here, or as having a distinct sense.

Pakaluk (2004: 259–60) understands *kosmos* as 'governor' or 'organizing principle' or 'regulating force'. He takes this to be a metaphor, appropriate to his understanding of *megalopsuchia* as 'a virtue which consists in a settled attitude of conversion to virtue', whose 'function would therefore naturally be described as overseeing and encouraging the development of the other virtues' (p. 60).

That suggested account of the virtue fails to do justice to its self-evaluative character as described above. In any case, the use of *kosmos* in the sense suggested appears to be confined to its occurrence as a title of certain magistrates in Crete (see LSJ s.v. III); Aristotle's employment of the word in that sense is restricted to that context (*Pol.* II. 10, 1272ª6 ff.). It is unlikely that he would have employed what is in fact a technical term without comment.

[11] Total virtue in its social aspect is explicitly identified with 'justice as a whole' and distinguished from the specific virtue of justice in V. 1. Had Aristotle intended to designate total virtue in yet another way as greatness of soul, it is hard to believe that he would not have been equally explicit.

Bae (2003) denies that the great-souled person possesses complete virtue, arguing that 'ornament of the virtues' means not 'ornament of all the virtues taken together' but 'ornament of any virtue' (i.e. of whatever virtue or virtues the great-souled person happens to possess). That contradicts 1123ᵇ26–30 and ᵇ35–1124ª4, esp. ª4: 'it is not possible (to be great-souled) without *kalokagathia*'. The discussion of Bae's paper by Stover and Polansky (2003) gives an excellent account of the virtue.

1124ᵃ4–5 'the great-souled person is concerned above all with honour and dishonour'. This has to be understood as 'greatness of soul is a reflexive attitude defined as an attitude to honour and dishonour', not as 'the great-souled person cares more about honour and dishonour than about anything else'.[12] For what follows makes it clear that the latter statement is false. See next note.

1124ᵃ5–20 The attitudes of the great-souled person to honour and dishonour are complex.

(i) Since the only things such people care about for their own sake are excellence and the fine, the only honours that matter at all to them are honours bestowed (a) by other excellent people (b) for excellence: (a) because excellent people are the only people whose opinion matters, (b) because excellence itself is the only thing worth caring about for its own sake, and therefore the only thing really deserving of honour. But since honour itself is something of less value than the excellence which merits it, the great-souled person, who recognizes its inferior value, will care about honour, even deserved honour bestowed by good people, only moderately (ᵃ6–9). In fact, the great-souled person, even though regarding honour as the greatest external good, cares comparatively little for the external goods (including honour itself) as a kind. Their presence is an agreeable enhancement of excellence, their loss or absence a cause for some, but not much, regret.

(ii) Honour bestowed by inferior people, and/or honours for inferior achievements, will not matter to the great-souled person at all.

(iii) Neither will dishonour, since the great-souled person will know that in his or her case it is undeserved. (It follows that it will always be bestowed by inferior people thinking the great-souled person deserving of dishonour. Hence, that is a further reason why the great-souled person will be indifferent to it.)

1124ᵃ20–ᵇ5 Aristotle here distinguishes from the genuinely great-souled person a class of people who are commonly but

---

[12] So Curzer (1990: 522; 1991: 147). (The latter article contains convincing rebuttals of a wide range of moral criticisms of Aristotle's great-souled person.)

    Schütrumpf (1989) accepts, wrongly in my view, that for the great-souled person the love of honour is 'the central quality which embraces all other virtues' (p. 18), and hence concludes that Aristotle's statement that not even honour is of (great) value to him 'destroys the basis of Aristotle's argument' (p. 20).

incorrectly thought to be great-souled. These are people who lack
virtue but possess external goods such as wealth or power, and
think (wrongly) that they are worthy of honour on the strength
of those. Like the great-souled person, they consider themselves
superior to other people, but unlike in the case of the great-souled
person, that relative evaluation is in their case false. Hence such
people are arrogant (^{a}29), in contrast to the genuinely great-souled,
who merely appear arrogant (^{a}20).

^{a}20–4:   'Good fortune . . . honoured by some people'. These sentences clearly express a view of greatness of soul which Aristotle
himself does not share, though it is shared by people who think
themselves worthy of honour for external goods and by those who
honour them.

^{a}25:   'In reality it is only the good person who is worthy of
honour'. This sentence, as Aquinas sees, unambiguously expresses
Aristotle's own view.

^{a}25–6:   'but the person . . . worthy of honour': it is not, however, totally clear whether (as Aquinas says in his commentary
on the passage) Aristotle shares the evaluation expressed in this
sentence. It is clear that his general theory of the good contains
the theses (a) that excellence of character and intellect ought to
be everyone's principal goal in life ($1098^a7–18$) and (b) that an
excellent person who has a sufficiency of external goods has a
more desirable life than an excellent person who lacks that sufficiency ($1100^b22–30$). So the person who has both excellence
and external goods is more to be congratulated than the person
who has excellence only. It does not, however, follow from that
that he or she is more deserving of honour; one can consistently
hold that, while people should be congratulated on their good luck,
they should be honoured only for their achievements, since only
the latter are up to them. Hence, since external goods are (predom-
inantly) a matter of luck, while excellence (especially excellence
of character) is up to the agent (cf. III. 5), good fortune does not
add anything to the agent's deserts, and is consequently no ground
for the agent's being more worthy of honour.

   It would, therefore, be consistent with the general thrust of his
ethical theory were Aristotle to dissociate himself from the evaluation expressed in this sentence by 'is regarded as more worthy

of honour'. Whether he does in fact do so in the context of this particular discussion is less clear.[13]

1124^{b}5–1125^{a}17   This catalogue of attitudes and types of behaviour characteristic of great-souled people has as its core their sense of self-worth, in the light of which they see most commonly prized goals as not worth pursuing, and many ways of behaving as beneath their dignity, in that they involve accepting a position of inferiority *vis-à-vis* another, or accepting that the behaviour and attitudes of others are a matter of concern to them.

Some comments on details follow.

^{b}8–9:   'since he does not hold ... any means whatever': i.e. in the view of the great-souled person it is not worth saving your life if you have to act discreditably in order to do so.

^{b}15–16:   Aristotle refers inaccurately to an episode in *Il.* 1. 503–10, where Thetis asks Zeus to support her son Achilles in his quarrel with Agamemnon. In our texts Thetis does mention (though very briefly) her previous services to Zeus, and does not mention kindnesses she has previously received from him. Aristotle's citations of Homer (doubtless done from memory) do not always correspond accurately to our texts; cf. notes on 1109^{a}32 and 1116^{a}34–5.

^{b}16–17:   According to Anon., the reference is to a Spartan embassy to Athens dated by the historian Callisthenes to 369 BC.

---

[13] I therefore disagree with Cooper's assertion (1989: 196) that Aristotle 'clearly says' that good fortune makes people more great-souled.

Irwin (1999b: 208–9) maintains that Aristotle thinks that possession of external goods is a legitimate ground of honour, on the grounds (a) that the distinction in I. 12 between what is praiseworthy (*epaineton*) and what is honourable (*timion*) implies that if one good is better and more complete than another, it is more honourable, and (b) that Aristotle believes that virtue combined with successful virtuous actions and other external goods is better than virtue alone (p. 209). I am not convinced that the discussion in I. 12 commits Aristotle to (a), since that discussion is (as Irwin acknowledges) concerned with the distinction between things which promote intrinsic goods (i.e. praiseworthy things) and intrinsic goods themselves (i.e. honourable things). The distinction between virtue alone and virtue accompanied by external goods is a distinction within the class of intrinsic goods. Even granted that only intrinsic goods are honourable, it does not follow that the greater of two intrinsic goods is more honourable than the lesser.

^{b}23: 'not to go for things which confer honour': i.e. not to go for things other than virtue, which confer honour according to ordinary valuations. Cf. 1124^a10-11.

^{b}23–4: 'where other people are in first place': the Greek verb *prōteuō* (from *prōtos*, 'first') may mean either 'be in charge' or 'excel'. Aristotle might intend either or both; the point is that the great-souled person avoids any situations where he or she has to accept an inferior position.

^{b}24–5: 'except where there is great honour or a great task to be done': the great-souled person will seek to perform virtuous actions, which bring deserved honour. On the question of how far the great-souled person will seek *to be honoured*, see note on 1124^a5-20, and the discussion of acting for the sake of the fine in commentary on 1105^a30-3.

^{b}30–1: Though Aristotle counts dissembling, i.e. insincere self-denigration, as one of the vices opposed to truthfulness (cf. 1108^a19-23, with note), he allows great-souled people to play down their merits in speaking to their inferiors. Presumably this connects with the point made at ^{b}22–3, that it would be vulgar, and therefore beneath their dignity, to display their superiority to their inferiors. Not merely must they not parade it, but they must even bend the truth to avoid displaying it.[14]

1125^a3-5: 'Nor does he bear grudges ... overlook them': this establishes the connection of greatness of soul with magnanimity in the modern sense. But the thrust of Aristotle's account indicates that the reason why great-souled people do not harbour grudges is that it is beneath them to do so, since doing so would involve acknowledging that they have been hurt or injured, and thus put in a position of inferiority. In so far as they forgive others, it is because they look down on them, whereas magnanimity in the modern sense often involves recognition of merit on the part of someone who has injured one.

^{a}8–9: 'unless to insult them': an alternative translation is 'unless in response to insults from them'. Stewart, Burnet, Gauthier/Jolif,

---

[14] I see no textual basis for Cooper's claim (1989: 197) that the great-souled person's *eirōneia* towards the many 'is not pretence but reticence'. Cooper does, however, have the support of Anon., who takes Aristotle's meaning to be that the great-souled person is not apt to proclaim his or her merits to all and sundry.

Ross rev. Ackrill/Urmson, Dirlmeier, and Rowe take the passage in the former sense (following Anon.), Irwin, Crisp, and Pakaluk (2004: 254) in the latter (following Aspasius and Aquinas). Natali sits on the fence with 'per insolenza', while recording both alternatives in his note (p. 483).

1125ᵃ17–33 The defects opposed to greatness of soul.

As with the defects opposed to magnificence (see note on 1123ᵃ31–3), Aristotle does not treat these defects as major flaws of character. He characterized the defects opposed to magnificence as *kakiai*, but said that they do not incur reproach. Here he says that people who manifest the defects are not bad (*kakoi*), though they have gone wrong (they are *hēmartēmenoi*, which in some contexts has the primary implication of having made a mistake, in others that of having been guilty of a fault).

ᵃ24–7: The lack of self-confidence which characterizes small-minded people leads them to fail to do fine things of which they are in fact capable. E.g. a small-minded person might avoid risking his life in combat in the mistaken belief that he was not courageous enough.

ᵃ32–4: Another case in which one of the opposed defects is further from the mean than the other; cf. note on 1122ᵃ13–16.

In contrast with his treatment of the defects opposed to generosity, Aristotle does not explain his belief that small-mindedness is worse than vanity. Perhaps the reason is the feature of the former discussed in the preceding note. Small-mindedness does harm, in that it prevents some people from acting virtuously, whereas vanity is merely ridiculous.

For *EE*'s discussion see III. 5. Rees (1971) and Irwin (1999*b*) compare the two discussions (the latter extending the comparison to *MM* I. 25).

BOOK FOUR

CHAPTER 4

1125ᵇ1–2 'as we said in our preliminary remarks': 1107ᵇ24–30.

1125ᵇ11–18 Cf. 1107ᵇ30–1108ᵃ1, with note.

^{b}11–13:   Cf. also 1109^{b}16–18.

^{b}13:   '[M]oderate' renders *sōphrōn*; cf. note on 1123^{b}5.

^{b}14–15:   Since Aristotle makes his point about the variable application of the term *philotimos* (lit. 'honour-loving', normally rendered in this volume 'ambitious'; see note on 1107^{b}30–1108^{a}1) on the strength of a general point about the application of terms formed from *philo-* (*philotoioutos*, 'lover of such-and-such'), I have here, exceptionally, preferred the translation 'honour-loving'.

1125^{b}18–21   Aristotle argues that, despite the lack of a name for the mean state with regard to honour, the existence of excessive and deficient states presupposes the existence of a mean.

1125^{b}21–5   Aristotle makes the same point about courage at 1108^{b}19–26. See note on that passage.

Comparison of this chapter with the preceding one raises the problem of whether Aristotle can properly admit as a virtue a mean level of desire for small-scale honour, i.e. the state of wanting such honour neither too much nor too little. For in his description of the great-souled person, who is the person of perfect virtue, Aristotle specifies that that person does not value such honour at all (1124^{a}10–11). And since the virtuous person is the proper judge of what is valuable and not (cf. 1113^{a}29–33, with note on 1113^{a}20–33), it should follow that such honour is not valuable at all. The parallel with the virtues to do with wealth does not help Aristotle here. There is a proper way of using wealth both on the larger scale of public munificence and on the smaller scale of private generosity, and the fully virtuous person will be correctly disposed in both ways. With regard to honour, on the other hand, the fully virtuous person has no ground to recognize anything other than virtue as an appropriate ground of honour (see commentary on the preceding chapter). It therefore follows that that person should have no desire at all for any honours other than those accorded for virtue. And since, by the principle just cited, the virtuous person's judgement is decisive on what is really valuable, it follows that no one should desire honours for anything other than virtue.

I think that the answer to this difficulty must be that in identifying the anonymous mean with regard to 'small-scale' honours,
Aristotle is pointing out, not an item in his own ideal evaluative
scheme, but a feature of our everyday evaluations. We do criticize some people for being overly concerned with honours and
distinctions of various kinds, and others for being insufficiently
motivated by that kind of consideration, and in looking at things
in that way we take it for granted that there is an appropriate
level of that kind of motivation, a level which is higher than
zero. We do think that it is appropriate to want the esteem of
others for achievements of various kinds, including those which
fall outside the Aristotelian scheme of excellences. We think that
way, of course, because we are not, in Aristotle's terms, great-
souled; if we were, we should regard many of the concerns that
do now motivate us as beneath us. No doubt being great-souled
is something which we should aspire to; but the standpoint of
the great-souled person, for whom nothing matters except excellence of character and intellect, is in fact far removed from that
from which most of us, most of the time, view the world and
ourselves.

But now, what should be our attitude to the thesis that the virtuous person is the proper judge of what is really valuable? One
possibility is to accept that some of our value judgements, even
some which are closely bound up in our day-to-day lives, are just
wrong. We are just wrong in thinking that it matters whether we
are elected to the local Rotary Club, or win an Olympic gold
medal, or are made an Honorary Fellow. As far as possible, we
should try to detach ourselves from all such things, and seek to
achieve greatness of soul. And as a result of achieving greatness of soul, we shall cease to count the virtue concerned with
small-scale honours as a virtue. Another possibility is to rela-
tivize the thesis that the virtuous person is the proper judge of
value. For people who do aspire to greatness of soul, the great-
souled person is the judge. But may there not be other levels of
goodness, on which someone of less exalted standards can still
count as being good enough to be the proper judge for people
like us?

There is no corresponding discussion in *EE*.

BOOK FOUR

CHAPTER 5

1125^{b}26 'anger': plural in the Greek. Cf. note on 1104^{b}3–5.

1125^{b}26–9 On the absence of pre-existing names for states to do with anger, cf. 1108^{a}4–9, with note.

States to do with anger provide another case where the mean is closer to one extreme than to the other; cf. 1108^{b}35–1109^{a}19, 1121^{a}19–30, 1122^{a}13–16, and 1125^{a}32–4, with notes. Aristotle explains why good temper is closer to the deficiency than to the excess at 1126^{a}2–3, adding further reasons at ^{a}29–31.

1125^{b}31–1126^{a}1 The standard specification of the conditions constituting the mean state; cf. 1115^{b}15–19 and the other passages cited in the note on that passage. Also 1126^{a}4–6, 9–11, 13–15, 26–8, 33–5, ^{b}5–6.

1126^{a}1–2 Presumably Aristotle is here reporting the common view; his own view (see above) is that good temper is closer to the deficiency than to the excess. It is only in the common perception (perhaps reflected, as Gauthier/Jolif suggest (ii. 301–2) in the ordinary connotation of the term *praos*) that good temper is *too* close to the deficiency.

1126^{a}3–4 'unanger': cf. note on 1108^{a}4–9.

1126^{a}6–8 'putting up with ... slavish': a verbal reminiscence of Plato, *Grg.* 483b.

1126^{a}8–13 On the variety of ways in which excess of anger may be manifested, cf. 1106^{b}16–24, with note.

The impossibility of being excessively angry in every way at once appears to be psychological rather than logical; from what follows it appears that Aristotle is thinking primarily of the psychological contrast between the hot-tempered person who flares up quickly and calms down equally quickly and the bitter person whose anger smoulders for a long time.

1126^{a}21 '[F]ury' renders *thumos.* cf. note on 1105^{a}7–8.

1126ᵃ26–7 'difficult': the adjective *chalepos* is cognate to the verb *chalepainein*, one of the two verbs (the other is *orgizesthai*, from *orgē*, 'anger') which Aristotle applies to being or getting angry. I have rendered *chalepainein* as 'be angry', and *orgizesthai* normally as 'get angry', chiefly to mark the fact that Aristotle uses two verbs rather than one. But there is no emphasis in his discussion on the contrast between being and becoming angry; irascible people get angry quickly (ᵃ13–14), but bitter people are angry for a long time (ᵃ20), and in each case the verb is *orgizesthai*, translated 'get angry' in the former passage and 'are angry' in the latter.

1126ᵃ28 'or': a variant reading in a single manuscript is 'or even'. Assuming the OCT reading it is not clear whether, as Anon. thinks, Aristotle distinguishes getting one's own back, i.e. exacting recompense, from punishment, i.e. inflicting further harm once recompense has been exacted. 'Or' may have the sense 'or in other words'. The variant reading demands the distinction.

1126ᵃ29–31 Two further reasons why excessive anger is further from the mean than deficient anger (a) we are more prone to the former, (b) it is socially more damaging. Cf. note on 1108ᵇ30–1109ᵃ19.

1126ᵃ31–ᵇ4 Cf. 1109ᵇ14–23.

ᵃ36–ᵇ2: Cf. 1107ᵇ31–1108a1, 1108ᵇ22–6, 1109ᵇ16–18.

ᵇ2–4: Repeats 1109ᵇ20–3.

ᵇ3: 'specify by reason'; alternatively, 'specify by one's principle'. Cf. note on 1103ᵇ32–4.

For *EE*'s discussion see III. 3.

BOOK FOUR

CHAPTER 6

Throughout this chapter 'offence' and its cognates render *lupē* and its cognates. Aristotle is talking about causing annoyance or offence, which are kinds of *lupē*. Cf. note on 1104ᵇ3–5.

1126ᵇ19–25 Though the social virtue which is intermediate between being ingratiating and being disagreeable has no name of its own, it most closely resembles friendliness, in that the person who has that virtue treats others in a friendly manner. The difference is that genuine friendliness, i.e. the attitude which true friends have to one another, involves an emotional attachment which is not implied by the nameless virtue.

We might well think that this discussion calls for the distinction between the relationship of friendship, which requires that the parties to that relationship are emotionally attached to one another in some degree (see e.g. 1156ᵇ7–30, 1158ᵃ8–14), and the social virtue of friendliness, which is a state of individual character, consisting in the standing disposition to treat others, whether friends or not, in a friendly way. Aristotle, however, makes no explicit distinction between friendliness and friendship, using the term *philia* for both.

1126ᵇ25–1127ᵃ6 The virtuous agent's relationships to others will be determined by his or her long-term aims: viz. to do what is fine and advantageous. Subject to these, and other things being equal, he or she will treat everyone in a friendly way, seeking to please them and avoid causing them offence. Inequalities, are, however, introduced by different degrees of association; for instance, it is not appropriate to be as considerate of strangers as of people one knows well.

It is noteworthy that Aristotle here identifies the virtuous person's long-term concern, not simply as with the fine, as he usually does (1115ᵇ12–15, 1120ᵃ23–4, 1122ᵇ6–7; *EE* 1230ᵃ27–9) but as with the advantageous and the fine. Cf. 1104ᵇ30–1105ᵃ1, with note. These should not, however, be seen as strictly independent goals. Clearly, even for the virtuous person, not everything advantageous is fine; e.g. good health is advantageous but not fine. But (a) the virtuous person will never pursue anyone's advantage at the expense of the fine, and (b) Aristotle's treatment of self-sacrifice suggests that the fine is the virtuous agent's *ultimate* concern (see discussion of IX. 8 in commentary on 1105ᵃ30–3 (pp. 89–90, 92)). It is probably best to see the fine as intrinsic value and the advantageous as instrumental value, possessed by what promotes or enhances the fine.

1127ᵃ11–12   Repeats 1125ᵇ24–5, with slight verbal modifications.

EE's discussion is a brief note, 1233ᵇ29–34.

BOOK FOUR

CHAPTER 7

1127ᵃ18–20   At 1108ᵃ9–30 Aristotle identified three sets of virtues and vices relating to social life, two concerned with pleasure and unpleasantness and one with truth and falsehood. Of those in the former class friendliness and its opposed vices, whose sphere is social life in general, have been discussed in the previous chapter; wit, whose sphere is the specific one of amusement, is the topic of chapter 8.

1127ᵃ23–4   '[S]traightforward' renders *authekastos*, lit. 'saying of each thing that it is it' (i.e. calling a spade a spade). Cf. *EE* 1233ᵇ39. The term is so understood by Burnet, Ross rev. Ackrill/Urmson, Irwin, Crisp, Dirlmeier, and Natali (following Aspasius and Anon.); Stewart, Gauthier/Jolif, and Rowe render 'appearing in one's own character' or 'being oneself' (i.e. being one's own man). Dirlmeier's note (p. 389) suggests that the term has both connotations in this passage.

1127ᵃ26–8   Aristotle distinguishes people with natural dispositions towards truthfulness and its opposed defects from those who deliberately behave in those ways for a specific purpose. By the latter he presumably has in mind people who are boastful or self-denigrating with an eye to some particular advantage; he does not explicitly distinguish people who deliberately cultivate those states of character from those who deliberately behave in those ways on particular occasions.

1127ᵃ31–2   The boaster is more blameworthy than the dissembler because boasting is offensive to others (1127ᵇ8–9), whereas a certain degree of self-denigration is a socially agreeable trait (1127ᵇ22–3, 29–31).

1127^a33–^b1   Honesty in agreements or generally in one's dealings with others is an aspect of the specific virtue of justice, the principal topic of Book V.

1127^b20   '[E]xpert' renders *sophos*, also 'wise, learned'. The text translated is a variant, found in various manuscripts, of the OCT text, which reads 'a seer, expert or doctor'. The latter is read by Aspasius and Anon., the former by Heliodorus; Aquinas recognizes the possibility of either reading, though his translator favours the latter.

1127^b25–6   Socrates: see note on 1108^a19–23.

1127^b28   The ostentatiously austere dress of the Spartans is given as an example of the kind of excessive down-playing which is itself a form of showing off.
    For *EE*'s discussion see 1233^b38–1234^a3.

BOOK FOUR

CHAPTER 8

The topic of this chapter is humour, in particular making fun of people, which the Greeks appear to have regarded as the basic kind of humour (cf. note on 1108^a35–^b6, with reference to Plato's discussion of comedy in the *Philebus*).[15]

1128^a1   Aristotle treats humour as a form of conversation, and throughout distinguishes the roles of speaker and hearer. There are standards of propriety for both, but those for the speaker are more restrictive; there are some things said in fun which it is proper for a respectable person to listen to, but not to say him or herself. Cf. ^a17–20, ^a28–9, ^a33–^b1.

1128^a2   Propriety in either aspect is relative to the company one is in.

---

[15] Cf. also *Poet.* 1449^a32–7, where the ridiculous, which is the subject-matter of comedy, is defined as a sort of harmless fault and deformity, and the definition of wit at *Rhet.* 1389^b11–12 as 'educated insolence' (on which, see Fortenbaugh (1968: 218–19)).

1128ᵃ10   Aristotle correctly connects the adjective *eutrapelos*, 'witty', with *eutropos*, lit. 'resourceful'. The etymological connection is that both are formed from the verb *trepō*, 'turn', hence having the basic meaning 'turning readily from one direction to another'. Aristotle uses that basic meaning to draw a parallel between the versatile play of ready wit and agility of bodily movement.

Since literal rendering of the two adjectives does not preserve the connection of Aristotle's thought, I render *eutropoi* as 'have their wits about them'.

1128ᵃ17   'Cleverness' renders *epidexiotēs*, lit. 'dexterity'.

1128ᵃ18   '[R]espectable' renders *eleutherios*: cf. note on 1118ᵇ4. Cf. ᵃ21, where the contrast, picking up the basic meaning of the term (cf. note on 1107ᵇ8–10), is with 'slavish'.

1128ᵃ23   '[V]ulgar language' renders *aischrologia*, lit. 'saying disgraceful things'; the term applies to obscenity and to vulgar abuse, both characteristic of Athenian Old Comedy, e.g. that of Aristophanes.

1128ᵃ25–7   At *EE* 1234ᵃ18–23 Aristotle says that the witty person should be defined as the one who make jokes which will please the person of good judgement, rather than as the one who does not offend the person made fun of. That criterion is extensionally equivalent to the former of the alternatives posed here, which is also preferred by Aspasius.

1128ᵃ29–32   The thought is that as there is a law against slander, so perhaps there ought to be a law forbidding some types of mockery. But the witty person needs no external restraint, since he or she will observe the proper restraint spontaneously.

1128ᵇ3–4   'But relaxation . . . in life': this emphasizes how inappropriate the attitude of the boor is; he has no time at all for what is in fact a necessary part of life.

1128ᵇ4–9   Cf. 1108ᵃ9–14.
For *EE*'s discussion see 1234ᵃ3–23.

BOOK FOUR

CHAPTER 9

1128ᵇ10–15   Cf. 1108ᵃ30–2. Shame is listed among the feelings at *EE* 1220ᵇ12–14; it does not figure in the corresponding list in *NE*, 1105ᵇ21–3. For the definition 'fear of disgrace' see *Rhet.* ῾1383ᵇ12–14; there the term defined is *aischunē* (see next note).

1128ᵇ15–21   Aristotle's view that shame is a feeling appropriate only for young people reflects the fact that the term *aidōs* also connotes modesty, the attribute of someone who is restrained, who does not flaunt him or herself (in particular, sexually) and who acknowledges the superior status of other, especially older, people. That style of demeanour was considered particularly appropriate for a young person; see especially Plato, *Charmides*, and the speech of the Right Argument in Aristophanes' *Clouds*, 961–1023.

On the other hand, the claim that shame is not appropriate in older people, or in good people generally, since they should not (and in the case of the latter do not) do anything of which they should be ashamed, assumes that shame is exclusively a reactive attitude to one's own past misdeeds, thereby neglecting the notion of *aidōs* as a sense of shame, in which it is in effect an aspect of the wider notion of *sōphrosunē* as soundness of mind (cf. note on 1123ᵇ5). Aristotle is right to say that the reactive attitude cannot be a characteristic of someone who is by his standards completely good. But *aidōs* as a sense of shame is not that attitude; rather, it is a sense of restraint inhibiting possible future action, a sense that one would be ashamed to do something like that. Since sensitivity to what it would be fine or noble to do necessarily involves comparison with what it would be disgraceful or shameful to do, Aristotle's insistence on that sensitivity as central to the motivation of the virtuous person ought to lead him to give a correspondingly prominent place to a sense of shame in that sensitivity. Cf. X. 9, 1179ᵇ7–13.

The lack of a distinction between the backward-looking reactive attitude and the forward-looking sense of restraint is reflected in Aristotle's treatment of the term *aidōs* as interchangeable with *aischunē*; the latter term, which is cognate to *aischos*, whose senses include 'disgrace' and 'ugliness', and *aischros*, 'disgraceful, shameful, ugly', primarily designates the reactive attitude. At ᵇ19–21 Aristotle says that we praise young people for being modest (*aidēmonas*), but that no one would praise an older person for being given to shame (*aischuntēlos*), because it is base deeds which are a source of shame (*aischunē*).

Anon. correctly distinguishes the backward-looking attitude (*aischunē*) from the forward-looking (*aidōs*) as follows: 'it seems that *aidōs* differs from *aischunē* in this way, that *aischunē* is for bad things that have been done, but *aidōs* is fear of disgrace at the thought of disgraceful deeds,' adding that Aristotle fails to attribute the latter attitude to the virtuous agent because he shifts from discussing *aidōs* to discussing *aischunē* (204. 7–11).

1128ᵇ28 'one is ashamed of what is voluntary': no doubt the primary reference is to voluntary actions, but one might be ashamed of a voluntary *pathos*, i.e. something's happening to one in accordance with one's will, e.g. being the consenting object of someone's lust. Cf. note on 1109ᵇ30–2.

1128ᵇ29–31 Here Aristotle does seem to recognize a sense of shame (*aidōs*; see above), whose characteristic expression is 'I should be ashamed were I to do anything like that'. (The verb for 'be ashamed' is *aischunesthai*; see above.) His reason for saying that that is not appropriate to the virtues is presumably that in his view the virtuous person would never even think of doing such things. But, as pointed out above, such thoughts are integral to the virtuous person's standing motivation to do things because it would be fine to do them or disgraceful not to (1116ᵃ10–12, 1117ᵃ17, ᵇ9; cf. 1115ᵃ12–14, 1116ᵃ27–9).[16]

1128ᵇ33–5 Aristotle discusses self-control, by which he means having bad desires but overcoming them by reason, in Book VII, 1145ᵇ8–20, 1146ᵃ9–18, ᵇ14–19, 1150ᵃ32–ᵇ1, 1151ᵇ23–1152ᵃ3, 1152ᵃ25–36. The connection between self-control and shame is presumably that a sense of shame helps the self-controlled person master his or her bad desires.

1128ᵇ35 This introduces the subject of Book V.
On shame *EE* has only a brief note, 1233ᵇ26–9.

---

[16] On the importance of shame in moral education see Curzer (2002).

In *EE* Aristotle asserts that the states of character discussed in *NE* IV. 6–9 are not virtues properly speaking, since they lack the element of choice; they are, rather, to be classified as feelings (1234^{a}24–8) or, more strictly as 'mean states having to do with feelings' (*mesotētes pathētikai*, 1233^{b}18). By the latter term Aristotle means the disposition to experience a certain feeling 'in a mean way', i.e. neither too much nor too little' (cf. his discussion of 'qualities having to do with feelings' (*pathētikai poiotētes*) in *Cat.* 9^{a}27–10^{a}10). Since being disposed to have feelings in that way is part of his account of virtue of character (cf. II. 6, esp. 1106^{b}16–24, with note) the reason why he does not count these dispositions as virtues must be that he takes it that they are purely natural, as distinct from virtues of character, which are acquired by habituation (II. 1).

We have seen that in *NE* Aristotle applies that analysis to modesty and to righteous indignation (1108^{a}31–^{b}6). In *EE* he applies it also to friendliness, truthfulness, and wit, which in *NE* are treated as virtues of character, without differentiation from the rest. Even in the case of the first two we have no reason to accept Aristotle's claim that the mean states are not acquired by habituation. If, as we suggested, the essence of modesty is having an appropriate sense of shame, in virtue of which one regards as shameful things which it is right to regard as such, then we should certainly expect that sense to be acquired by habituation, just as moral sensibility in general is acquired. Exactly the same seems true of righteous indignation.

With regard to friendliness, truthfulness, and wit, the distinction from virtues properly so called is even less plausible. None of these character-states is an emotion, nor is it plausible to see them as purely natural dispositions to feel emotions.[17] Though of course the conditions for the acquisition of one virtue differ from those for the acquisition of another, Aristotle gives us no reason to think that those states are not acquired by the same kind of process of habituation as are e.g. courage or generosity.[18]

---

[17] See Fortenbaugh (1968). He maintains, plausibly, that truthfulness and friendliness are not associated with any specific emotion (pp. 214–16), but holds that the same is not true of wit, since he counts a sense of humour as an emotion (pp. 216–21). Irrespective of whether we accept that classification, there is no reason to think that the proper disposition with regard to one's sense of humour is not acquired by habituation.

[18] Cf. Fortenbaugh (1975: 91–2); Gottlieb (1994: 11–12).

BIBLIOGRAPHY

A. TRANSLATIONS AND COMMENTARIES

ALEXANDER OF APHRODISIAS (fl. AD 200), *Alexandri Aphrodisiensis Scripta Minora: Quaestiones IV*, ed. I. Bruns, *Supplementum Aristotelicum*, 2.2 (Berlin, 1892), 117–63. Trans. R. W. Sharples, *Alexander of Aphrodisias, Ethical Problems* (London, 1990). Cited as 'Alexander'.

ANONYMOUS (AD ?2nd c.), *Anonymi in Ethica Nicomachea Commentaria*, ed. G. Heylbut, *CAG*, 20 (Berlin, 1892). Cited as 'Anon.'

AQUINAS, ST THOMAS, *In Decem Libros Ethicorum Aristotelis ad Nicomachum Expositio*, ed. R. M. Spiazzi, 3rd edn. (Turin, 1964). Cited as 'Aquinas'.

ASPASIUS (AD 2nd c.), *Aspasii in Ethica Nicomachea Commentaria*, ed. G. Heylbut, *CAG*, 19 (Berlin, 1889). Cited as 'Aspasius'.

BURNET, J. (1900), *The Ethics of Aristotle* (London). Cited as 'Burnet'.

CRISP, R. (2000), *Aristotle, Nicomachean Ethics* (Cambridge). Cited as 'Crisp'.

DIRLMEIER, F. (1969), *Aristoteles, Nikomachische Ethik*, 5th edn. (Berlin). (*Aristoteles, Werke in deutscher Übersetzung*, Band 6.) Cited as 'Dirlmeier'.

GAUTHIER, R. A., and JOLIF, J. Y. (1958, 1959), *L'Éthique à Nicomaque: Introduction, Traduction et Commentaire*, 2 vols. in 3 parts (Louvain and Paris). Cited as 'Gauthier/Jolif'.

HELIODORUS (date uncertain), *Heliodori in Ethica Nicomachea Paraphrasis*, ed. G. Heylbut, *CAG*, 19 (Berlin, 1889). Cited as 'Heliodorus'.

IRWIN, T. (1999a), *Aristotle, Nicomachean Ethics*, 2nd edn. (Indianapolis and Cambridge). Cited as 'Irwin'.

NATALI, C. (1999), *Aristotele, Etica Nicomachea* (Rome and Bari). Cited as 'Natali'.

OSTWALD, M. (1962), *Aristotle, The Nicomachean Ethics* (Indianapolis and New York). Cited as 'Ostwald'.

ROSS, D. (1980), *Aristotle, The Nicomachean Ethics*, rev. J. L. Ackrill and J. O. Urmson (Oxford, New York, Toronto, and Melbourne). Cited as 'Ross rev. Ackrill/Urmson'. This is the latest of several revisions of Ross's translation, which was originally published in 1925 in vol. ix of *The Works of Aristotle Translated into English* (Oxford). Readers should note that it is not identical with the revision by J. O. Urmson, published in 1975 and reprinted in J. Barnes (ed.), *The Complete Works of Aristotle: The Revised Oxford Translation* (Princeton, 1984).

ROWE, C. (2002), *Aristotle, Nicomachean Ethics* (Oxford). (With philosophical introduction and commentary by S. Broadie.) Cited as 'Rowe'.

STEWART, J. A. (1892), *Notes on the Nicomachean Ethics of Aristotle*, 2 vols. (Oxford). Cited as 'Stewart'.

B. OTHER WORKS

ACKRILL, J. L. (1974), 'Aristotle on *Eudaimonia*', *Proceedings of the British Academy*, 60: 339–59. Repr. in Rorty (1980: 15–33) and in Ackrill (1997: 179–200).

—— (1978*a*), 'An Aristotelian Argument about Virtue', *Paideia*, Special Aristotle Issue: 113–7. Repr. in Ackrill (1997: 222–9).

—— (1978*b*) 'Aristotle on Action', *Mind*, 87: 595–601. Repr. in Rorty (1980: 93–101) and in Ackrill (1997: 212–21).

—— (1997), *Essays on Plato and Aristotle* (Oxford).

ALLAN, D. J. (1953), 'Aristotle on the Origin of Moral Principles', *Actes du XIe Congrès Internationale de Philosophie*, 12: 120–7. Repr. in Barnes *et al.* (1977: 72–8).

—— (1971), 'The Fine and the Good in the Eudemian Ethics', in Moraux and Harlfinger (1971: 63–71).

ANNAS, J. (1981), *An Introduction to Plato's* Republic (Oxford).

ANSCOMBE, G. E. M. (1958), 'Modern Moral Philosophy', *Philosophy*, 33: 1–19. Repr. in *The Collected Philosophical Papers of G. E. M. Anscombe*, iii: *Ethics, Religion and Politics* (Oxford, 1981), 26–42, and in Crisp and Slote (1997: 26–44).

ANTON, J. P. and PREUS, A. (1991) (eds.), *Essays in Ancient Greek Philosophy*, iv: *Aristotle's Ethics* (Albany, NY).

BAE, E. (2003), ' "An Ornament of the Virtues" ', *Ancient Philosophy*, 23: 337–49.

BARNES, J. (1984) (ed.), *The Complete Works of Aristotle: The Revised Oxford Translation*, 2 vols. (Princeton).

—— (1999), 'An Introduction to Aspasius', in A. Alberti and R. W. Sharples (eds.), *Aspasius: The Earliest Extant Commentary on Aristotle's* Ethics (Berlin and New York), 1–50.

—— SCHOFIELD, M., and SORABJI, R. (1977) (eds.), *Articles on Aristotle*, ii: *Ethics and Politics* (London).

BOSLEY, R., SHINER, R. A., and SISSON, J. D. (1995) (eds.), *Aristotle, Virtue and the Mean, Apeiron* 28.4.

BOSTOCK, D. (1988), 'Pleasure and Activity in Aristotle's Ethics', *Phronesis*, 33: 251–72.

_____(2000), *Aristotle's Ethics* (Oxford).

BROADIE, S. (1991), *Ethics with Aristotle* (New York and Oxford).

_____(2003), 'Aristotelian Piety', *Phronesis*, 48: 54–70.

BROWN, L. (1997), 'What is "The Mean Relative to Us" in Aristotle's Ethics?', *Phronesis*, 42: 77–93.

BURGER, R. (1991), 'Ethical Reflection and Righteous Indignation: *Nemesis* in the *Nicomachean Ethics*', in Anton and Preus (1991: 127–39).

BURNYEAT, M. F. (1980), 'Aristotle on Learning to be Good', in Rorty (1980: 69–92). Repr. in Sherman (1999: 205–30).

CHARLES, D. (1995), 'Aristotle and Modern Realism', in Heinaman (1995: 135–72).

COOPER, J. (1975), *Reason and Human Good in Aristotle* (Cambridge, Mass., and London).

_____(1988), 'Some Remarks on Aristotle's Moral Psychology', *Southern Journal of Philosophy*, 27 suppl.: 25–42. Repr. in Cooper (1999: 237–52) and in Irwin (1995: 229–47).

_____(1996*a*), 'An Aristotelian Theory of the Emotions', in A. O. Rorty (ed.), *Essays on Aristotle's "Rhetoric"* (Berkeley), 238–75. Repr. in Cooper (1999: 406–23).

_____(1996*b*), 'Reason, Moral Virtue, and Moral Value', in M. Frede and G. Striker (eds.), *Rationality in Greek Thought* (Oxford), 81–114. Repr. in Cooper (1999: 253–80).

_____(1999), *Reason and Emotion: Essays on Ancient Moral Psychology and Ethical Theory* (Princeton).

COOPER, N. (1989), 'Aristotle's Crowning Virtue', *Apeiron*, 22: 191–205.

CRISP, R., and SLOTE, M. (1997) (eds.), *Virtue Ethics* (Oxford).

CURREN, R. (1989), 'The Contribution of *Nicomachean Ethics* iii 5 to Aristotle's Theory of Responsibility', *History of Philosophy Quarterly*, 6: 261–77.

CURZER, H. J. (1990), 'A Great Philosopher's Not So Great Account of Great Virtue: Aristotle's Treatment of "Greatness of Soul" ', *Canadian Journal of Philosophy*, 20: 517–37.

_____(1991), 'Aristotle's Much Maligned *Megalopsychos*', *Australasian Journal of Philosophy*, 69: 131–51.

_____(1996), 'A Defense of Aristotle's Doctrine that Virtue is a Mean', *Ancient Philosophy*, 16: 129–38.

_____(2002), 'Aristotle's Painful Path to Virtue', *Journal of the History of Philosophy*, 40: 141–62.

_____(2005), 'How Good People Do Bad Things: Aristotle on the Misdeeds of the Virtuous', *Oxford Studies in Ancient Philosophy*, 28: 233–56.

DAHL, N. O. (1984), *Practical Reason, Aristotle, and Weakness of the Will* (Minneapolis).

DARWALL, S. (2002), *Welfare and Rational Care* (Princeton and Oxford).

DEVEREUX, D. T. (1985–6), 'Particular and Universal in Aristotle's Conception of Practical Knowledge', *Review of Metaphysics*, 39: 483–504.

DI MUZIO, G. (2000), 'Aristotle on Improving One's Character', *Phronesis*, 45: 205–19.

DODDS, E. R. (1959), *Plato: Gorgias. A Revised Text with Introduction and Commentary* (Oxford).

DOVER, K. J. (1974), *Greek Popular Morality in the Time of Plato and Aristotle* (Berkeley and Los Angeles).

DUFF, A. (1987), 'Aristotelian Courage', *Ratio*, 29: 2–15.

ENGBERG-PEDERSEN, T. (1983), *Aristotle's Theory of Moral Insight* (Oxford).

ENGSTROM, S., and WHITING, J. (1996) (eds.), *Aristotle, Kant, and the Stoics: Rethinking Happiness and Duty* (Cambridge).

EVERSON, S. (1990), 'Aristotle's Compatibilism in the *Nicomachean Ethics*', *Ancient Philosophy*, 10: 81–103.

FORTENBAUGH, W. W. (1968), 'Aristotle and the Questionable Mean-Dispositions', *Transactions of the American Philological Association*, 99: 203–31.

—— (1975), *Aristotle on Emotion* (London).

FURLEY, D. J. (1977), 'Aristotle on the Voluntary', in Barnes *et al.* (1977: 47–60).

GAUTHIER, R. A. (1951), *Magnanimité: l'idéal de la grandeur dans la philosophie paienne et dans la théologie chrétienne* (Paris).

GOTTLIEB, P. (1994), 'Aristotle's "Nameless" Virtues', *Apeiron*, 27: 1–15.

HARDIE, W. F. R. (1964–5), 'Aristotle's Doctrine that Virtue is a "Mean"', *Proceedings of the Aristotelian Society*, 65: 183–204. Repr. in Hardie (1980: ch. 7). Revised version in Barnes *et al.* (1977: 33–46).

—— (1965), 'The Final Good in Aristotle's Ethics', *Philosophy*, 40: 277–95. Repr. in Moravcsik (1967: 297–322).

—— (1978), ' "Magnanimity" in Aristotle's Ethics', *Phronesis*, 23: 63–79.

—— (1980), *Aristotle's Ethical Theory*, 2nd edn. (Oxford).

HARE, J. (1988), ''Ελευθεριότης in Aristotle's Ethics', *Ancient Philosophy*, 8: 19–32.

HEIL, J. F. (1996), 'Why is Aristotle's Brave Man So Frightened? The Paradox of Courage in the *Eudemian Ethics*', *Apeiron*, 29: 47–74.

HEINAMAN, R. (1995) (ed.), *Aristotle and Moral Realism* (London).

HURSTHOUSE, R. (1980–1), 'A False Doctrine of the Mean', *Proceedings of the Aristotelian Society*, 81: 57–72. Repr. in Sherman (1999: 105–19) and in Irwin (1995: 279–94).

—— (1984), 'Acting and Feeling in Character: *Nicomachean Ethics* 3.i', *Phronesis*, 29: 252–66.

—— (1995), 'The Virtuous Agent's Reasons: A Reply to Bernard Williams', in Heinaman (1995: 24–33).

_____(1999), *On Virtue Ethics* (Oxford).

HUTCHINSON, D. S. (1986), *The Virtues of Aristotle* (London and New York).

IRWIN, T. H. (1978), 'First Principles in Aristotle's Ethics', in P. French, T. Uehling, and H. Wettstein (eds.), *Midwest Studies in Philosophy*, iii: *Studies in Ethical Theory*, 252–72.

_____(1980a), 'The Metaphysical and Psychological Basis of Aristotle's Ethics', in Rorty (1980: 35–53).

_____(1980b), 'Reason and Responsibility in Aristotle', in Rorty (1980: 117–55).

_____(1985), 'Aristotle's Conception of Morality', *Proceedings of the Boston Area Colloquium in Ancient Philosophy*, 1: 115–43. With Commentary by N. Sherman, 144–50.

_____(1988), *Aristotle's First Principles* (Oxford).

_____(1992), 'Eminent Victorians and Greek Ethics: Sidgwick, Green and Aristotle', in B. Schultz (ed.), *Essays on Henry Sidgwick* (Cambridge), 279–310.

_____ (1995) (ed.), *Classical Philosophy: Collected Papers*, v: *Aristotle's Ethics* (New York).

_____(1996), 'The Virtues: Theory and Common Sense in Greek Philosophy', in R. Crisp (ed.), *How Should One Live? Essays on the Virtues* (Oxford), 37–55.

_____(1999b), 'Algunas consideraciones sobre la concepción aristotélica de la magnanimidad', *Areté, revista de filosofía* (Departamento de Humanidades, Pontificia Universidad Católica del Perú), 11: 195–217.

_____(2000), 'Ethics as an Inexact Science: Aristotle's Ambitions for Moral Theory', in B. Hooker and M. O. Little (eds.), *Moral Particularism* (Oxford), 100–29.

JACKSON, H. (1920), 'Aristotle's Lecture-room and Lectures', *Journal of Philology*, 35: 191–200.

JOHANSEN, T. K. (1997), *Aristotle on the Sense-Organs* (Cambridge).

JUDSON, L. (1991), 'Chance and "Always or For the Most Part" in Aristotle', in L. Judson (ed.), *Aristotle's Physics: A Collection of Essays* (Oxford), 73–99.

KENNY, A. (1965–6), 'Happiness', *Proceedings of the Aristotelian Society*, 66: 93–102. Repr. in J. Feinberg (ed.), *Moral Concepts* (Oxford, 1969), 43–52; in Kenny, *The Anatomy of the Soul* (Oxford, 1973), 51–61; and in Barnes *et al.* (1977: 25–32). Entitled 'Aristotle on Happiness', in Kenny (1973) and in Barnes *et al.* (1977).)

_____(1978), *The Aristotelian Ethics* (Oxford).

_____(1979), *Aristotle's Theory of the Will* (London).

KORSGAARD, C. M. (1996), 'From Duty and for the Sake of the Good: Kant and Aristotle on Morally Good Action', in Engstrom and Whiting (1996: 203–36).

KOSMAN, L. A. (1980), 'Being Properly Affected: Virtues and Feelings in Aristotle's *Ethics*', in Rorty (1980: 103–16). Repr. in Sherman (1999: 261–75).

KRAUT, R. (1976), 'Aristotle on Choosing Virtue for Itself', *Archiv für Geschichte der Philosophie*, 58: 223–39. Repr. in Irwin (1995: 321–37).

——(1979), 'The Peculiar Function of Human Beings', *Canadian Journal of Philosophy*, 9: 467–78.

——(1989), *Aristotle on the Human Good* (Princeton).

——(1998), 'Aristotle on Method and Moral Education', in J. Gentzler (ed.), *Method in Ancient Philosophy* (Oxford), 271–90.

LAWRENCE, G. (2001), 'The Function of the Function Argument', *Ancient Philosophy*, 21: 445–75.

LEIGHTON, S. (1982), 'Aristotle and the Emotions', *Phronesis*, 27: 144–74. Repr. in Irwin (1995: 248–78).

——(1988), 'Aristotle's Courageous Passions', *Phronesis*, 33: 76–99.

——(1995), 'The Mean Relative to Us', in Bosley *et al.* (1995: 67–78).

LONDON, A. J. (2000–1), 'Moral Knowledge and the Acquisition of Virtue in Aristotle's *Nicomachean* and *Eudemian Ethics*', *Review of Metaphysics*, 54: 553–83.

McDOWELL, J. (1979), 'Virtue and Reason', *The Monist*, 62: 331–50. Repr. in Crisp and Slote (1997: 141–77) and in Sherman (1999: 121–43).

——(1995), 'Eudaimonism and Realism in Aristotle's Ethics', in Heinaman (1995: 201–18).

——(1996), 'Deliberation and Moral Development in Aristotle's Ethics', in Engstrom and Whiting (1996: 19–35).

MELE, A. R. (1981), 'Choice and Virtue in the *Nicomachean Ethics*', *Journal of the History of Philosophy*, 19: 405–23.

MEYER, S. S. (1993), *Aristotle on Moral Responsibility* (Oxford and Cambridge, Mass.).

——(1998), 'Moral Responsibility: Aristotle and After', in S. Everson (ed.), *Companions to Ancient Thought, iv: Ethics* (Cambridge), 221–40.

MIGNUCCI, M. (1981), "Ὡς ἐπὶ τὸ πολύ et Nécessaire dans la Conception Aristotélicienne de la Science', in E. Berti (ed.), *Aristotle on Science: The "Posterior Analytics"* (Padua), 173–203.

MILLS, M. J. (1980), 'The Discussions of Ἀνδρεία in the Eudemian and Nicomachean Ethics', *Phronesis*, 25: 198–218.

——(1985), 'Φθόνος and its Related Πάθη in Plato and Aristotle', *Phronesis*, 30: 1–12.

MOLINE, J. N. (1989), 'Aristotle on Praise and Blame', *Archiv für Geschichte der Philosophie*, 71: 283–302.

MONAN, J. D. (1968), *Moral Knowledge and its Methodology in Aristotle* (Oxford).

MORAUX, P., and HARLFINGER, D. (1971) (eds.), *Untersuchungen zur Eudemischen Ethik* (Berlin).

MORAVCSIK, J. M. E. (1967) (ed.), *Aristotle* (Garden City, NY).

MÜLLER, A. (1982), *Praktisches Folgern und Selbstgestaltung nach Aristoteles* (Freiburg and Munich).

OTT, W. R. (2000), 'A Troublesome Passage in Aristotle's *Nicomachean Ethics* iii.5', *Ancient Philosophy*, 20: 99–107.

OWENS, J. (1981), 'The Καλόν in the Aristotelian *Ethics*', in D. J. O'Meara (ed.), *Studies in Aristotle* (Washington), 261–77.

PAKALUK, M. (2004), 'The Meaning of Aristotelian Magnanimity', *Oxford Studies in Ancient Philosophy*, 26: 241–75.

PEARS, D. (1980), 'Courage as a Mean', in Rorty (1980: 171–87).

REES, D. A. (1971), '"Magnanimity" in the Eudemian and Nicomachean Ethics', in Moraux and Harlfinger (1971: 231–43).

REEVE, C. D. C. (1992), *Practices of Reason* (Oxford).

ROBERTS, J. (1989), 'Aristotle on Responsibility for Action and Character', *Ancient Philosophy*, 9: 22–36.

ROGERS, K. (1993), 'Aristotle's Conception of Τὸ Καλόν', *Ancient Philosophy*, 13: 355–71.

RORTY, A. O. (1980) (ed.), *Essays on Aristotle's Ethics* (Berkeley, Los Angeles, and London).

SANTAS, G. X. (1964), 'The Socratic Paradoxes', *Philosophical Review*, 73: 147–64. Repr. in Santas, *Socrates: Philosophy in Plato's Early Dialogues* (London, Boston, and Henley, 1979), 183–94.

——— (1993), 'Does Aristotle Have a Virtue Ethics?', *Philosophical Inquiry*, 15: 1–32. Repr. in Statman (1997: 260–85).

SCHÜTRUMPF, E. (1989), 'Magnanimity, Μεγαλοψυχία and the System of Aristotle's *Nicomachean Ethics*', *Archiv für Geschichte der Philosophie*, 71: 10–22.

SEDLEY, D. (2003), *Plato's Cratylus* (Cambridge).

SHERMAN, N. (1989), *The Fabric of Character* (Oxford). Shortened version of ch. 5 repr. in Sherman (1999: 231–60).

——— (1997), *Making a Necessity of Virtue* (Cambridge).

——— (1999) (ed.), *Aristotle's Ethics: Critical Essays* (Lanham, Md., Boulder, Colo., New York, and Oxford).

SIMPSON, P. (1991–2), 'Contemporary Virtue Ethics and Aristotle', *Review of Metaphysics*, 45: 503–24. Repr. in Statman (1997: 245–59).

SISKO, J. E. (2003), 'Touch, Taste and Temperance in *Nicomachean Ethics* 3.10', *Classical Quarterly*, n.s. 53: 135–40.

SORABJI, R. (1973–4), 'Aristotle on the Role of the Intellect in Virtue', *Proceedings of the Aristotelian Society*, 74: 107–29. Repr. in Rorty (1980: 201–19).

SORABJI (1980), *Necessity, Cause and Blame: Perspectives on Aristotle's Theory* (London).

STATMAN, D. (1997) (ed.), *Virtue Ethics: A Critical Reader* (Edinburgh).

STOCKER, M. (1986), 'Dirty Hands and Conflicts of Values and of Desires in Aristotle's Ethics', *Pacific Philosophical Quarterly*, 67: 36–61. Repr. in Stocker (1990*b*: 51–84).

——(1990*a*), 'Courage, the Doctrine of the Mean and the Possibility of Evaluative and Emotional Coherence', in Stocker (1990*b*: 129–64).

——(1990*b*), *Plural and Conflicting Values* (Oxford).

STOVER, J., and POLANSKY, R. (2003), 'Moral Virtue and *Megalopsychia*', *Ancient Philosophy*, 23: 351–9.

TAYLOR, C. C. W. (1988), 'Urmson on Aristotle on Pleasure', in J. Dancy, J. M. E. Moravcsik, and C. C. W. Taylor (eds.), *Human Agency: Language, Duty, and Value. Philosophical Essays in Honor of J. O. Urmson* (Stanford, Calif.), 120–32.

——(1990), 'Aristotle's Epistemology', in S. Everson (ed.), *Companions to Ancient Thought i: Epistemology* (Cambridge), 116–42.

——(2003*a*), 'Aristoteles über den praktischen Intellekt', in Th. Buchheim, H. Flashar, and R. A. H. King (eds.), *Kann man heute noch etwas anfangen mit Aristoteles?* (Hamburg), 142–62.

——(2003*b*), 'Pleasure: Aristotle's Response to Plato', in R. Heinaman (ed.), *Plato and Aristotle's Ethics* (London), 1–20. With reply by S. Broadie, 21–7.

URMSON, J. O. (1967), 'Aristotle on Pleasure', in Moravcsik (1967: 323–33).

——(1973), 'Aristotle's Doctrine of the Mean', *American Philosophical Quarterly*, 10: 223–30. Repr. in Rorty (1980: 157–70).

——(1988), *Aristotle's Ethics* (Oxford and New York).

VASILIOU, I. (1996), 'The Role of Good Upbringing in Aristotle's Ethics', *Philosophy and Phenomenological Research*, 56: 771–97.

VLASTOS, G. (1991), *Socrates, Ironist and Moral Philosopher* (Cambridge).

WHITE, S. A. (1992), *Sovereign Virtue: Aristotle on the Relation between Happiness and Prosperity* (Stanford, Calif.).

WHITING, J. (1988), 'Aristotle's Function Argument: A Defense', *Ancient Philosophy*, 8: 33–48.

WIGGINS, D. (1975–6), 'Deliberation and Practical Reason', *Proceedings of the Aristotelian Society*, 76: 29–51. Revised version in Rorty (1980: 221–65).

——(1995), 'Eudaimonism and Realism in Aristotle's Ethics: A Reply to John McDowell', in Heinaman (1995: 219–31).

WILLIAMS, B. (1993), *Shame and Necessity* (Berkeley, Los Angeles, and Oxford).

——(1995), 'Acting as the Virtuous Person Acts', in Heinaman (1995: 13–23).

WINTER, M. (1997), 'Aristotle, *hōs epi to polu* Relations, and a Demonstrative Science of Ethics', *Phronesis*, 42: 163–89.

WOODS, M. J. (1986), 'Intuition and Perception in Aristotle's Ethics', *Oxford Studies in Ancient Philosophy*, 4: 145–66. Repr. in Woods, *Four Prague Lectures and Other Texts* (Prague, 2001), 83–113.

YOUNG, C. M. (1980), 'Virtue and Flourishing in Aristotle's Ethics', in D. J. Depew (ed.), *The Greeks and the Good Life* (Fullerton, Calif.), 138–56.

——(1988), 'Aristotle on Temperance', *Philosophical Review*, 97: 521–42. Repr. in Anton and Preus (1991: 107–25).

——(1994), 'Aristotle on Liberality', *Proceedings of the Boston Area Colloquium in Ancient Philosophy*, 10: 313–34. With comment by J. D. Blankenship, 335–44.

INDEX OF PASSAGES CITED

GENERAL INDEX

(Figures in bold type refer to the Translation.)

Made in the USA
Las Vegas, NV
08 January 2022

40883211R00166